Sandringham Days

THE **DOMESTIC LIFE** OF THE **ROYAL FAMILY** IN **NORFOLK**, 1862–1952

JOHN MATSON

For
Mary
Colin, Andrew and Nicola
and their children

'The lights in my life'

By the same author:

Dear Osborne: Queen Victoria's Family Life on the Isle of Wight
Pressganged! – A musical for young people (words and lyrics)
Stories

First published 2011
Reprinted 2012

The History Press
The Mill, Brimscombe Port
Stroud, Gloucestershire, GL5 2QG
www.thehistorypress.co.uk

© John Matson, 2011

The right of John Matson to be identified as the Author
of this work has been asserted in accordance with the
Copyrights, Designs and Patents Act 1988.

British Library Cataloguing in Publication Data.
A catalogue record for this book is available from the British Library.

ISBN 978 0 7524 6582 1

Typesetting and origination by The History Press
Printed in Great Britain
Manufacturing managed by Jellyfish Print Solutions Ltd

CONTENTS

ACKNOWLEDGEMENTS

I warmly acknowledge the permission of Her Majesty Queen Elizabeth II to use previously published material from the Royal Archives, together with photographs from the Royal Collection, selected with the valuable help of Miss Frances Dimond, MVO. The assistance of Lady de Bellaigue, Registrar of the Royal Archives and more recently, Lady Roberts, and also the staff at the Royal Archives and the Photographic Collection is also much appreciated.

I am grateful to Sir Julian Loyd, KCVO, until 1991 the Queen's agent at Sandringham, for the very valuable assistance he gave me, allowing me to see more of York Cottage than would otherwise have been possible, and to visit the reclaimed area of land beyond Wolferton. His successors, Mr John Major, MVO and Mr M. O'Lone, have corrected errors in the preface and afterword and provided me with some useful illustrations of the house. My thanks to Mr R.S. French for helpful advice and information and for a most interesting tour of York Cottage. I appreciate the help offered by Lady Roberts and the staff at the Royal Archives and the Photographic Collection.

I would like to thank Lord Wigram of Clewer for permission to make use of the letters from his mother and a copy of her portrait by Oswald Birley. His kindness and hospitality made my search for material from that period of King George V's reign a real pleasure. I am indebted to Mr R. Verner-Jeffreys for the loan of letters from Prince George during his service in the Royal Navy and a copy of a letter from Queen Victoria to George, Duke of Cambridge in 1864 from which extracts have been taken.

I greatly appreciated the comments of the late C.M. Baker of Wellington College and W.L. Fryer. E.R. Sibbick, MVO has an encyclopaedic knowledge of the period and his advice and criticism have enabled me to avoid a number of pitfalls. Opinions, where not otherwise acknowledged, are my own, as are residual errors and omissions. My wife, Mary, and our daughter, Nicola, have devoted much time to the work in progress and suggested a number of amendments, which are incorporated. Our sons Colin and Andrew have kept the computer running and Lorna Mitchell's help proved very welcome.

Mr R. Hedley Walker of the Wolferton Station Museum generously gave me unrestricted access to the exhibits which he and his family collected over many years. This unique display added a valuable dimension to 'Sandringham life', enabling us to envisage the reception of Royal and important persons on the 'Downside' platform. The letters in this book are reproduced by his kind permission. The present owner, Mr Richard Brown, generously escorted us round his restoration work, including his discovery of Queen Alexandra's original garden.

Mrs Diana Coldicott kindly lent me a number of books for a prolonged period, and I am grateful to the librarian and his assistants at the Farnham Branch of the Surrey County Library for their help in obtaining material. Mr D.S. Brooks, librarian at Lord Wandsworth College, read the script and made a number of helpful suggestions. As Librarian he was most accommodating over the matter of prolonged loans. Mr John Moulding, a former shepherd, provided some interesting first-hand information on the estate during the reign of King Edward VII.

I would also like to thank everyone at The History Press for all their hard work.

I acknowledge with thanks the permission of the following for permission to use extracts from works quoted in the Bibliography:

Battiscombe, G., *Queen Alexandra* (Constable & Co., 1969)

Buxton, A., *The King in his Country* (Longmans, Green & Co., 1955)

Cathcart, H., *Sandringham* (W.H. Allen, 1964)

Donaldson, F., *Edward VIII* (Widenfeld & Nicholson Ltd., 1974)

Hepworth, P., *Royal Sandringham* (Wensum Books Ltd., 1978)

Gore, J., *King George V. A Personal Memoir* (John Murray, 1949)

Airlie, M., Countess of, *Thatched with Gold: Memoirs* (Hutchinson & Co., 1962)

Magnus, P., *King Edward the Seventh* (John Murray, 1964)

Nicholson, H., *King George V* (Constable & Co., 1952)

Ponsonby, A., *Henry Ponsonby* (Macmillan & Co. Ltd, 1942)

Pope-Hennessey, J., *Queen Mary* (George Allen & Unwin, 1959)

Wheeler-Bennett, J.W., *King George VI, His Life and Times* (Macmillan & Co. Ltd, 1958)

PREFACE

Sandringham, the private property of the Queen, is a large estate in Norfolk of some 20,000 acres comprising woodland, farmland, saltings on the edge of the Wash, and land reclaimed from the sea. Apart from the visitor centre there are a number of prosperous industries – a fruit farm, market garden, sawmill, the Royal Stud, a country park and nature trail. Within the estate are seven villages where about 10,000 acres are farmed by tenants. The house and gardens are opened to the public for much of the summer and provide a glimpse of a Royal and private home.

Such a visit raises many questions: how did this property come into the possession of the Royal family? How did they spend their time here? What kinds of problems and difficulties beset them over the past 150 years? Until recently the rusty chains of a child's swing hung from a tree near York Cottage and invited us to wonder about the children who grew up here, and what they did in later life.

Sandringham was purchased for the then Prince of Wales in 1862 and was, in effect, his creation. King George V was born there and for him it was perhaps more 'home' than it had been even for his father. He adopted the lifestyle of a country gentleman and said of Sandringham that it was 'the place I love best anywhere in the world'. King Edward VII was more cosmopolitan in his tastes than his son and enjoyed the fascinations of London life – in one week he visited the theatre twice, a circus once, spent the next day shooting and then went off to Homburg – and the attractions of Paris, Marienbad and Biarritz almost as much. He was a restless traveller and greatly enjoyed his visits to the continent. How then did he, when Albert Edward, Prince of Wales, come to own such a derelict estate in a region so inhospitable and so remote from those centres of enjoyment?

York Cottage was given to Prince George by his father on his marriage to Princess Victoria Mary of Teck in 1893. For the first seventeen years of his marriage the Prince lived there happily as a leisured country gentleman. On his accession as King George V in 1910, the Cottage remained his Norfolk home while his mother, Queen Alexandra, lived in the Big House nearby, almost alone in a mansion of 300 rooms, until her death in 1925. What caused this apparent anomaly?

It seems a natural progression from these questions to a consideration on the influences that shaped the lives of those who made Sandringham their home. Some of them are to be found here, and perhaps this account of domestic life in Norfolk will encourage readers towards the rewarding biographies of the successive owners, including the current Royal family, but they are beyond the scope of this narrative, which therefore closes with the death of King George VI in 1952. Accounts of the Queen's inheritance of the estate and the private lives of her family there are best left to other hands.

Note: It was the wish of King Edward VII and Queen Alexandra that their private correspondence should be destroyed after their death, which was dutifully fulfilled by Viscount Esher. There are many areas, therefore, where their thoughts and feelings can only be surmised. Queen Victoria's journal exists only in a form edited by her daughters, with passages omitted as they thought fit. Many of her letters, however, have been edited and published and in their characteristically forthright manner of expression there is much evidence of her relationships with her family. The private papers of King George VI and Queen Elizabeth II are, of course, inaccessible.

Note: Members of the Royal family change their titles in accordance with their rank and situation. For example, Princess Maud of Wales, youngest daughter of King Edward VII and Queen Alexandra, became Maud, Princess Charles of Norway on her marriage and, on her husband's election to the Norwegian throne, Queen of Norway. Similarly, King Edward's second son, born Prince George of Wales, became Duke of Cornwall in 1901; and later that year he became Prince of Wales; and on the death of King Edward VII in 1910, King George V. The tables below may be helpful.

A slight confusion may arise over the use of the name 'Bertie'. It was Queen Victoria's family name for Albert Edward, Prince of Wales and used by her until the day of her death and by his siblings. It was also given to Prince Albert (later King George VI), and used by his relatives.

The Children of Queen Victoria and Prince Albert

1. **Princess Victoria** (1840-1901). Princess Royal; married Prince Frederick William of Prussia in 1858. She was later Crown Princess of Prussia and Empress Frederick of Germany. Eight children; the eldest became Kaiser Wilhelm II.

2. **Prince Albert Edward**, (1841-1910) – known as 'Bertie'. Prince of Wales. Married Princess Alexandra of Denmark in 1863. Six children: Prince Albert Victor, died in 1892; Prince George, married Princess Victoria Mary of Teck, later **King George V**, died in 1936; Princess Louise, married Earl of Fife; Victoria; Maud, married Prince Christian of Denmark, later Queen Maud; and Prince Alexander John (died same day). In 1901 he became **King Edward VII**.

3. **Princess Alice** (1843-1878). Married Grand Duke of Hesse-Darmstadt in 1862; two sons and three daughters.

4. **Prince Alfred** (1844-1900) – known as 'Affie'. Duke of Edinburgh. Married in 1874, to Princess Marie of Russia; one son and four daughters.

5. **Princess Helena** (1846-1923) – known as 'Lenchen'. Married in 1866 to Prince Christian of Schleswig Holstein; three sons (two survived) and two daughters.

6. **Princess Louise** (1848-1939). Married the Marquis of Lorne in 1871, later Duke of Argyll. No issue.

7. **Prince Arthur** (1850-1941). Duke of Connaught; married Princess Louise Margaret of Prussia in 1879; one son and two daughters.

8. **Prince Leopold** (1853-1884). Married Helena, Princess of Waldeck-Pyrmont, in 1882. One son and one daughter. He suffered from haemophilia.

9. **Princess Beatrice** (1857-1944). Married Prince Henry of Battenberg in 1885; three sons, one daughter.

The Children of King Edward VII and Queen Alexandra

Albert Victor, (1864-1892), known as Eddy. Born on 8 January at Frogmore, two months premature; died on 14 January 1892.

George (1865-1936). Born on 3 June at Marlborough House, London, one month premature. Duke of York, 1892; Prince of Wales, 1901; **King George V**, 1910. He died at Sandringham on 20 January 1936.

Louise (1867-1931). Born on 20 February at Marlborough House. Married Alexander Duff, Earl of Fife (created Duke) in 1889. Died in January 1931.

Victoria (1868-1935). Born on 6 July at Marlborough House. Died 3 December 1935.

Maud (1869-1938). Born on 26 November at Marlborough House. Married Prince Charles of Denmark in 1896. Queen Maud of Norway, 1905. Died 20 November 1938.

Alexander John (1871). Born on 6 April at Sandringham. Lived one day.

The Children of King George V and Queen Mary

Edward (1894-1972), known as David. Born 23 June at White Lodge, Richmond. Prince of Wales, 1910; **King Edward VIII,** January 1936, abdicated December 1936; created Duke of Windsor 1937; married Wallis Simpson 1937; died in Paris 1972.

Albert (1895-1952), 'Bertie'. Born on 14 December at Sandringham. Duke of York, 1920; married Lady Elizabeth Bowes-Lyon, 1923; **King George VI** 1936; died at Sandringham 1952.

Mary, Princess Royal (1897-1965). Born on 25 April at Sandringham. Married Viscount Lascelles, later Earl of Harewood, 1922. Died 1965.

Henry (1900-1974). Born on 31 March at Sandringham. Created Duke of Gloucester 1928. Married Lady Alice Montagu-Douglas-Scott in 1935. Died in 1974.

George (1902-1942). Born on 20 December 1902 at Sandringham. Created Duke of Kent in 1934. Married Princess Marina of Greece 1934. Killed on active service in 1942.

John (1905-1919). Born on 12 July at Sandringham. Died at Wood Farm, Sandringham in 1919.

CHAPTER ONE

EARLY DAYS OF A PRINCE

S hortly before Easter in 1863, a round-faced, slight young man and his bride of less than a month descended from their carriage at the extraordinary brick and stone porch of Sandringham Hall. The porch itself was an incongruent addition to the white stucco front of the house, and around and beyond the building stretched some 7,000 neglected acres of the estate. The young man was Albert Edward, Prince of Wales – and consequently heir to the throne of England – and his lovely bride was Princess Alexandra of Denmark. They were moving into their own home after a week's honeymoon at Osborne on the Isle of Wight, which had been lent to them by Queen Victoria. This event signalled their entry into an independent lifestyle and by any standards they must be considered a singularly fortunate couple. Yet the Prince's twenty-one year road to this point in his life had not always been easy and, if we are to understand his feelings as he took up residence at the Hall, we should pause to trace his early life.

Two years earlier the Prince, then nearly twenty years of age, was completing his education, to which he had displayed a steady resistance to the system devised in his childhood by Baron Stockmar, the confidant of Queen Victoria and Prince Albert, the boy's parents. 'If he does not like books he must be made to like them,'[1] wrote the Baron, who had gained a remarkable ascendancy over the Royal parents. He was convinced that they were too young to direct their eldest son's education, and that it was their 'sacred duty' to consult the most eminent persons in the land. Frivolity of any kind was a corrupting influence: the example of the sons of George III must be avoided at all costs; and Stockmar's scheme must have satisfied the most anxious parent. Five hours of study a day was to be imposed and 'an attempt was made to mould him, in isolation from his contemporaries, into a moral and intellectual paragon.'[2] Such a system appealed to the parents, who were only too conscious that their son would in all likelihood one day succeed his mother.

At the age of seven and a half, the Prince of Wales commenced his education under a team of tutors headed by a Mr Henry Birch, and quickly found himself in an atmosphere of unrelenting pressure. He would have enjoyed shorter hours and longer holidays had he been at any normal preparatory school in the country. Relaxation came only on Sundays and birthdays, and when the Court moved from London or Windsor. Mr Birch's task was unenviable: his pupil's behaviour was erratic, varying from insolence to apathy, and the tutor noted that 'the want of contact with other boys' and lack of competition accounted for many of his problems. There was little of what might be termed positive encouragement, yet he still had an affectionate and amiable disposition.

Mr Birch was succeeded by Frederick Gibbs, a fine scholar, who obeyed the first instructions of his Royal employers and increased his charge's labours to six and even, at one time, seven hours a day. The Queen told Gibbs to observe him closely, noting that he 'hangs his head and looks at his feet, and invariably within a day or two has one of his fits of nervous and unmanageable temper.'[3] That these were signs of acute exhaustion was confirmed by extracts from Gibbs' diary in 29 January 1852:

> Mr Leitch the drawing master came. P. of W. very angry with P. Alfred and pulled his hair brandishing a paper-knife...
>
> Feb 28. I had to do some arithmetic with the P. of W. Immediately he became passionate, the pencil was flung to the end of the room, the stool was kicked away and he was hardly able to apply at all... Next day... he became violently angry because I wanted some Latin done.[4]

Mr Birch's diagnosis of the Prince's problems was not shared by the Queen. Both she and Prince Albert were suspicious of the morality of boys in general. Occasionally, at Windsor, a few very carefully selected pupils from Eton were invited to the Castle where, in Prince Albert's presence, they would listen to improving talk. Prince Albert, one of these boys noted, seemed 'a proud, shy, stand-offish man, not calculated to make friends easily with children. I was frightened to death of him.'[5] Understandably, Prince Albert's own early life in Germany had been in sharp contrast to the democratic ways of an English boarding school, and he viewed the pupils of Eton with distrust.

Inevitably, cracks began to appear in this harsh régime. More than one of the Prince's tutors warned of the effects of this unremitting pursuit of excellence: 'You will wear him out early,'[6] wrote Dr Voisin, and Dr Becker, Librarian to the Prince, reported that the outbursts of 'blind destructive rage' were the result of 'too great and continuous strain upon a young mind and body.' He had tried, he said, both kindness and severity:

…kindness had elicited no response but severity had invariably caused gusts of elemental fury in which 'he takes everything that is at hand and throws it with the greatest violence against the wall or window… or he stands in the corner stamping with his legs and screaming in the most dreadful manner.'[7]

The parents themselves suspected that all was not well with their son and some attempt was made to relate his studies to military matters, in which he displayed interest and intelligence. The Queen believed that the precocious brilliance of her eldest child, the Princess Royal, reflected adversely on her son, who was conscious of his intellectual inferiority.

Gibbs himself, though loyal to the parents – he considered his daily reports to them a 'very happy arrangement' – sometimes felt that the pressure exerted on the Prince of Wales, and scarcely less so on Prince Alfred, his younger brother, was unreasonable.[8] Prince Albert had told him 'that it must not be supposed that our stay there (at Balmoral) was to be taken as a holiday; that the Princes had had mistaken notions about this; but that henceforth work must be done diligently." I told the Queen that I thought we had made a mistake.' It is not surprising that the Prince's conduct was unsatisfactory: six or seven hours of study left him bewildered and exhausted, and with a life-long aversion to reading. The parents had set their goals too high; the Prince was only too aware that their approval depended on his ability to excel. Gibbs pressed for more opportunities for the Princes to meet their contemporaries, but the resulting visits to Eton were a dismal failure[9]: they were unused to the kind of social intercourse encountered at the College and were rude and over-bearing to other boys. Naturally, the parents, anxiously watching the results, misunderstood both causes and effects and laid the blame on their children. As far as the Queen was concerned, perfection was embodied in her husband and there must be something wrong with her son if his aspirations were not his father's.

Despite the Prince's capacity for affection, so often remarked by others, it was not sufficiently often returned by his parents. Their anxiety prevented them from showing much approval of his positive virtues. The Queen was honest enough to admit that she found 'no especial pleasure or compensation in the company of the elder children… only very occasionally do I find the rather intimate intercourse with them either agreeable or easy.'[10] This was partly, she explained, because she felt really at her ease only in the company of Prince Albert and, also, because she had grown accustomed to having to carry out so much of her work alone. It was rare for her to write, after one of her walks with the sixteen year-old Prince, that she found him 'very amiable and sensible.'[11]

There was another side to his childhood, of course. Despite all the work there was a holiday atmosphere at Osborne, the villa on the edge of the Solent where the Queen was perhaps happiest. There was a private beach where Vicky, the Princess Royal, would wander barefoot, looking for shells for her collection: there were games and parties at the Swiss Cottage, and sea-bathing. It was here that the Queen found respite from the work which beset her elsewhere. When the Prince of Wales was seven, a Maid of Honour wrote: 'The whole Royal family, children, Queen and all seem to be out the whole day long...(The Queen) draws a good deal, and walks about and enjoys herself. The children dine and tea in the garden, and run about to their hearts' content.'[12]

Such was the upbringing of the young Prince, a boy of great charm, and of an affectionate and forgiving nature. It seems that he never bore his long-suffering tutors a grudge for the punishments so often inflicted on him. But his future remained unclear: how he was to occupy the very considerable time before he should succeed his mother – she was only twenty-two at his birth – was a problem never satisfactorily solved. When he was fifteen he was sent abroad to broaden his experience and to improve his command of French and German. There he attracted attention by his good looks and charm. He was taken about London and accompanied his parents on Royal occasions. The parents fell back on the well-tried tradition that the eldest son should go into the Army, which was his own greatest wish – not as a profession, the Queen reminded him – but he could learn in it. At sixteen he was given an annual allowance of £100, and permission to choose his own clothes: here was freedom indeed!

Immediately after the Prince's seventeenth birthday Mr Gibbs resigned, unlamented by his pupil and unregretted by his employers. 'Poor Mr Gibbs certainly failed during the last 2 years entirely, incredibly, and did Bertie no good,' the Queen wrote.[13] A year later she was fearing that 'the greatest improvement would never make him fit for his position'[14] and trembled to think of dying while there was so much to be done for her son. As it turned out, it was Prince Albert who was so soon to die, leaving uncompleted the purchase of Sandringham for his son.

The education of the Prince of Wales continued after Mr Gibbs' departure with a spell at both Oxford and Cambridge, where he was accompanied by an entourage headed by Colonel Bruce. His four terms at Oxford were interrupted by a highly successful tour of Canada and the United States, which greatly increased his confidence and impressed his parents. This was followed by a course of training with the Grenadier Guards at the Curragh Camp, near Dublin; to the Prince's resentment he was given the rank of Colonel, for he had not earned it. At this time two further plans were being hatched by the Queen and Prince Albert. The Prince was to have a residence of his own, and a wife: 1861 was to prove a fateful year.

These two objectives, simultaneously pursued, were occupying Prince Albert's mind when news reached him that his son had been the victim of a practical joke by his brother officers at the Curragh, who had smuggled an actress, Nellie Clifden, into his quarters. The Queen and the Prince were shocked and humiliated: worse, it revived all their old fears that in the Prince of Wales the immorality of the Hanoverians would return to haunt them. If the Queen was horrified, the news came to the Prince Consort as a near-mortal blow. His own forebears had not been above reproach and both he and the Queen had worked for twenty years to restore the public image of the monarchy that had, before her accession, become so tarnished. Now failure seemed to stare him in the face. Unwell, and with the Queen prostrated with grief over the recent death of her mother, the Duchess of Kent, Prince Albert sat down to write to his son, now at Cambridge, that 'this woman can drag you into a Court of Law and there... she will be able to give before a greedy multitude disgusting details of your profligacy... and to break your parents' hearts.'[15]

Later, Prince Albert travelled to Cambridge to talk to his son, and came away heartened by his contrition. But he was fast becoming too ill to bring to fruition the plans he had laid for a home and marriage for his eldest son. The purchase of an estate at Sandringham in Norfolk was under negotiation, and the question of a bride was now in the forefront of his mind.

For some time the Courts of Europe had been ransacked in search of a suitable Princess. Prussian ties were strong but the only really eligible candidate there for the hand of the Prince of Wales had been turned down by him after inspecting her photograph. It was the Princess Royal, now Crown Princess of Prussia, who put forward the claims of Princess Alexandra of Denmark, though her name had been mentioned to the Prince Consort by Walpurga Paget, wife of the British Minister in Copenhagen, as early as 1860. Discreet enquiries were made and the outlook seemed encouraging. Meetings were arranged and, after an encounter in Speyer Cathedral – scarcely an appropriate setting for a romance, perhaps – the Prince was able to write: 'I can now candidly say that I think her charming and very pretty.'[16]

It became apparent, however, that the Prince, despite his attraction to the Princess, was unduly hesitant about bringing matters to a conclusion: 'A sudden fear of marriage, and, above all, of having children which for so young a man is so strange a fear, seems to have got hold of him,' the Queen complained to her daughter.[17] In turn, the Prince Consort in his efforts to bring about the marriage offered his son a second opportunity, the Prince of Wales having expressed a wish to meet the Princess in England. 'You must clearly understand,' he wrote, 'that this interview is obtained... in order that you may propose to the young lady if she pleases you on further acquaintance as much as she did at first.'[18] But this visit never took place: for some time in indifferent health and seriously overworked, Prince Albert fell victim to the typhoid that lurked in the primitive drains of Windsor Castle, where he died on 14 December.

The distraught Queen sought refuge from the world at Osborne, but not even her grief could distract her from the continuation of Prince Albert's plans for their son. 'His wishes – his plans – about everything... are to be my law! I apply this particularly as regards our children – Bertie, etc – for whose future he had traced everything so carefully.'[19] The immediate future was to have included a tour of the Near East; accordingly, he departed in February 1862, accompanied by his Governor, Colonel (later General) Bruce. In following Albert's 'plans' there was some ambivalence in the Queen's mind, for she would thus be spared 'a constant contact which is more than ever unbearable to me.'[20] She was convinced that the Curragh affair had fatally undermined her husband's health, and her dislike of her eldest son at this time became obsessive. 'I never can or shall look at him without a shudder,' she wrote. He 'does not know that I know all – Beloved Papa told him that I could not be told all the disgusting details.' She added ominously, ' I believe firmly in all Papa foresaw.'[21]

Nevertheless, the plan for the Prince's marriage was pursued. Princess Alexandra's parents must in all honesty be informed of the Curragh affair, but the Queen was distressed by the apathy shown by her son. The initial hesitancy had been explained by his lapse at the Curragh; what could be the reason for any further delay? 'If Bertie turns obstinate,' she declared, 'I will withdraw myself altogether and wash my hands of him.' She was well aware that her second son, Prince Alfred, though only eighteen, would be more than willing to offer for the – as yet unseen – Princess. 'Affie,' she wrote, 'would be ready to take her at once and really if Bertie refuses her I would recommend Affie's engaging to marry her in three years.'[22] Meanwhile, Affie was in disgrace; he had become involved with a girl in Malta in 1862 which, coming so soon after the Nellie Clifden affair, left the Queen shattered. Not long afterwards she wrote: 'We do all we can to keep him from Marlborough House as he is far too épris of Alix to be allowed to be much there without possibly ruining the happiness of all three... Affie has not the strength of mind or rather of principle and character to resist the temptation...'[23]

In truth, the Prince of Wales was deeply distressed by his father's death, and he felt a strong sense of guilt. He had his defenders, however: his sister, the Crown Princess of Prussia, wrote to the Queen on his behalf, and others suggested that this had been but a 'youthful error which very few young men escape.'[24] True enough, but it was not a line likely to appeal to the Queen, who felt that the Prince's morality was even more her concern now that Prince Albert was no longer there to guide him. The Prince was truly contrite, not least for the pain he had caused his parents, he now needed time to recover and the Near East tour did much to raise his spirits, so that the Queen, meeting him on his return, found him 'immensely improved', and ready for the next step. [25]

The 'next step' was to be another meeting with the Princess. The Queen was to visit her uncle Leopold, King of the Belgians, at Laeken, and she was much moved by her first sight of her future daughter-in-law who, in deference to the Queen's mourning, wore a simple black dress. The Queen gave her a sprig of white heather from Balmoral which had been picked by the Prince. It was a scene of tremulous emotion: '...the dear child looked so affectionate and kindly at me,' the Queen recorded.[26] Later, the Royal parties met in Brussels and nearly a week afterwards, back at Laeken, the Prince proposed – and was accepted, at once and without hesitation.

It was, of course, an arranged match, inasmuch as it was made with no clear expectations of mutual affection before marriage. It was highly expedient, too, for the Prince to be seen to be settled and raising a family. The Princess had been brought up in an impoverished household, and in the utmost simplicity: the step to becoming the Consort of the future King was an impressive one. The Princess's grandfather, Frederick VI, had been a patriarchal figure in Denmark; as his people were his 'family', so the importance of family life was stressed and nowhere more so than in the Yellow Palace at Copenhagen, with its unassuming façade and front door opening straight onto the pavement, where Alexandra was born on 1 December 1844. She was the second of the six children of Prince and Princess Christian. It was a happy, easy-going and affectionate family circle, not intellectual but full of high spirits; and within it the Princess grew up, unaffected and unspoilt. Even in early childhood her beauty was remarked on, and recently the Crown Princess of Prussia had written to her father the following glowing account:

'She is a good deal taller than I am' (the Crown Princess was a little more than five foot), has a lovely figure but very thin, a complexion as beautiful as possible. Very fine white regular teeth and very fine large eyes – with extremely prettily-marked eyebrows. A very fine well-shaped nose, very narrow but a little long – her whole face is very narrow, her forehead too but well shaped and not at all flat. Her voice, her walk, carriage and manner are perfect, she is one of the most ladylike and aristocratic people I ever saw.[27]

From all the reports which flowed in to the Queen, the Princess was indeed the paragon of virtue she appeared at first sight, possessing all the qualities the Queen sought in a bride for her son. Her beauty, which the Crown Princess had considered '...not really a necessity, only a pleasant ginger-bread'[28] was what immediately struck the beholder, but her kindness, warmth and charm quickly became apparent. Her father described her simply as 'a good child, not brilliant, but with a will of her own,'[29] which on the whole satisfied the Queen, who nevertheless had hoped for a young lady with 'brains' to improve the Prince's mind. She could not but agree with the father: 'very clever I don't think she is', she was to write soon after the wedding.[30]

With such a contrived match, in which the protagonists were moved to meet and to separate like puppets on strings, speculation about their true feelings for each other may be justified. It seems that the Prince, who had had little time to consider his future and for whose occupation no provision whatever had been made, and moreover was not easily going to forget the Curragh affair, was compliant and impressionable. After seeing this lovely creature in their brief time together in Belgium, he was very ready to persuade himself that he was in love, as he wrote only three days after his offer of marriage had been accepted: 'I did not think it possible to love a person so much as I love her.'[31] As for the Princess, she must have been captivated by the prospect of marriage to the most eligible bachelor in Europe – a young man with great charm and powers of attraction, and heir to a great kingdom. Simple and artless as she was, she was ready to enter matrimony with so glittering a prize. Whatever love was lacking in these early days, it is certain that they discovered much happiness in each other's company as they prepared for their wedding.

CHAPTER TWO

MARRIAGE – 1863

Engagements can be a trying time for young lovers and that of the Prince of Wales and Princess Alexandra proved no exception. There was every kind of obstacle to prevent another meeting before the wedding which had been fixed by the Queen, somewhat arbitrarily and against considerable opposition, for 10 March. The Princess' parents naturally wished to inspect their future son-in-law and, like their Danish subjects, felt slighted when they were told peremptorily by the Queen that this was not to be. Politically, it was inexpedient, for war between Denmark and Germany was imminent, but in reality the Queen did not wish to encourage closer relationships with Princess Christian's family; rather she wished to become better acquainted with Alexandra and to instruct her in her future role. She accordingly summoned her to Osborne in November, 1862 – Prince Christian was to stay only two nights, and her mother was not invited at all. It was plain that the Queen was not seeking further acquaintance with the Danish relatives, which the Princess resented. The Prince of Wales of course was absent: the Queen had sent him to join the Crown Prince and Princess of Prussia on a Mediterranean cruise, to be well out of the way.

The visit was a distinct success. The Princess and her father were met at as they landed at the pier in Osborne Bay by Princess Helena ('Lenchen') and the nine-year old Prince Leopold who, as his sister was left sitting in the carriage with a heavy cold, had to do the honours. When the Princess stepped ashore, however, all formality was forgotten. She bent down and warmly kissed the Prince, thus enslaving him for life. The Queen, with the Princesses Louise and Beatrice, met the visitors in the hall: 'At last, at 9, dear Alexandra arrived with her father, looking very lovely and well. A gleam of satisfaction for a moment shone in my heart as I led "our" future daughter upstairs to her room.'[32]

The bereaved Queen was charmed by the Princess's warmth and affection. A week after her arrival she was the subject of unstinted praise:

I can't say how I and we all love her! She is so good, so simple,
unaffected, frank, bright and cheerful yet so quiet and gentle that her
umgang (companionship) soothes me. Then how lovely... this jewel!
She is one of those sweet creatures who seem to come from the skies to
help and bless poor mortals and brighten for a time their path![33]

In her journal the Queen wrote on the same day: 'How Albert would
have doted on her and loved her!'

This visit, which ended at Windsor, was terminated by Princess
Christian insisting that her daughter should return home for her
eighteenth birthday. Chagrin was evident on both sides; in England there
was no wish to relinquish one who had 'done much to rouse the poor
dear Queen who seems dotingly fond of her',[34] and in Denmark Princess
Christian was smarting from the treatment both she and her husband
had received, which was undeniably shabby. Nevertheless, despite the
increasing tension between Denmark and Prussia, the arrangements
for the wedding continued. Yet even here a difficulty arose: the Queen
wished her son to be married as soon as possible; any unnecessary
delay only inflamed her distrust of the Prince, whom she described as
'a very unpleasant element in the house.'[35] Her feelings verged on the
pathological: she decided that the Princess' parents would have to be 'told
all', and she feared 'dear Alix is under a complete delusion.'[36] But a March
wedding would occur in Lent; in April the Queen wished to be on hand
for the birth of Princess Alice's first baby; May was voted 'unlucky' by the
Royal family and June was too far off. The Queen fell back on March
and, when objections to a Lenten wedding were raised by the Church,
she brushed them aside in her own inimitable way, replying that she was
ready to break a custom 'only in use among the higher classes',[37] adding
that 'Marriage is a solemn holy act *not* to be classed with amusements.'
Thus, on 10 March 1863, the marriage took place in St George's Chapel,
Windsor Castle.

Throughout this period, negotiations had been proceeding for the
purchase of the Sandringham estate by the Prince of Wales. The property
at this time belonged to Spencer Cowper, Lord Palmerston's stepson, but
he was to all intents and purposes an absentee landlord and the estate had
been much neglected. The price, £220,000 for the entire estate of some
7,000 acres, including five farms, was considered by many to be excessive
but Palmerston, the former arch-enemy of the Queen and the Prince
Consort, was delighted. Knowing Queen Victoria as well as he did, and
aware that she was insistent that 'Albert's plan for Bertie' should be carried

out to the letter, Palmerston was assured of a sale, and guided her towards a bad buy with great skill.

In truth, Sandringham had possessed only one distinct advantage in Prince Albert's eyes: it was sufficiently remote from the distractions and temptations of London. He did not live to discover that the delights of both the capital and Newmarket Heath came within increasingly easy reach of his son with the advent of improved rail services and the motor car. With some misgivings he had conceded that his eldest son should set up his own establishments and approved the purchase of Sandringham and the bestowal of Marlborough House on the Prince of Wales as his London home.

The Prince had accumulated during his minority some £600,000 from the revenues of the Duchy of Cornwall, and his total income from all sources was little less than £100,000 per annum. Apart from the purchase price, a further £60,000 was released from the Duchy to be spent on improving the property, and a similar sum was withdrawn for 'outfit'. For the rest of his life the Prince spared no expense so far as Sandringham was concerned, and it was not until the turn of the century that improvements could be made without dipping further into reserves.

On his first visit to Sandringham, in February, 1862, the twenty-year-old Prince must have viewed the property with mixed feelings. The asking price would not have meant much to him: the negotiations were being carried out by Sir Charles Phipps, Keeper of the Privy Purse, and by Mr White, the Queen's private solicitor who accompanied him. At Lynn, where the line then ended, he was met by Edmund Beck, the agent at Sandringham and a friend from Cambridge named Bagge, who lived in the area. This fact alone must have commended the estate to the Prince, and a further consideration was the relative proximity to Sandringham of Blankney Hall in Lincolnshire, the home of Henry Chaplin, the 'Magnifico' who, as undisputed leader of university society at Oxford, had extended his friendship to the somewhat timid Prince. Chaplin, who had inherited great wealth and an estate of 25,000 acres after his father's death, lived in the grand style as an undergraduate, hunting six days a week during terms and attending Chapel in hunting dress inadequately concealed by his surplice. It was precisely Chaplin's air of assurance and independence which appealed to the Prince, who was accommodated in his own establishment at Frewin Hall, and supervised by his Governor, who had to approve the Prince's acquaintances and entertainments. The Prince's admiration of Chaplin was to develop into a life-long friendship.

An amusing story is related about Chaplin. He was summoned before Dean Liddell, who said: 'My dear Mr Chaplin, as far as I can gather you seem to regard Christ Church as a hunting box. You are hardly ever in College, and I must request you, unless you change your habits, to vacate your rooms.'

'But, Mr Dean, what do you expect me to do?'

'Do?' replied the Dean, 'you must go in for an examination.'

'My dear Mr Dean, if only you had told me before, I should have taken the necessary steps; but when is there one?'

'In three weeks,' was the curt reply. He passed Mods with distinction.[38]

The Prince Consort had investigated over a score of properties for his son, including Newstead Abbey, the former home of Lord Byron – of whom the Queen disapproved – but he had not visited any of them. At Sandringham, the dilapidated appearance of the estate might have encouraged the young Prince to seek elsewhere had there not been a powerful cabal in his entourage ready to exert persuasion. Perhaps none was needed, for he was mindful of his mother's hostility and would have been reluctant to run counter to her wishes. The Prince's father had died less than two months previously, and the dreadful scenes in the Blue Room at Windsor Castle still haunted him. There had been his introduction to his prospective bride, Princess Alexandra; and again, the vista of independence was dangled enticingly before his eyes after a boyhood spent for the most part in stultifying seclusion.

The Hall itself had little to recommend it; standing on a wooded escarpment overlooking the Wash and built nearly 100 years previously on the site of a former house, it consisted of two oblong three-storey blocks erected back to back under a slate roof. More recently, a porch on the eastern side and a conservatory at the southern end built of an injudicious mixture of local carstone and brick had been added; both were designed by Samuel Teulon, whose work became notorious for its extreme ugliness. The western side of the house overlooked a lake. Beyond the gardens lay the estate, where the land was poor and the soil utterly exhausted. Only pine trees, bracken and rabbits flourished. It seems that the Prince really had very little choice in the matter; had his wishes been consulted other properties with prospects of better value for his money might have been more seriously considered, but the approval of the Prince Consort had been all that was needed for the exorbitant asking price to be accepted. That the rent-roll represented a mere 3 per cent of the cost mattered not at all, and the Queen was in no mood to recommence the search. In her eyes, Bertie's matrimonial future was a far more pressing concern.

That negotiations were already in an advanced state is apparent from the fact that the purchase was completed by the end of February 1862, when the Prince was absent on his tour of the Near East. At the beginning of September he was at Sandringham with instructions for the improvement of his property. Park House was built near the little church for Sir William Knollys, the Comptroller of the Prince's Household in succession to General Bruce, his former Governor, who had died soon after returning from the tour. Later, in 1961, it was the birthplace of Diana, Princess of Wales. A large, rambling house in its own grounds it had been leased to the 4th Baron Fermoy, the Princess' grandfather, by King George V. There was a further Royal connection: Lord Fermoy's wife, Ruth, was a Woman of the Bedchamber and one of the inner circle around Queen Elizabeth the Queen Mother. Later still, the house became a hotel for disabled ex-servicemen.

Additional stabling at Sandringham was designed by the architect, Mr Humbert, who had previously been approved by the Prince Consort for some of his own schemes, including the rebuilding of Whippingham Church, near Osborne. A week later, the Prince of Wales proposed to Princess Alexandra and soon afterwards he was back at Sandringham directing Mr Humbert with a new intensity, for by now things were falling into place; there was a bride for the home that was to be his personal property, and as such it possessed a charm never attained by Marlborough House.

The wedding duly took place on 10 March at Windsor. The bride was attended by 'eight as ugly girls as anyone could wish for' and perhaps the singing so soon after his death of a chorale composed by Prince Albert was unwise, for the Queen and her entire family wept openly. A reception was held at the castle, the Queen, unready to join the large throng, noted, 'I dined alone'. Arrangements for the return of the guests to London were defective: the trains were overcrowded; Disraeli, the Prime Minister, was glad to sit on his wife's lap. Afterwards, the Prince and his bride spent a week at Osborne, where they were visited by the Crown Princess of Prussia. She wrote to the Queen:

> It does one good to see people so thoroughly happy as this dear young couple are. As for Bertie, he looks blissful. I never saw such a change, his whole face looks beaming and radiant... Darling Alix looks charming and lovely and they both seem so comfortable and at home together.[39]

Leaving Osborne, the Prince and Princess stopped briefly in London to call on Alix's parents before moving to Sandringham, the home that they both grew to love and to which Alix was to withdraw for the last years of her life.

They found the house habitable, though smelling of plaster and paint, for walls had been knocked out to enlarge some of the rooms. Elsewhere, on the estate, cottages were being improved, farm buildings restored and roads were under construction. Phipps, the Keeper of the Privy Purse, wrote to Knollys complaining of the increasing expense of Sandringham. The Prince, he declared, displayed 'a Royal impetuosity in expecting improvements to be carried out at once.'[40] Though the Princess was delighted with her new home, and might revel with unaffected simplicity in the rural delights of Norfolk, where everything that was their own could only please the eye, others were not so happy. Lady Macclesfield wrote bitterly that there were:

> ...no fine trees, no water, no hills, in fact no attraction of any sort... It would be difficult to find a more ugly or depressing place... The wind blows keen from the Wash and the Spring is said to be unendurable in that part of Norfolk. It is, of course, a wretched hunting country... As there was all England to choose from I do wish they had had a finer house in a more picturesque and cheerful situation.[41]

Queen Victoria naturally remained aloof from all opinions but there must be some doubt whether, in the event, Prince Albert would have wished to proceed with the purchase of such a run-down property at such enormous expense. But he had never inspected the estate; Lord Palmerston's recommendation and its remoteness from the temptations of London had been sufficient to induce him to give instructions for the purchase. The Prince Consort had spent wisely and carefully on the Royal estates at Osborne and Balmoral, and had laboured to invest the income from his eldest son's Duchy of Cornwall shrewdly, at the same time increasing the income itself from £16,000 to £60,000 per annum. But the Queen was in no fit state to seek further guidance so soon after the Prince Consort's death: she believed that her brain was being taxed to the limits of endurance. When faced with a difficulty or opposition, she would tap her forehead meaningly, murmuring, 'My reason, my reason!'[42] She was convinced that she was constantly overburdened with work; even twenty years later she was to write: 'If she had not comparative rest and quiet in the evening she would most likely not be alive.'[43] Ironically, having encouraged the purchase of Sandringham, she thought the house 'unlucky', and only visited it twice. Guests have from time to time shared Lady Macclesfield's views: Diana, Princess of Wales, as a child disliked visiting the house, while James Pope-Hennessey thought it 'exposed, depressing and unrelievedly ugly.' The first visit of the 'Waleses', as they became known, was a distinct success, unmarred by any mishaps, though the previous December, during a rabbit-shoot, a local newspaper reporter, sneaking in disguised as a beater, was nearly shot in the leg by the Prince. The Royal couple were given a warm reception by the local residents, with the Hunt in their scarlet coats and children with flowers and flags. One of the earliest guests was Dean Stanley, who explained the English Communion service to the Princess in the Drawing Room. 'She was most simple and fascinating,' he wrote, 'so winning and graceful, and yet so fresh and free and full of life.'[44] A small dance was held, and the custom of the afternoon walk to view improvements and alterations began; there was always something new to be seen, and it became a tradition continued years later by King George V after Sandringham passed into his hands. The Royal couple actively hunted and on occasion the Meet was held at the Hall, with breakfast in the house before drawing the coverts on the estate.

The Prince's land to the west was unsuitable for hunting, comprising acres of pine trees and bracken hiding a network of rabbit warrens and sloping down to the salt-marshes and tidal creeks beyond Wolferton where it merged almost imperceptibly into the Wash. Here were pheasant, snipe and woodcock, whose erratic flight proved an irresistible attraction for King George V. The marshes and pools were the habitat of the wild duck which became the object of a studied approach by King George VI. The remaining three sides of the estate consisted of flattish, open farmland around Dersingham, Anmer and West Newton, leading to more undulating country before sloping down to the sea at Brancaster, where the dunes reach out towards the sandbanks off the coast. Pheasants lurked in the plantations and coverts, partridges roamed the open ground and hedgerows and, whilst hunting was an attraction, especially in those early days, Sandringham became famous for the shooting: in the season 1899–1900 over 12,000 birds were shot on the estate.

It had early been made public that the Prince had purchased Sandringham for the shooting, and this was to become the focal point of entertainment at Sandringham. Almost every other consideration was subordinated to this: copses, coverts and plantations were cleared and reset for the rearing of game birds: no expense was too great. In other matters the Prince played the part of the benevolent country squire, and improvements to his tenants' accommodation ran away with vast sums of money. With Marlborough House, the Prince's London residence, also to be included in the reckoning of his entertainment, it was small wonder that he was reported to be exceeding his income by £20,000 per annum within a few years of taking the estate in hand.

In October 1863, the Prince and Princess held their first large house party. After following the Queen to her customary retreat at Balmoral, they returned to Norfolk to await the arrival of the 'special' at Wolferton Station, whither the line from Lynn had only recently been completed. The Princess's parents and her sister Princess Dagmar were invited with other guests, including Lord Granville and the Duke of St Albans. Another custom was established that year: the celebration of the Prince's birthday on 9 November. It was to become one of the highlights of the Sandringham year, centred on one of the best shoots – the 'Horseshoe'. The Queen, who had followed the first year of her son's marriage with some anxiety, was relieved to hear from Lord Granville that life at Sandringham resembled that at Balmoral in Prince Albert's time: 'I naturally rejoice truly to hear this,' she commented, '...and the country has looked and longed to see you both follow that course with great anxiety and how they will rejoice to see that realised! Let us hope that in serious subjects such as reading this will gradually follow. This letter is meant for beloved Alix too naturally.'[45] Alas, her hopes in this respect were not to be fulfilled. The Princess had beauty, she had intuition and sympathy and charm, but she was not intellectually gifted. Neither of the young couple ever enjoyed reading as a pastime and it is more likely that Lord Granville's report was based more on what he knew the Queen would like to read, than on a strict regard for accuracy. The Queen's anxiety about them had not been ill-founded; the ceaseless round of engagements during their life in London had attracted her attention, and it was then that she began to discover other defects in her daughter-in-law. 'She never does anything but write,' complained the Queen. 'She never reads' and 'I fear the learning has been much neglected and she cannot either write or I fear speak French well.'[46] She remarked too on the affliction which was to have so significant an effect on Alix's later life: 'Alas, she is deaf and everyone observes it, which is a sad misfortune.'[47] So it was to prove; her husband was a natural philanderer with a low boredom threshold and he was powerfully attracted to beautiful, intelligent and amusing women for the entertainment and companionship which his wife, increasingly, was unable to provide. Over the years she was to retreat from the lively and brilliant social scene which she had so much enjoyed and seek a solitary life at Sandringham, where her increasing deafness was less of a handicap, within her own loyal household.

It was not quite a coincidence that the new railway line from Lynn to Hunstanton was opened almost simultaneously with the purchase of

Sandringham by the Prince of Wales, but it was none the less an agreeable addition to the amenities of the estate. The great age of steam had become firmly established by the time of the Prince's birth and, during his early years, a network of railways was spreading out across the quiet English countryside. In 1856, a railway from Lynn to the rapidly developing resort of New Hunstanton was projected: Cromer had been fashionable since the beginning of the century; the land was flat, though subject to tidal inundation, and the work, once started, was completed in a year. The first train ran on 3 October 1862, some seven months after the Prince of Wales had alighted at Lynn to view Sandringham Hall. When he brought his bride to Sandringham in April 1863, the couple were able to travel on to the simple halt at Wolferton, little more than a mile down the hill from the Hall.

For some years the Royal family had been enthusiastic rail travellers. The train was far quicker, and cheaper, than by horse and carriage, with its halts for changes of horses. Rail was already safe and dependable. Queen Victoria plied regularly between London, Windsor, Gosport (change for Osborne House) and Ballater (for Balmoral). The advent of the railways changed not only her lifestyle and habits, but also those of nearly everyone else. Families could now venture further from their homes in the course of a day than many of their forebears had done in a lifetime; the expanding middle class could afford the seaside holidays which had their origin in the approval given to sea-bathing by King George III's physician, who declared it healthy and beneficial to the system. The Prince Regent had patronised Brighton, formerly the little village of Brightelmstone, by building his oriental Pavilion there; and now the remote coast beyond the Fens had become accessible.

For the Prince of Wales the railway from Sandringham, which now linked at Lynn with the main line to London, provided inestimable benefits. His own restless nature found satisfaction in the ease with which he could enjoy the attractions of the capital. It was possible for him to break his holiday in Norfolk, travel to London for an engagement and return to Sandringham the following day without the least fatigue. Moreover, guests could come and go with ease; large house-parties gathered and dispersed twice a week with their hordes of servants and mountains of baggage in a way which would not have been possible before the advent of the train. A special train could be hired for about 5s a mile – not an exorbitant expense – and at short notice. The journey took 2½ hours.

For many years this small line ran profitably. In due course it became absorbed into the Great Eastern Railway, and the facilities at Wolferton were improved. On the London-bound side new buildings were erected in 1876. They were not elaborate: it was not the prince's habit to wait for trains. The opposite, or 'Down', side became a subject for some controversy. The line was doubled in 1898 and the Great Eastern Board decided, with some reluctance, to spend £8,000 on the building of a suite of Royal waiting rooms. It was a wise decision, for the Midland and Great Northern Line ran on the other side of the estate and would have been glad to attract the Prince's patronage.

The need for Royal waiting rooms on the Down side perhaps needs some explanation. If the Prince or Princess were arriving, they would not have been likely to spend time in the waiting room with members of their own Household before driving to Sandringham. Their main function, therefore, was to provide suitable accommodation for the reception and entertainment of Royal, and often related, visitors. After the initial greetings on the platform, the Royal party would pass into the small hall, the ladies and gentlemen retiring to their separate suites to left and right. In fine weather tea was sometimes served in a private garden. The room used by the Prince and, later, by him as King Edward VII, was furnished in a manly style, with a settle covered in red leather round the fireplace. There was a table with decanters, and suitable lavatory accommodation installed in an adjoining room which, with the rest of this area, was panelled. The door fittings were gold-plated and the glass in the windows was frosted to deter the curious.

On the right of the hall was the Princess' room, decorated in her favourite shade of blue. Here she entertained Queens and Empresses with tea and conversation. During this interlude servants had been busy piling luggage into wagons to be taken to the house and unpacked to be ready for the arrival of the Royal visitors. When all had been completed the two parties merged again to enter their carriages in the station approach where, on special occasions, a guard of honour from the Norfolk Yeomanry were drawn up. There were outriders and postillions, and the whole cavalcade swept up the hill towards the gates of the Hall.

The scale of the welcome accorded to visiting Royalty could vary considerably. The Prince of Wales was a thoughtful host and nothing was omitted which could reasonably be expected. Queen Victoria's first visit to her son's home reflected an air of terrible urgency. She was met by Prince Alfred and two gentlemen from the Prince's household, who wasted no time in escorting her up to the house, where her husband was fighting for his life.

The Queen's second visit afforded the Prince an opportunity of welcoming his mother in a more fitting style (for which he had been waiting, one suspects, these twenty-five years). This was the occasion of the engagement of Princess Louise of Wales to the Earl of Fife in 1889. The Prince was at the station to welcome the Queen; tubs of flowers and a red carpet brightened the platform. A large crowd had gathered and the Hunt was present to provide a splash of colour with their red coats, together with crowds of people on foot, on horseback and in carriages. Even though Queen Victoria never paid another visit to Sandringham, she was gratified by this demonstration of affection and respect by her son.

CHAPTER THREE

CHILDREN

There were some inconsistencies in Queen Victoria's hopes and fears. Since her mother's death in 1861 she had been in mourning, and then became inconsolable after the Prince Consort's death nine months later. She had suffered the shock of her eldest son's escapade at the Curragh and of a similar incident involving her second son, Prince Alfred, when he was stationed with the fleet in Malta. She felt desperately alone. Yet, since she had withdrawn from public life the Prince had not only undertaken duties on her behalf but had also become, for lack of other employment, the acknowledged leader of Society – that Society which the Queen had always disapproved of as 'shallow, idle and frivolous.' Their sole aims in life, she declared, were pleasure-seeking and dissipation. The Prince defended himself and his 'set' as strongly as he could:

> With regard to what you say about the Aristocracy... I quite agree that in many instances amusement and self-indulgence, etc predominate, but it is hard to say that all are so. I know of so many instances where those of the highest rank are excellent country gentlemen – are Chairmen of Quarter Sessions, Magistrates, etc, and the ladies attend to their duties also.[48]

The pre-eminence of the Prince and Princess in London society was a foregone conclusion and they were whirled into a ceaseless round of glittering engagements, centred on Marlborough House. The gossip columns reported carriages queuing for a mile to discharge their passengers, of dancing well into the small hours and entertainment on a lavish scale. 'Bertie and Alix left Frogmore today,' wrote the troubled Queen, 'both looking as ill as possible. We are all seriously alarmed about her. For although Bertie says he is so anxious to take care of her, he goes on going out every night till she will become a skeleton, and hopes there cannot be.'[49] 'Hopes' this time revolved around an heir.

Much as the Queen deplored the pace that Bertie set – and Alix so willingly followed – she was reluctant to find any serious employment for her successor on the throne, a problem that only until recently remained unsolved. A year after his marriage she wrote to her cousin, the Duke of Cambridge★: 'I entirely agree with your wishing Bertie to take an interest in the Army and to get him to feel that life is not merely for amusement.' She hoped that 'he could be made to work and be found fault with if he made mistakes.' He could be under the command of the general commanding at Aldershot and learn to command a brigade. She was adamant that he should not in any way be put on the same footing 'as his beloved great Father was or I am... Bertie should never be put more forward than is necessary.'[50] In her case, the Queen had serious reservations about Bertie's lack of discretion, and he was never to be given access to confidential papers. When an attempt was made to harness his energies by giving him an insight into the Foreign Office, Lord Clarendon noticed that a confidential memorandum had been seen circulating at the dinner table. He saw the solution to the problem as 'most difficult' and noted that the Prince's interest in the affairs of a House of Lords Committee lasted no more than a day. There was certainly an element of jealousy in the Queen's decision to deny him a position of responsibility, yet she deplored his seemingly useless existence. In 1871, Colonel Ponsonby, the Queen's Private Secretary, noted: 'Quite right to let H.R.H. know what is going on – but as the direction of affairs is not in his hands it does not appear to be necessary to submit confidential drafts for his consideration before they take effect.' His restless nature and need for occupation in the absence of intellectual interests ensured for him the leisure in which to indulge his highly developed capacity for enjoyment. Ponsonby wrote of the Prince: 'Nothing can be more genial and pleasant than he is for a few minutes. But he does not endure. He cannot keep up the interest for any length of time and I don't think he will ever settle down to business.'[51] Mr Gladstone commented: 'What we want is not to supply him (the Prince) with the means of filling a certain number of hours: we should seek to give him a central aim and purpose which may... gradually mould his mind and colour his life.'[52] The situation was aggravated by his abundant natural energy; his worst enemy was boredom and his mind, untrammelled by few serious considerations, was taxed only by the need to find constant occupation. As King, though, when his Secretary sometimes had difficulty in diverting him from social commitments and getting him to attend to State affairs, after some initial reluctance he would look up with his charming smile and say, 'Yes, I see this is important,' draw up his chair and give the matter his full attention. His abilities should never be underestimated; he put his charm

★ HRH The Duke of Cambridge was also Commander-in-Chief of the British Army.

to good use when his influence helped to establish the *entente cordiale* with France – his love of Paris and all its attractions, his fondness of the company of beautiful and intelligent women, his readiness to be amused all ensured that he was a familiar and welcome figure.

But 'hopes' there were, despite the Queen's pessimism; the Princess was pregnant, a condition that gave her little discomfort. The Crown Princess of Prussia visiting Sandringham that winter of 1863, wrote:

> This seems a charming place so quiet and country-like, and a delightful house furnished with great taste and comfort. Bertie and Alix seem to like it very much and to be very happy and comfortable. Dear Alix seems very thin but looking well; she shows her condition very little though her figure is much changed already – she seems perfectly well, has not an ailment of any kind or sort to complain of and has a very fresh colour.[53]

The Princess continued in good health and spirits and subordinated her pregnancy to her pleasure. On 6 January 1864, in very cold weather, while spending Christmas at Frogmore in the Home Park at Windsor, she went out to watch the skating on Virginia Water, despite some warnings of incipient labour. She returned home and there gave birth, two months prematurely, to Prince Albert Victor.

The Queen was much distressed at the manner of the small Prince's arrival into the world. He weighed only 3¾lbs, and his grandmother complained that nothing had been made ready. The layette was described: 'A basket (contents wanting)'. The child's names she had arranged herself. The parents were not unnaturally upset: 'I felt rather annoyed when told that you had settled what our little boy was to be called before I had spoken to you about it'.[54] Her interference went further: she wished her uncle, the King of the Belgians, 'to speak strongly and frighten Bertie… to make him understand what a strong right I have to interfere in the management of the child…and that he should never do anything about (him) without consulting me.'[55]

Some years later Queen Victoria's 'interference' took a practical turn when she refused to allow the Prince and Princess to take the little Princess Louise with them to spend Christmas in Denmark. She had reluctantly allowed the two young Princes to travel but argued that it was selfish of the parents to risk the health of Louise. The Prince of Wales wrote to the Queen in strong terms:

> I regret very much that you should still oppose our wishes but as you throw responsibility entirely on Alix if we take Louise, I naturally shall share it and have not the slightest hesitation or fear in doing so… her whole

life is wrapt up in her children – and it seems hard that because she wishes (with a natural mother's pride) to take her eldest children with her to her parents' home every difficulty should be thrown in her way, and enough to mar the prospect, and when Vicky and Alice come here nearly every year with their children... it seems rather inconsistent not to accord to the one what is accorded to the others.[56]

If the Queen had not previously perceived her lack of logic in the matter of her grandchildren's travel, she could not fail to do so in the face of this frontal attack. She capitulated, contenting herself with finding fault with the composition of the suite accompanying the Prince and Princess. So, in December 1868, whilst Sandringham was being rebuilt, the Royal couple with their three eldest children set off for Denmark.

The family of the Prince and Princess of Wales increased with the birth of Prince George on 3 June 1865 – like his elder brother, somewhat before his time – and once again Queen Victoria missed the event. 'It seems that it is not to be that I am to be present at the birth of your children,' she wrote fretfully to the parents.'[57] Whilst she was delighted that the succession was thus made doubly sure (and how fortunate that was), she was about to enter a period of contention with the Princess, who was recovering from her confinement and, at the same time, undergoing considerable personal stress. Princess Alexandra was fiercely loyal to her native Denmark and was deeply disturbed by the misfortunes of some of her relatives who had been dispossessed of their lands by the annexation of the provinces of Schleswig and Holstein by Prussia. The Queen could sympathise with her but, with her own Germanic antecedents and with her eldest daughter now the Crown Princess of Prussia, her loyalties must at least have been divided. A possible coolness at this time in their relations was exacerbated by the Queen's criticism of her grandchildren's upbringing, stemming from her daughter-in-law's independence of mind. The Queen, mindful of 'her right to interfere' complained to the Crown Princess: 'Alix and I never will or can become intimate: she shows me no confidence whatever especially about the children.'[58] She may well have felt slighted; after all, with nine children living and the youngest only eight years old, the Queen could claim to be expert in these matters, and might reasonably have expected to be consulted. When Prince George was nearly eighteen months old, the Crown Princess wrote to her mother suggesting that she should give more time to seeing Alix:

I know Alix has the greatest wish to be now and then alone with you. She says she is not amusing, she knows, and she fears she bores you, but she loves you so much, and it seems to be a little ambition of hers to be alone with you sometimes. It was Bertie who told me this and it quite touched me.[59]

It was an appeal which could not fail to touch the Queen's warm heart also, and the Crown Princess' advice was at once acted upon and proved sound. 'I have taken a nice walk and drive with dear Alex and nothing could be nicer or dearer than she is,' she wrote from Windsor. 'It is quite charming to see her and hear her. She looks delicate. I do love her dearly.'[60] For the moment the 'fast' life which the Princess led, which so worried the Queen, was forgotten.

Some months later the Princess returned to Marlborough House feeling unwell following a visit to Sandringham. She complained of pains and a chill, and was clearly no better when the Prince, who had been to Russia to attend the wedding of his sister-in-law, Princess Dagmar, joined her in London. He left almost at once to attend a steeplechase and a dinner, returning home the next day to find the Princess in great pain and suffering from rheumatic fever. A few days later, and still in frightful pain, she gave birth to her first daughter, Princess Louise, without anaesthetic, since this relief was judged to be unwise in view of her illness.

The Princess was exhausted and her condition gave the Queen great anxiety when she visited Marlborough House a week after the baby's birth. The Prince, perhaps encouraged by the optimistic reports from the doctors, took his wife's illness lightly. Never good in a sickroom and oppressed by inactivity, he shut his eyes to what he did not wish to see. His inattentiveness towards the Princess was much resented by Lady Macclesfield:

> The Princess had another bad night, chiefly owing to the Prince promising to come in at 1.0 a.m. and keeping her in a perpetual fret, refusing to take her opiate for fear she should be asleep when he came! And he never came until 3.0 a.m. I hear nothing but general indignation at his indifference to her and his devotion to his own amusements.[61]

Certainly the Prince at this juncture shows up in a bad light. Easily bored, he still played no part in the affairs of State, the Queen distrusting his discretion. He seemed doomed to a life of idleness, although this was exactly what the Queen explicitly deplored.

The illness ran its course and it was not until the summer that the Princess was well, but the fever left her with a stiff knee for the rest of her life. She bore the handicap with great gallantry, often referring to it lightly and refusing to allow it to hinder her activities. Her saddle was changed for riding and she continued to dance and skate: the 'Alexandra limp' was instantly copied in fashionable circles. There were other difficulties; the Prince had dallied with well-known beauties whilst on his travels, though it is impossible to say how much his wife knew about his infidelities. What was known throughout the country, however, was that her husband had not chosen to remain with her during her illness but had sought his own pleasure; it was a humiliating thought. The Prince continued to find entertainment within a very fast set: on one occasion he and his companions loosed a carted deer in Harrow, chasing it through Wormwood Scrubs before the kill in the goods yard at Paddington Station. His evening amusements included visits to pleasure gardens in Chelsea; an elderly lady, whose grandfather had kept an all-night stall by Vauxhall Bridge, related that the Prince used to stop his hansom cab to buy a hot potato, usually in the very small hours.

There was yet another difficulty for the troubled Princess: her hearing, which had always been defective, deteriorated further as a result of her illness and tended to isolate her from the company which so often surrounded her. The louder people talked to her, the greater their embarrassment, especially in public, so that they tried to avoid such encounters. The Princess, straining to hear, might misunderstand what was being said and, conscious of the difficulties which might ensue, tended more and more to withdraw into her own silent world. She hated using an ear-trumpet, in those days the only aid for the deaf. For the rest of her life she was afflicted by noises in her head, causing additional stress. Princess May of Teck was perceptive enough to understand the consequences of deafness, especially to the First Lady in Society, since the Queen had withdrawn from public life. 'It makes me quite sad and she looks so pathetic sometimes, trying to hear what we are saying and laughing about,' she wrote.[62] The Princess was quick to appreciate such thoughtfulness: 'Whenever I am not quite *au fait* on account of my beastly ears you always by a word or even by a turn towards me make me understand – for which I am most grateful as nobody can know what I have to go through.'[63] She developed a trick, when there was a burst of laughter at mealtimes, of waving and smiling to indicate that she had heard and was amused.

The Princess did not greatly value intellectual achievements, as did Princess May, and we know that she did not care for reading. Rather, she retained a childlike simplicity: perhaps her deafness caused her to fall back on that which was familiar and secure. Lord Esher, though, gave her credit for much more: 'Her cleverness has always been under-rated, partly because of her deafness,' he wrote; 'in point of fact she says more original things and has more unexpected ideas than any other member of the family.'[64]

Gradually, the pleasures of a fashionable, social life began to wear thin as the Princess found herself increasingly unable to play a full part in her husband's activities. She surrounded herself with her horses and dogs and a strange menagerie of animals at Sandringham. Her devotion to her children was almost suffocatingly affectionate. In the circumstances it was natural that her country home increasingly became the focus for her interests.

The Princess' illness caused her husband to review the situation at Sandringham. The house had long been thought damp and Norfolk winters can be harsh. Sir James Paget, surgeon to the Princess, had thought the rheumatic fever was caused by dampness, and there was no alternative but to rebuild. Although, as we have seen, £60,000 had been earmarked for alterations and improvements, the entire property had been very much neglected and the money spent on the house had shown little return. After only four years, the Prince decided that the old Hall was to be demolished to make way for an altogether more substantial residence.

The architect he retained was A.J. Humbert, whom he already knew through the work he had carried out on Whippingham Church, on the edge of Queen Victoria's estate at Osborne. A number of designs for the new house were submitted and the demolition of the old house began early in 1868 after the family had spent Christmas at Park House. The Prince then rented Houghton Hall, a splendid mansion in the district, until the new house was ready for occupation, if not entirely completed, for the Prince's birthday on 9 November 1870. It was, reported the Duke of Cambridge, a great improvement on the old house; certainly different as it 'seems quite dry'. If the Victorian, Elizabethan style with a trace of Dutch influence was not wholly successful, it was because Humbert's original design, broadly a copy of Blickling Hall in Norfolk, was compromised by the Prince's wish to incorporate the traditional gables and bays of the old house. It was perhaps nobody's fault that its appearance became inextricably linked with large Victorian hotels and railway stations. Almost inevitably, it proved too small. Such was the Prince's hospitality that, whenever the family were in residence, the house was nearly always full. Guests usually brought their own personal servants, valet and lady's maid, with them, and these too had to be accommodated. In an attempt to make room for them all, the Prince built the 'Bachelors' Cottage' a little to the south of the house but, as time went on, this simply would not do. After Sir William Knollys' death, Park House was used as additional accommodation for guests and the Prince's household.

Humbert died in 1877, at the age of forty-five, to be succeeded as the Prince's architect by Colonel R.W. Edis, who designed the ballroom at Sandringham, completed in 1884, and the wings at the south end of the house. The dark-red brickwork contrasts with the lighter tone of Humbert's design, but the Prince wished the new building to blend with Teulon's conservatory which forms the dividing line between the two. Perhaps it was not a happy decision; the adjacent structures could never blend in to a single entity. It has been claimed that Edis was not a qualified architect; in fact, he became known as the builder of the Inner Temple Library, was President of the Architects' Association, knighted and appointed Deputy Lieutenant for Norfolk.

The family of the Prince and Princess of Wales continued to increase with the arrival of Princess Victoria and Princess Maud at intervals of some eighteen months. The youngest child was Prince Alexander John, who lived only one day, to the deep distress of his parents, and was buried in the churchyard at Sandringham.

The upbringing of the Royal children was so markedly different from that of the offspring of Queen Victoria and Prince Albert that it was almost bound to meet with the disapproval of their grandmother. 'They are such ill-bred, ill-trained children I can't fancy them at all,' she wrote indignantly in 1872.[65] Guests at Sandringham had mixed views; those who subscribed to the dictum that children should be seen but not heard could only observe with astonishment the freedom with which they mingled with the grown-ups. Whilst Queen Victoria overtly criticised the 'Wales' children, and Lady Geraldine Somerset could describe them as 'wild as hawks' and 'rampaging little girls'[66], others, who perhaps had the opportunity of becoming more closely acquainted, saw them as devoted to each other and to their parents, and Princess Louise, the eldest, was reported on diversely as 'very sharp, quick, merry and amusing' and 'devoid of looks and charm.'[67] The two Princes were fortunate in having a 'nursery attendant' who was devoted to their welfare. Charles Fuller accompanied them wherever they went and until his death in 1901 was a faithful correspondent with Prince George.

That they were a closely-knit family cannot be doubted. Their mother adored them almost to suffocation: whilst she never seemed completely to grow up, her children were simple and unaffected, but in some respects appeared to languish in a childhood world. Princess Louise celebrated her nineteenth birthday with a children's party. Queen Marie of Rumania noted that they seemed to 'express themselves in a minor key'; one gained the impression from their conversation that 'Life would have been very wonderful and everything very beautiful if it had not been so bad.'[68] All those in the immediate family circle were referred to as 'dear'; outside it everyone was 'poor'. Their nicknames were 'Toots, Gawks and Snipey'. Princess Maud, also known in family circles as 'Harry', was something of a tomboy, larding her speech with schoolboy slang culled from an unknown source. High spirits and practical jokes were part and parcel of Sandringham life. Prince George, writing to his mother years after the event, recalled how they squirted each other with soda-water siphons; a visitor at the Sandringham dinner table described how he felt his leg being pinched by a small plump hand and, peering under the table, discovered the laughing face of one of the Princesses. A young midshipman visiting Sandringham was given a mince pie filled with mustard to eat: shrieks of laughter greeted his discomfiture. There was sliding downstairs on teatrays and high jinks in which the Princess of Wales joined as merrily as anyone. After all, just such frivolous amusements had been a matter of course at her home in Denmark.

This freedom and informality, so far from the traditional rules of decorum, was not favoured by the Queen. She deplored the lack of routine and system in the lives of her grandchildren, and some of her reluctance to let the Princess of Wales travel abroad with her children may be traced to this. On one issue, however, she could agree with her daughter-in-law: 'that is,' she wrote, 'great simplicity and an absence of all pride, and in that respect she has my fullest support.'[69]

The lifestyles of the Queen and the family of her eldest son were diametrically opposed. The Queen had retired into a seclusion that at times was almost complete: she felt absolutely unable to perform public duties, to the extent that there were calls for her abdication; such was the people's view of a monarch who was never seen to fulfil her office. Conversely, the Prince and Princess of Wales lived an admittedly hectic social life; though the Prince suffered waves of unpopularity whenever scandals surfaced, they were to some degree mitigated by the simple and unaffected admiration of the general public for the Princess. Her calm, her poise and serenity in the face of adversity in her domestic life excited enormous sympathy. The presence of the heir to the throne on important occasions avoided by the Queen showed the public that the dynasty was very much alive and possessed an unequivocal ability to enjoy itself which warmed their hearts. It was seldom that the Prince remained long in the country's 'bad books'. His easy, affable charm and friendly nature, and his constant need for occupation and entertainment ensured continuing public interest. Today, the Press would have described him as 'colourful'. It was, largely, a happy family; the children adored 'Motherdear' and found the comfortable affection of their father irresistible. The Prince was not lightly to be crossed – he had an explosive temper and his angry bellow could be heard through the house – and it is possible to give credence to the apocryphal tale that George V once said: 'I was afraid of my father.' It is more likely that the languid, indolent Prince

Eddy, in almost every respect the reverse of his restless, energetic father, felt an awe bordering on fear, contributing to a sense of inferiority which time did nothing to diminish.

These children, who were very much part of the family scene, spent much of their time at Sandringham, where the boys' tutor, the Revd John Dalton, tried to improve their minds. In 1874, when the Princes were nine and ten, he wrote to Queen Victoria:

> They are living a very regular and quiet life in the country at Sandringham, and keeping early hours, both as to rising in the morning and retiring to rest at night; they ride on ponies an hour each alternate morning, and take a walk the other three days in the week; in the afternoon they take exercise on foot; while as regards their studies, writing reading and arithmetic are all progressing favourably; music, spelling, English History, Latin, Geography and French all occupy a due share of Their Royal Highness' attention, progress in English History and Geography being very marked.[70]

We may well believe that Mr Dalton was writing in his most diplomatic vein, and that probably the parents were not at that time in residence at Sandringham. Had they been, there would almost certainly have been disruptions in their studies at any time when they were needed by their mother, who could be impulsive and capricious in her demands on her children. There was by no means always the regularity in their routine that Mr Dalton described. Contrary to expectations, though, the Princess of Wales took a surprisingly realistic view of her children's education. Brought up herself in a close, impoverished family in Copenhagen, she took a carefully calculated look at what she wished for her own. Writing to Mr Dalton in April, 1877, she stressed what seemed to her most important, aside from any possible academic considerations, in the boys' upbringing:

> One thing I must ask you, especially now I am away, to pay great attention to their being obedient and obeying the moment they are told. Also let them be civil to everybody, high and low, and not get grand now they are by themselves, and please take particular care they are not toadied by the keepers or any of those around them.[71]

In November of the same year, she wrote with perceptible self-reproach: 'I cannot help thinking that under these circumstances it is most inadvisable that they should have all these extra treats and excitements which you always used to tell me at home disturbed their minds for the next day.'[72]

Mr Dalton was nothing if not a conscientious tutor – mindful of the responsibility attached to his task of educating the sons of the future King, he took his duties seriously. The routine he imposed upon his pupils was not so very far removed from that of Mr Gibbs but its effect on the young Princes differed, in that the parents were good-natured and affectionate; there was less of the anxiety which had informed the decisions of the Queen and Prince Albert and led to such inflexibility. Even so, in Mr Dalton's *Journal of Weekly Work*, Prince George, there are echoes of the schoolroom of the previous generation.

Week ending 2 September 1876: 'Prince G. this week has been much troubled by silly fretfulness of temper and general spirit of contradiction.'

23 September: 'Prince George has been good this week. He shows however too much disposition to find fault with his brother.'

14 October: 'Too fretful; and inclined to be lazy and silly this week.'

As the weeks passed, further comments emphasised the 'self-approbation... which was almost the only motive power in him.'

The timetable itself would seem daunting enough for today's ten and eleven-year olds. The Princes:

> ...would rise at seven and prepare their Geography and English before breakfast. At eight came a Bible or History lesson, followed by Algebra or Euclid at nine. There then ensued an hour's break for games and thereafter a French or Latin lesson until the main meal, which took place at two. The afternoon was occupied by riding or playing cricket and after tea would come English lessons, music and preparation. The two Princes were put to bed at eight.

Happily there were no signs of the nervous and mental exhaustion which had reduced the Prince of Wales to passionate screaming. There is nothing in these reports which might have caused alarm: they read like those of many a spirited schoolboy who is testing his surroundings. Indeed, Mr Dalton, writing some years later, found himself missing the liveliness of his charge and wrote to Prince George, then serving on HMS *Canada*: 'We miss your voice so at meals: they all sit round the table and eat and never say a syllable. I never knew such a lot... Oh, dear!'[72]

The two Princes were remarkably dissimilar: Prince Albert Victor, born in a hurry after that skating party on the ice at Virginia Water, and two months before his time, was a quiet, delicate-looking child. 'Very backward,' Queen Victoria commented, 'though a dear good little thing... I can't help being anxious about it.'[72] He continued to cause a good deal of anxiety in one way or another throughout his life. Prince George, though again a premature baby, seemed cast in a different mould: he was a sturdy, healthy and lively little boy, described as a 'jolly little pickle', and was as high-spirited as Prince Eddy, was as apathetic and backward. There was as much quarrelling as might be expected between two brothers born only eighteen months apart, and their mother wrote to Mr Dalton asking him to put a stop to their bickering and strong language, and to their habit of interrupting conversations.

When Prince George was twelve, there arose inevitably the question of the next stage of the Princes' education. Queen Victoria favoured Wellington College, for the Prince Consort had been deeply involved in this memorial to the late Duke. Mr Dalton had reservations about this plan: Prince Eddy would find himself among boys who were academically ahead of him, and his attention could not be brought to bear sufficiently ever for him to have a chance of catching up, 'his mind being in an abnormally dormant condition'.[73] The Prince of Wales more prudently opted for the Navy, which offered a practical bias to the cadets' education. For a while it seemed that neither of these alternatives would come into effect, for Prince Eddy caught typhoid; but he recovered and went on to join Prince George on board HMS *Britannia*, the old wooden training ship, at Dartmouth. There, the Princes found themselves being treated much the same as the other 200-odd cadets, except that they slung their hammocks in a small space some 12ft square behind a bulkhead and were attended by a footman from Sandringham and accompanied by Mr Dalton, who dined with the captain. Where the footman dined is unfortunately not recorded. The cadets' food was atrocious. The Princess of Wales, unpractical but mindful of domestic happiness, ordered pictures of Sandringham and family photos to be arranged in this limited space. She missed her sons terribly and guessed, with a mother's sure reasoning at their homesickness. 'I hate to go past your dear rooms,' she wrote, 'where I have so often tucked up my dear boys for the night.'[74] Writing to Queen Victoria she lamented: 'It was a great wrench – but must be got through... poor little boys, they cried so bitterly.'[75] His father felt the parting from his younger son no less acutely: 'On seeing you going off by the train yesterday I felt very sad and you could, I am sure, see that I had a lump in my throat when I wished you goodbye... I shall miss you more than ever, my dear Georgy... Don't forget your devoted Papa, A.E.'[76]

The Queen still had her misgivings, but at least she was grateful that they would be removed from the society of the Marlborough House set, those 'fast and fashionable people' who lived only for their own pleasure, and whose ways she so openly deplored.

Prince George adapted easily to the ways of the Navy; he was bright, friendly and cheerful, and was healthily involved in the cadets' normal activities, passing his examinations and pleasing Mr Dalton. He confessed that he missed home desperately, which was understandable, for he had been ill-prepared for the Spartan conditions of life aboard a training ship. The bullying by senior cadets was rife: new arrivals were ordered to smuggle sweets and butterscotch called 'stodge' aboard ship, and were punished when caught by the ship's petty officers. 'It was our money,' Prince George complained, 'and they never paid us back.'[77] Teams of younger boys were forced to carry seniors bodily up the long hill from the landing-place to the sports ground ashore.[78] These practices were abandoned only when the training hulks were decommissioned and cadets commenced their careers at Osborne. Prince Eddy, though, drifted on with his brother, largely unresponsive to the life around him; and for whom learning was a painfully slow business – there was even talk of withdrawing him from training. They were sent to sea on two cruises in HMS *Bacchante* and on the conclusion of the second the brothers separated, Prince George continuing with his training, whilst Prince Eddy was to prepare for life at Trinity College, Cambridge. No one expected much to come of this venture, but it was hoped that the experience would be useful. 'He sits listless and vacant,' Dalton reported.[78] He was prepared at Sandringham for entry by J.K. Stephen, a brilliant young don, but the omens were unpromising: 'He hardly knows the meaning of the words to read,' Stephen wrote.[79] There were some natural disadvantages; he had inherited something of his mother's deafness (due to otosclerosis), and he had arrived into the world two months before his time. The problems were identified well before he contracted typhoid, but the fever cannot have improved his constitutional apathy. After Cambridge, Prince Eddy joined the Tenth Hussars. He liked the uniform but evinced not the smallest interest in Army manoeuvres or the complexities of parade-ground drill – though he showed a certain aptitude for whist – and thought his Colonel a fool. His despairing parents could only look around for a suitable wife.

Prince Eddy's twenty-first birthday on 8 January 1885 was celebrated at Sandringham in the grand style. After he had been given his presents:

> …he received addresses and deputations in the Ball Room, to all of which he made very suitable replies and did it very well, in a simple manner, without appearing nervous. All the retainers, headed by Beck and Jackson, passed by in procession and gave him hearty cheers, and then Sanger's Circus shuffled past, before a performance which we attended after luncheon and which was given by the Prince to the labourers on the

Estate and children of the several schools hereabouts... Dinner at 8.15 in uniform. At which I gave Eddy's health, who replied very nicely, though in but very few words. The day finished with a great Ball, 600 invitations, the Gentlemen in uniform, which looked extremely well, in the new Ball Room, which lights up extremely well.[81]

While the Princes were away from home, a problem arose in the nursery. A 'Mrs' Walkley ('Mrs' was a courtesy title, normally accorded to housekeepers and senior female staff) was suspended from her duties and sent away by the Princess of Wales; it seemed that she had a drink problem and was disobedient. After her departure from Sandringham a number of items belonging to the Prince and Princess were missed and later found in her home. Such difficulties were common in Victorian mansions with many domestic staff; later, as we shall see, there were problems, though of a different nature, at York Cottage, but Mrs Walkley had inspired affection in the children, and there is a tone of genuine regret in the Princess' firm letter:

Sandringham, Norfolk
January 25th, 1881
My dear Walkley,
I have long intended to write to you but I have had so much to do lately that I could not find time – I am very glad to hear from yr letter that you are feeling better. I am sure the quiet atmosphere does you good – the Children are all well. We miss you and often speak of you. Partings are always so painful! I hope you will now settle down comfortably with yr parents to whom I am sure you will be of great help and comfort. But I must ask you now, my dear Walkley to send for all your things from Marlborough House without delay otherwise I shall be obliged to ask Mrs Dodds to forward them to you directly – you see dear Walkley as you have now left our service, it would be much better for you to have all yr things and not to leave them at Marlborough House to be disturbed by others so pray have this done at once. Later in the year I will ask you to come and see us but at present it would be too painful as it would only involve fresh parting – so goodbye dear Walkley – let me hear again what yr future plans are and how you are getting on – With the Children's best love, Yrs sincerely

Alexandra[81]

CHAPTER FOUR

THE HOUSE PARTY

The restless nature of the Prince of Wales demanded constant occupation, and he liked nothing better than to fill his house with friends. There was an easy conviviality during the daytime, followed by dinner, and activities and entertainments in the evening, and he exerted his considerable charm to ensure the comfort and contentment of his guests. The big house was often full to overflowing, and it was not long before the Prince gave Humbert orders for a 'Bachelors' Cottage' to be built beside the lake to the south of the house.

Visitors arrived by rail which was an essential adjunct to the house parties, and without which the estate would have remained seriously isolated from the capital. Three classes of carriages ranged from the opulent to the open-topped and primitive, but facilities improved steadily over the period with the advent of dining cars. Special trains provided remarkably good value for the money, even as late as the 1930s. The Great Eastern Railway's account for operating Royal trains over a year between St Pancras and Wolferton amounted to £513 for the passengers and £10 for parcels.

It was a long-established tradition that the Royal family spent Christmas at Sandringham; it was continued by King George VI and into the reign of the present Queen. After the Second World War, the branch line to Hunstanton, like so many others throughout the country, could no longer be considered viable. Freight was not carried after 1965 and in the following year the Royal train went no further than King's Lynn. The last train to run was the 10.29 a.m. 'Up' on 3 May 1969. The need for economy and the age of the motor car had finally triumphed.

Guests arriving at Wolferton Station were driven up to the house in carriages, finding themselves put down in the *porte-cochère*. Their luggage, comprising many trunks and smaller pieces, was brought up on carts to the house, where the unpacking was done by valets and ladies' maids. At this time the ladies wore gowns reaching to the ground; their hats, too, worn throughout the day but discarded for dinner, were becoming larger and more elaborate. Many brought riding dress, for the Princess was a keen horsewoman, and heavy warm clothing for walks on the estate and following the guns. Gentlemen too brought changes of costume for the activities organised by the Prince. Entering the house, guests often discovered the family in the Saloon, a fine, lofty room, which was the social centre at that time of day, and were liable to find themselves placed on the weighing-machine just inside the door, next to a large baboon which held in its outstretched paw a salver for visiting-cards. They were often taken to their rooms by their host or hostess who would stir the fire for them and see that all was in order. Bishop Magee wrote that after a long journey by train he arrived:

> ...just as they were all at tea in the entrance hall and had to walk in all seedy and dishevelled... and sit down beside the Princess of Wales, with Disraeli on the other side, and sundry lords and ladies around the table... I find the company pleasant and civil, but they are a curious mixture. Two Jews... an ex-Jew... a Roman Catholic... an Italian Duchess; a set of young Lords and a bishop...

Later, 'we are all to lunch together in a few minutes, the children dining with us.'[82]

This juxtaposition of disparate characters occasionally worried the Prince's neighbours and, sometimes, even fellow guests who were more accustomed to conventional gatherings. Czar Nicholas II encountered people at Sandringham the like of whom he scarcely believed to exist, and it was noted that he tended to avoid them as much as possible. They were carefully chosen, however, for their ability to entertain and amuse the Prince – and for the similarity of their interests. Reuben Sassoon, one of three brothers who were deriving immense wealth from their industrial empire in India, was well-known for his fascination for the turf; Baron Hirsch, owner of enormous estates in the Balkans, had constructed a railway through his lands to Constantinople; the Rothschilds and Sir Ernest Cassel were financiers. Their wealth was a source of envy to the Prince, who often had reason to be grateful to them for financial advice and, on occasion, relief from temporary embarrassment.

His demand for entertainment was insatiable; whilst he was punctilious in returning hospitality and sensitive to the necessity of entertaining as a duty, the spectre of boredom lurked and required constant vigilance: woe betide the luckless lady seated beside the Prince at dinner if his fingers began to drum on the table; it was an infallible sign of a wandering attention and she would not be invited again. Other regular visitors included the Marquess of Hartington – heir to the Duke of Devonshire and nicknamed 'Harty-Tarty' – as well as the Duke of St Albans, Christopher Sykes, and the Marquis de Soveral, the Portugese Minister in London. Universally popular, de Soveral, called 'the blue monkey' on account of his complexion and blue-black hair and vivacity, was an excellent talker and always welcome at receptions, even by the husbands of his mistresses. The Prince once forgot to invite him, only rectifying the omission at the last moment, and on his arrival told him that he knew he need never wait for an invitation; de Soveral instantly replied, 'I was just setting out, Sir, when your telegram arrived.'

The arrival in the vicinity of the Maharajah Duleep Singh provided an agreeable diversion from the more conventional circle around the Prince. In 1849, after an uprising, the former ruler of the Punjab, which he had inherited in his infancy, found that his territory had been annexed by Britain, which had sent troops to his aid. In return for a generous pension, the young man surrendered his rights and settled in England. Queen Victoria was much interested in him, as she was indeed in all things Indian, and he was soon in Royal favour. Still in his early twenties, he purchased the 17,000 acre Elveden estate in Norfolk, with Government money, and became a welcome visitor to Sandringham. He spent freely, transforming his house into an oriental palace; and his engaging personality and dark good looks ensured his success with women. At race meetings his appearance added a touch of oriental glamour to the scene. But by 1880 he had exhausted his resources; he was encumbered with a wife and six children, and unable to extract an increase in his allowances from the Government. He settled for a time in Paris, subsequently moving about Europe, until his death following a fit, at the early age of fifty-five.

In 1883, Lord Sandwich noted some fifteen guests who attended the Prince's birthday celebrations at Sandringham. There were shoots every day, 'and he received innumerable presents from all sorts and kinds of people, and there was a ball, which lasted until 4 a.m.'

The ladies were constantly changing their clothes – and dressing could be a lengthy operation. These periods of seclusion provided a welcome relief from the interminable conversation and gossip, and from the constriction of the tightly-laced corsets by Worth, which made the 'hour-glass' figure popular even before the new century. In this exclusive circle everybody knew everybody else; many were related to each other. It was a society that enjoyed immense wealth and unique privileges over everybody else and took them for granted. It was a society carefully designed to perpetuate itself, for one of its prime functions was to provide opportunities for matchmaking. Noble blood there was in plenty and mothers shrewdly calculated how to secure it for their daughters. They met each other at Chatsworth and Holkham, Studley Royal and Mentmore Towers; at the races at Ascot, Epsom and Newmarket; on the water at Henley and Cowes and on the promenades of Biarritz, Nice, Cannes and Paris. Their enormous houses were a statement of wealth and power, often derived in the previous century from the extraction of minerals, especially coal and iron to meet the demands of the huge expansion of the Industrial Revolution, and also the sugar plantations of the West Indies. Newcomers were admitted only after the most minute enquiries into their backgrounds and breeding, interrogations proceeding ruthlessly behind a front of friendly, enquiring smiles. The rules governing etiquette were strict and comprehensive; gaucheries were not lightly overlooked and could end in ostracism. To be labelled 'encroaching' was social death; on the other hand 'a pretty-behaved girl' would be sure to find herself a guest at other, almost exactly similar, occasions. Previously, of course, she would have been 'Presented' at Court; which was the essential first stage towards acceptance. It was a circle diminished almost to extinction by its sheer extravagance – and by the impact of the First World War, after which things would never be the same again; social barriers had been penetrated and the cost of maintaining their vast houses had become prohibitive. Servants were fewer and were aware of their scarcity value. Only too often, large estates lacked an heir; the entire coterie of wealthy, intelligent and aristocratic young men surrounding Lady Diana Manners, daughter of the Duke of Rutland, was destroyed on the Western Front in 1914. In the aftermath of the Second World War the class which for many years had dominated society was further eroded by the crippling effect of high taxation, scarcity of luxuries and lack of staff still willing to enter domestic service. All this resulted in the demolition of many great houses.

Although dinner, at which the ladies wore their tiaras and the men stiff-fronted shirts and their orders and decorations, was an elaborate affair, it was not the lengthy meal one might have expected. The Prince ate rich food voraciously but drank little. He worked his way steadily through as many as twelve courses and then asked why there was no cheese. Apart from an increasing girth he appeared to suffer no ill effects. After the ladies had withdrawn from the table, it was not long before the gentlemen met them again in the drawing-room, for the Prince found himself at a disadvantage in the company of men who had often been at the same schools and came from the same background – though the social background of his guests could sometimes be diverse in the extreme. When the fingers drummed and the heavy eyelids drooped, it was time to move. Besides, the Prince had arranged everything for the evening's amusements with his customary care. There was music, cards and billiards – after Teulon's conservatory had been converted – and dancing, and the bowling alley was in constant use. There were frequent tours of the house, for the Prince was never happier than when he was escorting his friends round his property, either in or out of doors. Often, the Prince retired to play cards with a few select friends; baccarat, which was at that time illegal, was among his favourite. The Royal couple became known for the late hours they kept: one exhausted visitor noted, 'We were in the bowling alley until two o'clock this morning.'[83] Guests were not expected to retire until after their host and hostess. Once, General Probyn, elderly and unwell, had sought the refuge of his bed, only to be summoned downstairs as his presence had been missed. On this occasion the Prince apologised for troubling the old gentleman. Those who knew the ropes found ways and means of catching up on their sleep.

The mornings started quietly enough. Mr Asquith described the extraordinary care lavished on guests in the Edwardian era. While staying at Lord Rothschild's he was awakened by the sound of a maid laying the fire at the end of his bedroom, just as a trolley was wheeled in by two footmen.

'Will you take tea, coffee, or a peach off the wall, Sir?'

'Tea, please.'

'Indian, China or Ceylon, Sir?'

'Indian, please.'

'Milk, cream or lemon, Sir?'

'Milk, please.'

'Jersey, Hereford or Shorthorn, Sir?'[84]

The Prince was an early riser but other members of the Royal family did not generally appear until midday. Breakfast was at ten o'clock, when an abundance of dishes were available on the sideboard, from which everyone helped themselves. Porridge could be eaten standing, to be followed by bacon, eggs, kidneys, spare ribs, kedgeree or kippers from the row of chafing dishes. Guests who had been to Sandringham before were aware that they could be in for an active morning, and a full and satisfying breakfast was a good start to a cold day in windswept Norfolk. The long dining-room table had been replaced by smaller tables, so that the guests could sit where they wished – there was a pleasant informality at this time of day.

Sometimes the Norfolk Hunt met at Sandringham, and ladies and gentlemen arrived for their stay with riding habits and hunting attire in the massive trunks which accompanied them. Not so very many years had passed since the earliest days of steeple-chasing, and the younger men and some of the ladies, including the Princess, were often hard and adventurous riders.

In the afternoons there was always something to do. The Prince was unhappy if anyone was unoccupied, but he could be satisfied by being told that a visitor would be watching some activity, perhaps ice-hockey on the lake, or later, during his reign, walking round the golf-course with the players. The thought of an afternoon spent with a book distressed him, and one was encouraged to be out and about. When the ladies returned from watching the gentlemen's afternoon sport, they changed from their warm tweeds, so necessary for winter, into elegant tea-gowns. And so the round continued until it was time to dress for dinner. The house-parties generally lasted three or four days; there was much hospitality to be repaid, and often the carriages rolled away down the drive to Wolferton Station, returning later to collect another houseful of visitors. You had to be on your toes, for 'Sandringham time' was half an hour ahead of the rest of the country: you had to leave the Hall at 2.30 p.m. in order to catch the 2.15 p.m. at Wolferton. The Prince had copied the idea from Lord Leicester at Holkham, who was among the first of the daylight-saving exponents. Queen Victoria was indignant when she first encountered the phenomenon during her visit in 1871. 'It's a wicked lie', she declared roundly, and as a special concession, the clocks were put back to Greenwich Mean Time for her second visit.[85]

The shoots on the estate provided the focus for the house-parties in the autumn and winter months. The Prince continued to spend heavily on the establishment of coverts for the birds and in employing a posse of keepers to ensure that nothing was allowed to interfere with the rearing of game on an impressive scale. The rights of tenants were too often disregarded and his 'perfect passion' for the sport clouded his judgment. 'Nothing made him more angry than the slightest opposition to it.'[86] The feud between the Prince and a widow who was also a tenant farmer at Sandringham has been recorded in great detail, and the facts remind one forcibly of William the Conqueror's destruction of whole villages in the New Forest for the improvement of his hunting – such is the misuse of power.

Louise Cresswell, with her husband Gerard, took up the tenancy of Appleton Farm on the estate, just when it was passing into the Prince of Wales' hands, and together they had great hopes for their new landlord. He arrived at the farm, inspected the rat-ridden premises energetically, and

built them a new house. The situation promised well; the Prince was gracious
to his new tenants, receiving them at Sandringham and greeting them affably.
But Gerard died within three years. He had been depressed by his inability
to improve a run-down and neglected holding, and in part, at least, his failure
can be attributed to the interference of the Prince's keepers. These men
patrolled the fields, forbidding the clearing away of weeds and planting trees
and shrubs, their aim being to rear as many birds as the land would hold. Hares
were imported and wrought havoc among the crops. The Cresswells were
in despair. Protest would have incurred the Prince's displeasure. Eventually,
goaded beyond endurance, Mrs Cresswell submitted an account of £575 for
damages, of which less than half was paid; she was never to see the balance.
Afterwards, there was more trouble; the widow had already displeased the
Prince, but this was as nothing to the fury with which he greeted a report
that seventy-one pheasants had been killed by her. After a close enquiry, the
losses were attributed to a fox, but Louise had felt the force of Royal anger
at close quarters. There were times, however, when the Prince exerted all his
charm: Louise was invited to a ball at Sandringham; she became a frequent
though somewhat reluctant guest at the house, but troubles were never far
away. Damage to land and crops by rabbits and hares continued, and swathes
were cut across her land by the keepers. The Prince's agent was the root cause
of the troubles. In his efforts to please his master, he treated the tenant farmers
with scant respect and went to some trouble to avoid interviews with Louise,
who once appeared brandishing a bunch of ruined mangolds, as evidence of
the depredations of the animals.

Partridge driving created the greatest havoc on tenants' land. Secure
in the knowledge that they were working for the Prince, the village boys
rampaged across the fields, breaking fences and gates and damaging crops: for
the Cresswells it was heart-breaking. After Louise left Appleton★, she wrote:

> I would have stayed and fought through everything if the money losses
> that were forced upon me had not brought me to a standstill... An old
> friend offered me enough capital... to start afresh, concluding, of course,
> that arrangements would be made at Sandringham which would give
> me a fair chance of success. Not one concession would they make in
> game, rent, labour or anything that would enable me to accept this
> offer... I was leaving because I could not remain unless I killed down the
> Prince's game from Monday morning till Saturday night, and reserved
> Sunday for lecturing the Agent.

★ Louise was not an easy tenant, but there faults on both sides. *vide 'The Prince's Thorn'*
by Mary Mackie.

As agriculture in general was moving towards a depression, Louise Cresswell found herself bankrupt, and in 1880 she emigrated to America.

The Prince of Wales unfortunately inherited the sporting traditions of his father and the Coburgs. Prince Albert had been criticised in the Press for holding 'battues', in which animals were forced into an enclosure and shot at close range. The practice deeply offended the English sporting instinct, being considered a barbarous affair. For Albert Edward the concept of number was paramount; though a good shot himself his passion for large bags enabled him to leave the difficult birds for others; besides, shooting never held quite the same fascination for him as racing. The coverts were designed so that birds would be driven out by the beaters in great numbers to fly low over the ground. On one occasion in Wolferton Wood, after a hare drive, the animals were lying thickly on the ground, some wounded and screaming. A visitor, Charles Kingsley, who had been the Prince's Tutor at Cambridge, walked up to the guns and denounced their lack of feeling. The Prince was, for once, much abashed. It was for the future King George V to learn the satisfaction of achieving the 'difficult killing of a high-flying bird.'

To be fair to the young Prince, he lacked guidance in these matters; enjoying the lavish entertainment by some of the wealthiest in the land; he and his lovely Princess were the most sought-after guests in the world of fashionable Society, which set examples which Albert Edward could only attempt to emulate. At Holkham, for instance, in his own county of Norfolk, the game room was the largest in the country: the Prince at once had one built at Sandringham on the same scale. 'Bags' of two thousand birds were not uncommon, and the Prince felt that his own guests should have the same opportunities as they would find on neighbouring estates. In November 1872, the Duke of Cambridge spent some days at Sandringham and recorded: 'In spite of much rain had one of the finest days' sport I ever saw, killing 1,766 head of game, of which 1,083 were pheasants and 68 partridges, besides hares and rabbits.'[87] As late as 1913 King George V and his eldest son were present at Hall Barn, owned by Lord Burnham, when over 4,000 birds were killed in a single day. Even the King, who was no less an enthusiast than his father, having himself shot over a thousand head, was moved to say to the Prince, 'Perhaps we went a little too far today, David.'[88]

On 28 November, he wrote:

My dear Macduff,
I hope it will suit you to pay us a visit from the 14th to the 19th of next month – & I trust that your plans for leaving England may not prevent

us from having the pleasure of seeing you – I propose having three day's (sic) shooting and one day's hunting during that week. Hoping that you have had good sport in Scotland with the smaller game.

I remain,

Yours very sincerely,

Albert Edward

It was within this tradition that the Prince of Wales conducted the shooting at Sandringham. The arrangements were elaborate, the entertainment lavish:

A complete silence having been secured for miles around, the day was ushered in by a procession of boys with blue and pink flags... a band of gamekeepers in green and gold, with the head man on horseback, an army of beaters in smocks and hats bound with Royal red, a caravan for the reception of the game and a tailing off of loafers to see the fun, for H.R.H. is very good-natured in allowing people to look on at his amusements, provided they do not interfere with them... [89]

At about eleven o'clock the Royal party arrives in a string of wagonettes, and range themselves in a long line under the fences or behind the shelters put up for that purpose, each sportsman having loaders in attendance with an extra gun or guns to hand backwards and forwards, to load and re-load. The boys and beaters are stationed in a semi-circle some distance off, and it is their place to beat up the birds and drive them to the fences, the waving flags frightening them from flying back. On they come in ever increasing numbers, until they burst in a cloud over the fence where the guns are concealed. This is the exciting moment, a terrific fusillade ensues, birds dropping down in all directions, wheeling about in confusion between the flags and the guns, the survivors gathering themselves together and escaping into the fields beyond. The shooters then retire to another line of fencing, making themselves comfortable with campstools and cigars until the birds are driven up as before, and so on through the day...[90]

After Mrs Cresswell had returned to visit Sandringham once more, in 1886, she settled down in the United States and wrote an account of her life entitled *Eighteen Years on the Sandringham Estate*. Appleton was given to Princess Maud, the youngest daughter of the Wales', on her marriage to Prince Charles of Denmark. The house held many happy associations for her, and even when she and her husband succeeded to the Danish throne as King Haakon and Queen Maud, she continued to make frequent visits. 'She was a lovely woman,' said Hubbard, the gardener who had worked for her for forty years. 'This was her real home, she loved this place.'[91]

There was nothing static about Sandringham; there was always something new to be seen. As the years passed, one novelty was succeeded by another: an aviary replaced a monkey house; a pit containing Charlie and Polly, two black bears (one of which was once released, to everyone's consternation, by a house-party guest) was filled in after its inhabitants had been disposed of in 1889. Kennels were built to house the Princess' motley collection of dogs, sometimes as many as sixty, which she and her guests visited and fed. Beyond Appleton a water tower had been erected; later the electricity generating plant could be inspected; walled gardens appeared, together with the enormous range of glasshouses built with the winnings and stud fees of Persimmon. The Princess took her guests to see the Craft Schools for boys and girls to learn trades on the estate. There was the black ram to visit: this fortunate animal had been rescued from ritual slaughter by the Princess during her visit to Egypt in 1869. It was sent on to Sandringham where it enjoyed a bachelor existence to a ripe old age. In the course of the Egyptian tour the Princess also acquired, in a similarly impulsive gesture, a ten-year old Nubian boy named Ali Achmet, who had loosely attached himself to the Royal camp at Wadi Halfa. The child was engaging but amoral: at Sandringham, where his duties included serving coffee, he stole guests' property and alienated himself from the servants. The end came when he was discovered to have borrowed one of the Prince's guns, which was bad, and had broken it, which was far worse, and was sent away into the service of the Rector of Sandringham. As an experiment, this venture was a failure; even its value as an act of charity is debatable.

During the re-building of the house the lake on the western side was filled in, to be replaced by flower gardens. New lakes were created further to the south, the larger with magnificent rock features. Improvements were made to the estate: in 1884 the Sandringham Club at West Newton was built as a recreation centre for men and the older boys in the village, many of whom were already working on the estate by the time they were allowed to use the Club at the age of fourteen. Beer-drinking was limited to a daily pint. Soon afterwards, another such Club was opened at Wolferton.

The Prince's hospitality was legendary: not only did he lavishly entertain the nobility in the district, but his guests included diplomats and foreigners whom he had met during his frequent journeys abroad. At his house-parties the Prince required only that his guests should be entertaining and entertained. His tastes were, however, expensive; a

number of his friends, including Christopher Sykes, heir to Sledmere, a
large estate in Yorkshire, were brought to the verge of ruin in their efforts
to match his pace. His restlessness was remarkable; perhaps it was the
product of an active mind too little employed: 'a perpetual search in the
daytime of hours he had lost the night before.'[92]

The vicissitudes of betting whetted the Prince's appetite for racing
which, in later life, was to become a passion. In his first year of marriage
he paid a visit to Epsom to watch the Derby. He was accompanied by
Sir Frederick Johnstone, an established owner, and Henry Chaplin. Almost
from the moment he entered the grandstand to the enthusiastic cheers of
the huge crowd, the excitement of the turf possessed him and Sandringham,
managed by Lord Marcus Beresford, and his string of racehorses brought
him some major successes: three times winner of the Derby, in 1896 with
Persimmon, in 1900 with Diamond Jubilee and, in 1909, with Minoru.
In 1900 – a great year – he won the Grand National with Ambush II. His
racing interests brought him into contact with the leading figures of the
turf; he had his own quarters in the Jockey Club at Newmarket and he was
always to be seen in the Paddock, the Grandstand or the Royal Box, portly
in frock coat and top hat, cigar or cigarette in hand, often accompanied
by Chaplin, whose air of nonchalant authority never deserted him, even
when, ruined by gambling, he was forced to sell Blankney Hall, the family
home. Sir Frederick Johnstone also dissipated his large fortune and was
forced to sell up. Another victim of his own colossal extravagance was the
Marquis of Hastings, who died at the age of twenty-six, having squandered
two large estates on the turf. He could scarcely be said, however, to have
been within the Prince's circle, for his wife, Lady Florence Paget, the tiny,
exquisite 'Pocket Venus', had eloped with him, leaving her fiancé, Henry
Chaplin, outside a shop waiting for her to appear. Such duplicity could
only exile the pair from the Prince's favour.

Ascot Week was to become the highlight of the Royal racing calendar,
with the Prince driving up the course followed by his guests at Windsor
Castle. The reception accorded him varied – after the Mordaunt
case, he was greeted with hisses and boos. Queen Victoria, perhaps
misunderstanding the nature of the week's races, begged him to forego
his attendance on two of the days, lest he gave the appearance of being
unduly attracted to the sport. The Prince replied tersely that he could
not well leave his friends to look after themselves. 'Allow me to use my
discretion in these matters,' he wrote.

It was this search for excitement that led him to indulge in gambling.
'Games of chance appealed to his love of adventure.' Whilst at times he

risked heavy stakes at cards, he protested that he seldom played high: he played whist with Mr Gladstone for 'shillings and half-a-crown on the rubber'[93]. It seems he never lost much above £100 pounds in an evening's play, but one of his debtors took four years to amass a sum in settlement of £1,025. It was unfortunate that the Prince was addicted to baccarat, at that time illegal. He took his own set of counters with him on his travels, and the exposure of this practice during the Tranby Croft affair gave the Press an excuse to accuse him of setting a bad example to the nation.

Queen Victoria's dislike of Society was no mere prejudice: it was grounded on an accumulation of evidence that it was selfish, idle and promiscuous. Her fears that her eldest son and daughter-in-law would fall into the numerous pitfalls that awaited them were fully justified. They were young enough to be led so that, although they were the acknowledged leaders of Society, they were influenced by those who were used to its ways. Infidelity was rife; within this charmed circle there were few secrets, but waywardness must never be allowed to become a scandal. Diana Cooper remembered her mother allotting the guests-rooms at Belvoir Castle for a large house party: 'Lord Kitchener must have this room and then, of course, Lady Salisbury must be here;' and then later in the evening: 'If you are frightened in the night, Lord Kitchener, dear Lady Salisbury is just next door.'[94] Within its closed ranks, gentlemen's mistresses were known and admitted: *maisons à trois* were commonplace and accepted; a convention that the Prince found wholly agreeable. He himself not only enjoyed an affair with Alice Keppel towards the end of his life, with the compliance of her husband, George, but he also favoured many other women during his travels on the continent. In the Mordaunt case, he was cited by Harriet Mordaunt herself as one of the young men of the 'fast set' who might have fathered her child. Harriet's father declared her insane; certainly her behaviour became increasingly irrational.

In the divorce case which followed, the Prince was subpoenaed and a number of his letters were read in court, though they contained nothing of an improper nature. There was a good deal of sympathy for Harriet Mordaunt and the Prince did not come out of it well. The Queen accepted that her son was innocent but had always deprecated his involvement with these 'idle, highborn beings' and hoped that the trial would teach him a lesson. She wrote that the affair was 'painful & lowering' and felt that it had done nothing to diminish her worries about the Prince's propensity for indiscretion which, some twenty years later, prompted a sporting paper to state that 'there was nothing whatever between the Prince of Wales and Lily Langtry', followed the next week by an apparently unrelated remark: 'Not even a sheet'. Whilst it was generally considered that the Royal family were not 'fair game', the Prince's infidelities brought unwelcome publicity upon himself. It was doubly unfortunate that, just at this time, the Queen, through her retirement from public life, had left the Monarchy open to charges of neglect of duty, while there was also a wave of anti-Prussian feeling resulting from that war with France.

It goes without saying that the chief activities of the House Party were male-orientated. They centred on sport, of course – racing, hunting, shooting, fishing; moving about the country to follow whatever game was in season. Their womenfolk followed dutifully, accompanied by their personal servants, but few occupations were provided specifically for them. Outdoors, they played croquet and tennis and, later, golf. The Princess of Wales often took her guests to the dairy at Sandringham to help make Devonshire cream and butter – echoes of Marie Antoinette of France and her circle. Escape to the 'simple life' had its attractions but it was small wonder that gossip and promiscuity flourished in such an uncreative environment. Sundays were spent in comparative tranquillity, everyone attending morning service in the church, the Prince arriving just before the sermon and scrutinising the crowded pews to ensure that the local tenants were present. He made it known that 'he liked his people to attend, just as he himself did.' There was the compulsory tour of 'new works' and improvements during the afternoons to rouse the torpid and fill the long hours between luncheon and tea. Towards midnight, the Prince always brightened visibly and, as the clock struck, hurried off to impel his guests into renewed activity.

CHAPTER FIVE

1870 – 1871 YEARS OF CRISIS

The years when the Prince of Wales was 'in waiting' for his accession to the throne were seldom without interest, but these, while he was still under forty years of age, were to prove exceptional. His extraordinary vitality, panache and love of sport and excitement ensured the public's continuing fascination with his activities which were not, however, wholly devoted to pleasure. He complained to Queen Victoria that it was impossible to satisfy the endless demands on his time to undertake engagements, since she herself had withdrawn from public life after Albert's death. Though light enough in the early days, the many requests forced him to winnow the merely frivolous or selfish from those of genuine importance, such as the opening in 1865 of the Crossness Pumping Station on Bazalgette's great Metropolitan Sewerage undertaking.

It was while Sandringham was being rebuilt that the Prince of Wales became involved in a Society divorce case. Early in 1870, Sir Charles Mordaunt filed for divorce from his young wife, Harriet, on the ground of adultery with two of the Prince's friends and, on the basis of some letters from the Prince to Lady Mordaunt, he was subpoenaed to appear as a witness.

This was an unwelcome intrusion into the Prince's private life, and he therefore consulted the Lord Chancellor, who agreed that the letters were harmless and advised him to write at once to the Queen, who also strongly supported him, only asking him to be more circumspect in his private life. The outcome was never in doubt. The divorce petition failed since Lady Mordaunt's family declared her to be insane.

The publicity surrounding the case shed a damaging glare on the Prince's lack of judgment, just at a time of increasing public unrest. He and the Princess were hissed in the street and booed at the theatre. The Queen was an invisible figurehead and, after nine years of secluded widowhood, in danger of becoming largely unknown. Mr Gladstone noted that 'while the nation has confidence in... the Sovereign, the Throne may be regarded as

safe, but' – remembering the excesses of the late Hanoverians – 'the revival
of circumstances only half a century old…might bring about its overthrow.'

Such were the relations between the Monarchy and the nation in 1871.
The Prince and Princess of Wales had spent some weeks with the Queen
at Balmoral, and on their return south early in November they stayed with
Lord Londesborough, arriving at Sandringham to celebrate the Prince's
thirtieth birthday on 9 November. Soon afterwards the Prince became
ill, and on the 23rd the Queen was informed that her son had contracted
typhoid. Several of Lord Londesborough's guests had also caught the
disease, and the Earl of Chesterfield had died. The Prince's groom, Blegge,
was also taken ill as they returned from Londesborough Lodge.

As the fever pursued its course, the Princess and her Lady of the
Bedchamber, Lady Macclesfield, had to grapple with the problems created
by the arrival of relatives and well-wishers. Princess Alice, who, since
her marriage to Prince Louis of Hesse-Darmstad, had taken a practical
interest in hospitals and the care of the sick, was at first warmly welcomed,
but before long her managing ways caused irritation. 'We are all furious at
seeing our Princess sat upon and spoken of as if she had not sense enough
to act for herself,' Lady Macclesfield wrote.[96] As for the Princess of Wales
herself, she was becoming 'deadly tired' with the strain and lack of sleep.
She would retire into the Prince's dressing room for a few hours at a time,
so that she was always at hand if need be. When the Prince entered on long
periods of delirium, the Princess was kept from his room as far as possible,
for his ravings were 'very dreadful' to hear, full as they were with names
and indiscretions.[97] The delirium left him, but returned from time to time.
Pillows were thrown into the air, and once the Princess was knocked
over as she attempted to crawl into his room on hands and knees, so that
he would not see her, as the doctors believed that her presence excited
him. 'The dear Princess behaves admirably, she does not disguise the truth
from herself, but her self-control and composure are perfect, she never
thinks of herself and is so gentle and considerate to everyone as ever,'
Lady Macclesfield commented.[98] On a sharper note during that period
of calm, when it seemed that the patient was recovering, she mused, 'But
how Princess Alice is to be rooted out it is not easy to see… Suffice it is
to say for the moment that she is the most awful story-teller I have ever
encountered, meddling, jealous and mischief-making. For a short time she
is everything that is charming, but the less one knows of her the better.'[99]

The Queen had never visited Sandringham. She deplored the 'fast
set' who formed the innermost circle of the Prince's friends, and since
the Prince Consort's death ten years previously, she seldom broke her

established routine of journeying between Windsor, Osborne and Balmoral. But now it was time to put her own inclinations aside. 'Better accounts from Sandringham,' the Queen recorded on 29 November:

Quieter, mind clearer. Nourishment taken well. I was nervous and agitated at the thought of this sad journey... At eleven I left (Windsor)... Reached Wolferton after three. Affie, Sir William Knollys and Colonel Ellis met me there, and a quarter of an hour's drive brought us to Sandringham. The road lay between commons, and plantations of fir-trees, rather wild-looking, flat, bleak country. The house, rather near the high-road, a handsome quite newly-built Elizabethan building, was only completed last autumn. Dear Alix and Alice met me at the door, the former looking thin and anxious, and with tears in her eyes. She took me at once through the great hall upstairs to my rooms, three in number.

I took off my things and went over to Bertie's room, and was allowed to step in from behind a screen to see him sleeping or dozing. The room was dark and only one lamp burning, so that I could not see him very well. He was lying rather flat on his back, breathing very rapidly and loudly. Of course the watching is constant, and Alix does a great deal herself. Dr Gull came in, saying they were a little more anxious, as the pulse and temperature were higher. I remained until about ten and then went to my room.[100]

The Prince's illness continued to cause anxiety, By the 1 December – the birthday of the Princess of Wales and a muted occasion – the Prince had regained consciousness and the Queen was encouraged to think she could safely return to Windsor. She had made a good impression on Lady Macclesfield: 'charming, so tender and quiet', but the presence of so many of the family was not conducive to peace and quiet: 'really the way in which they all squabble and wrangle and abuse each other destroys one's peace.'[101]

On the 5 December, back at Windsor, the Queen received a guardedly optimistic report from Jenner, though the Prince could not yet be said to be out of danger. On the 8th, however, the Queen wrote in her journal:

Was dreadfully alarmed... the telegram I received at quarter past eight said: 'The Prince passed a very unquiet night. Not so well. Temperature risen to 104. Respirations more rapid. Dr Gull and I are both very anxious.' [This was from Jenner.] When I got up saw Dr Marshall, who said it was very grave, occurring at this stage of the illness, and he thought, if I wanted to go to Sandringham, I should do so today.

At three Louise and I started on our melancholy journey. Reached Wolferton at half past seven, Sir William Knollys meeting us and handing me a note from Sir William Jenner, saying condition no worse, but that was all he could say. Got into a brougham with Louise and Affie [who had joined the Queen at Victoria Park] and drove in deep snow and hard frost up to Sandringham. Nobody at the door but Lady Macclesfield, who said that dear Bertie was very bad. Went up at once to the room. The doctors were there, Alix and Alice on either side of the bed, and poor dear Bertie breathing rapidly. I naturally only peeped for a moment, and then remained behind the screen. The state was very critical but not hopeless, the doctors said...[102]

The Duke of Cambridge, the Queen's cousin, wished to join the family at the Prince's bedside but, much to his chagrin, had been advised to remain in London for the time being. 'Alfred,' the Prince's younger brother, 'came to see me in great distress,' wrote the Duke. 'Poor boy! He is going at once to Sandringham. I telegraphed for leave to go down myself, for I felt most miserable. I decided upon going down in the morning at all hazards.'[103] The following morning he received a telegram saying he might come and immediately ordered a special train which brought him to Sandringham at 1.30 p.m:

Found on arrival that the day had been so far quiet. I lunched with the young people, who are all here, Louise, Beatrice, Alfred, Arthur, Leopold; then saw Alice, whom I thought looking very ill and much distressed; then dear Alix, who was wonderfully calm and self-possessed, but looking better than I had anticipated. Later on I saw the Queen, who was calm and anxious...The anxiety of the Household, high and low, is intense...

The Duke of Cambridge, the Queen's cousin, caused a good deal of alarm by complaining of a bad smell, and ascribing it to the drains. Sir Henry Ponsonby wrote:

Cambridge has been full of talk but old Knollys says he utterly refuses to discuss military matters and converses on nothing but drains...This afternoon the Duke thought there was a bad smell in the library where we were sitting and when Francis Knollys came in and said he smelt it, the Duke jumped up and said, 'By George, I won't sit here', and went about smelling in all the corners...There may be a bad smell but I don't perceive it.[104]

Eventually, a gas leak was discovered and peace was restored. The Duke's preoccupation with the drains was natural enough. The 'Great Stink' of 1848 had been caused by the almost non-existent sewerage in London and the pollution of the River Thames. The Prince Consort had been carried off by typhoid, and the drains at Windsor Castle had been found to be in an appalling condition; bad sanitation at Londesborough Lodge had almost certainly been the prime cause of the Prince of Wales' illness. Often, a bad drainage system led to polluted wells, whence the microbe found its way into the drinking water. The Queen, writing to her daughter in Prussia, commented: 'I do not think this place wholesome and the drainage is defective – though he did not catch the fever here but at Scarborough. The poor groom is very ill, I went to see him on Thursday.'[105] Soon afterwards she was enlarging her views: 'I think the house very unhealthy – drainage and ventilation – bad; bad smells in some rooms – of gas and drains.'[106] Not so many years earlier she had thought the house 'unlucky'.

Royal etiquette demanded that when the Queen was taking a drive or walking, others should stay out of sight. Sir Henry Ponsonby, the Queen's Private Secretary, told his wife that when out walking with Prince Alfred's equerry:

We were suddenly nearly carried away by a stampede of Royalties headed by the Duke of Cambridge and brought up by Leopold, going as fast as they could... They cried out 'The Queen! The Queen!' and everyone dashed into the house again and waited behind the door until the road was clear. When Haig and I were alone we laughed immensely. This is that 'one-ness' we hear of.[107]

The patient's condition continued to cause great alarm and anxiety, and indeed the entire nation could not fail to be aware of the dread lying deep in the Queen's heart; namely, that the tenth anniversary of the Prince Consort's death from typhoid was but a few days off.

On the 11th the Duke of Cambridge wrote:

The awfulness of this morning, I shall never, never, forget as long as I live. Between six and seven the General (Sir William Knollys) knocked at my door to say we were sent for to the house. I rushed out of bed, dressed hurriedly, and ran to the house in intense agony. The morning was desperately cold and the damp rose from the snow on the ground. On arrival found all assembled near the dear patient's room... However, towards ten matters seemed rather to mend, at all events to quiet down.[108]

Certainly, the whole family, summoned while it was still dark, feared the worst. The Queen recorded:

At half past five I was woke by a message from Sir William Jenner saying dear Bertie had had a very severe spasm... I saw him at once, and he told me the spasm had been so severe, that at any moment dear Bertie might go off, so that I had better come at once... It was very dark, the candles burning, and most dreary. Poor dear Bertie was lying there breathing heavily, and as if he must choke at any moment... The talking was incessant, without a moment's sleep. Dr Gull said he was much alarmed.[109]

The crisis continued for two more days. Indeed, that it had not ended by this time with the Prince's death was in itself a notable achievement. Dr Gull, later to be knighted, had risen through sheer ability from a humble background to become in due course Physician-in-Ordinary to the Queen. As a Fellow of the Royal College of Physicians his treatment of the Prince, assisted by Sir William Jenner, brought him a baronetcy and considerable prominence. That the Prince had survived the fever this far was no doubt due as much to his natural resilience and zest for life as to the ministrations of his doctors. In this he was as unlike his father, the Prince Consort, as possible; for he, before his fatal illness at Windsor, had once remarked to the Queen: 'I am sure, if I had a severe illness, I should give up at once, I should not struggle for life.'[110]

But to return to Queen Victoria's chronicle of her son's illness:

Sandringham, 13th Dec. 1871. – This really has been the worst day of all, and coming as it has so close to the sad 14th, filled us and, I believe, the whole country with anxious forebodings and the greatest alarm. The first report early in the morning was that dear Bertie seemed very weak, and the breathing very imperfect and feeble... There had been no rest all night, from the constant delirium... Got up and dressed quickly, taking a mouthful of breakfast before hurrying to Bertie's room. Sat nearby on the sofa, but so that he could not see me. Remained a long time.

Strolled round the house and pleasure grounds for a short while. It was raw and damp and thawing all day.

Returned to Bertie's room and, whilst there, he had a most frightful fit of coughing, which seemed at one moment to threaten his life!.. Poor dear Alix was in the greatest alarm and despair, and I supported her as best I could. Alice and I said to one another in tears, 'There can be no hope.' He turned round and looked wildly at me saying, 'Who are you?' and then, 'It's Mama.' 'Dear child,' I replied. Later he said, 'It is so kind of you to come,' which shows he knew me, which was most comforting to me... I left again when Alix and Alice, who had been resting a little, came in.[111]

The day continued to be full of foreboding. As the Prince's condition deteriorated Princess Alice, with memories to call upon of her father's death in the Blue Room at Windsor ten years before, said, 'It is the death rattle – I have heard it before.' As a last resort, the doctors called for old champagne brandy and rubbed the patient's body with the spirit, which appeared to revive him. Queen Victoria resumed her journal:

When I returned I found dear Bertie breathing very heavily and with great difficulty. We were getting nearer and nearer to the 14th, and it seemed more and more like ten years ago, and yet it was very different too. After going to my room to have some dinner, went straight back, and the doctors told me they hoped dear Bertie was really a little better. He had had a few minutes sleep, was talking less loudly, and the breathing was less rapid. The condition was still very serious and alarming, but not hopeless. Went rather relieved back to my room.[112]

Elsewhere in the country, the nation waited anxiously for news. For all that the Prince had been booed and hissed when he appeared in public as a witness in the notorious Mordaunt divorce case of the previous year, his nearness to death was something else again. He was, after all, heir to the throne. News came, reduced to bathos in Alfred Austin's immortal lines:
  'Flash'd from his bed, the electric tidings came:
  He is no better, he is much the same.'[113]

All was not entirely easy, either, among the watchers at Sandringham: the Princess of Wales resented the managing ways of Princess Alice, though she was, in fact, a capable nurse. Members of the Royal family sat about, they could only speculate on the outcome and sense the crisis that was going on upstairs. Matters were not made any easier by the fact that not all members of the family were on good terms with one another. There was not enough for them to do; no one felt like taking active exercise of a cheerful nature with so serious a drama being enacted in the house. Sandringham itself was packed. Needless to say, the Queen's arrival with her retinue ensured that the house, already full, was crammed to overflowing; and it was reported that Princess Louise and Princess Beatrice had to share a bed.

The next day, the anniversary of the Prince Consort's death, brought the turning point: '14 Dec.– The dreadful anniversary, the 10th, returned again,' wrote the Queen.

> It seems impossible to believe all that time has passed. Felt painfully having to spend the day away from Windsor, but the one great anxiety seems to absorb everything else. Instead of this day dawning upon another death-bed, which I had felt almost certain of, it brought the cheering news that dear Bertie had slept quietly at intervals... the respiration easier, and food taken well...
>
> Breakfasted with Beatrice and Leopold, and then went over to dear Bertie. When I stood near the screen, he asked if that was not the Queen, and asked me to go up to him, which I did. He kissed my hand, smiling in the usual way, and said, 'So kind of you to come; it is the kindest thing you could do.' He wanted to talk more, but I would not allow him, and left... It seems hardly possible to realise the day and to feel that on this very day our dear Bertie is getting better instead of worse! How deeply grateful we are for God's mercy! Walked a little with Louise, very muddy and slushy, and the snow all disappearing. Went to see after dear Bertie, who was going on well, occasionally dozing and talking far less. What a relief... All satisfactory the last thing at night.[114]

Sir Henry Ponsonby, the Queen's Private Secretary and wisest of counsellors, took a more moderate view of the drama and sought to reduce the tension. He wrote to his wife: 'There seems to be a determination with some people to make the worst of everything... Stephy (the Duchess of Roxburghe) turns up her eyes and tells me wondrous horrors ending up by saying the Queen was by no means happy. 'Dear me,' I said, 'you surprise me, as I have just had a message as to whether Princess Beatrice and even some of the others might go tomorrow. Stephy considerably taken aback went to bed.'[115]

On the 15th, the doctors in attendance issued an optimistic bulletin: 'His Royal Highness has slept quietly through the night and there is some abatement of the gravity of the symptoms.' The Prince's life had indeed been saved: it was his groom, Charles Blegge, who died, and whom the Queen herself had visited. The Princess genuinely grieved for him; she paid for his tombstone in the little churchyard where her infant son was buried, with the inscription: 'The one is taken, the other left'.

The improvement in the Prince's condition continued and, after this harrowing ordeal, with its nightmare memories of the Prince Consort's death at this very time of year, the Queen was able to return to Windsor. There was a relapse, however, on the 17th, and once again the Queen journeyed to Sandringham. Departing from her invariable custom since the Prince Consort's death, she spent Christmas at Windsor; it was to be an *al fresco* festival, which 'would be spent very quietly with only one tree for ourselves and no élatage of dishes etc.'[116] Writing to her daughter, Vicky, the Queen reported: 'Another person, a woman who helped in the kitchen, has now got the fever.'[117] On the 27th, the Queen set off again for Sandringham on reports of high temperature and rapid pulse. 'They fear some deep seated inflammation somewhere and certainly it is very anxious.'[117] Severe pain in his leg caused further anxiety. The Prince was indeed very seriously ill, and only superb nursing and his own robust constitution enabled him to survive.

The children of the Prince and Princess of Wales had been sent to Osborne in the care of Mr Dalton. Their mother wrote:

My own darling little Eddy,
Mama sends a thousand thanks for all the very nice little letters, and is so glad to hear from Mr Dalton that Eddy is a good little boy. Mama is so glad that dear little Eddy has been going on praying God for dear Papa's recovery and the Almighty God has heard our prayers, and darling Papa is going to be quite well again and very soon we hope you may all come home again to see dear Papa once more! Mama is so glad her little Chicks will spend a happy and merry Christmas with dear Grandmama, and Mama sends you each a little Christmas card with many good wishes for Christmas and the New Year, which I hope will begin brightly and happily for all of us, and that my little Eddy will try and become a very good obedient boy. Remember me kindly to Mr Dalton with many thanks for all his letters, kiss Grandmama's hand, and give my love to Uncle Leo and Aunt Beatrice.
Ever your loving Mama,
Alix.[118]

On the 31st, the Queen was able to write, 'How I pray the New Year may see him safely on the road to recovery!'

Her wish was fulfilled. Alix was able to discern a real change in her husband. He was a man, full of life and energy, who had faced death, and he had been frightened. Now that he had been granted a reprieve, he could clearly perceive and appreciate not only the simple things of life, but also the goodness and devotion of a wife whom he had too often neglected. She wrote:

> Oh dearest Louise, you who knew what I suffered and saw my utter despair and misery – you would hardly know me now in my happiness. We are never apart and are enjoying our second honeymoon. Never, never can I thank God enough for all His mercy when He listened to my prayers and gave me back my life's happiness. [119]

The Duke of Cambridge returned to Sandringham at the beginning of February and was surprised by the rapid improvement in the Prince's health. 'Nothing could be nicer or more affectionate than he was... I really was more gratified at seeing his general condition than I could have believed possible after such an illness.' The following morning 'the Prince rode out, for his first ride, with dearest Alix, who looks happy and well, Alfred, myself, and some of the gentlemen.' [120] Shortly afterwards the Prince and Princess went down to Osborne to be reunited with their children. He was, for a time at least, a changed man. The Queen wrote to the Crown Princess of Prussia that 'he was quite himself again, only gentler and kinder than ever; and there is something different which I can't exactly express. It is like a new life – all the trees and flowers give him pleasure, which they never used to do... He is constantly with Alix, and they seem hardly ever apart!!!!' [121]

On the 27th, a Thanksgiving Service was held at St Paul's. The Queen, who had virtually retired from public life since Prince Albert's death, was a reluctant participant. 'I cannot deny,' she wrote to the Duke of Cambridge on the eve of the service, 'that I look with considerable dread to the dreadful fatigue of tomorrow, which I think will be too much for Bertie, and for which I am not feeling either very equal... we must hope that we shall have fine weather and my good people will be gratified.' [122] As it turned out, the crowds were enormous and the Queen and her son were delighted. Her reception taught her the importance of being seen – a major factor in the success of the monarchy, as it had never been enough to be reported unveiling statues and cairns in memory of the

Prince Consort in the remote Scottish Highlands – and encouraged her to resume her public engagements.

There was, too, an unexpected side-effect from the occasion. The under-current of republicanism had made sturdy growth recently. Sir Charles Dilke's lectures on the expenses of Royalty had aroused huge indignation, the disappearance of the Queen from public life and the successful re-establishment of the French Republic had combined to give the movement a fresh impetus. But the crowds' loyal enthusiasm which greeted the emergence of the Queen from her seclusion and the Prince's recovery dealt republicanism a severe blow.

The Prince's illness revealed other facets of his wife's character: her kindness and her courage. She was as much aware of the gravity of Blegge's condition as she was of her own husband's. She visited him, consulted with the doctors about him and, when he died, saw his parents and attended his funeral. Though her own birthday on 1 December was neglected, she remembered Lady Macclesfield's, two days later, with a gift of jewellery and an affectionate note. The Queen, whose feelings about her daughter-in-law tended to vary, was full of admiration for her selflessness. As for her courage, she had to endure what must have been serious humiliation when the Prince, in his delirium, shouted and swore, pouring out his indiscretions – which she would have wished to keep to herself. Now they were common knowledge, at least among her husband's family. All this had to be borne, too, in the presence of the doctors and nurses. The Princess was becoming used to her husband's infidelities – she had long since called him her 'naughty little man' – but they were endurable whilst there was at least an element of discretion in the conduct of his affairs; what she could not accept was public knowledge of scandals with which he was associated. With her lameness and deafness, her fortitude and devotion to a wayward husband, her generosity of spirit and lack of jealousy, the Princess revealed herself as a woman with remarkable qualities which, in any attempt to reach an assessment of her, should not be underestimated.

CHAPTER SIX

MARRIAGES

Of the five surviving Wales children, Princess Louise, the eldest daughter, was the first to marry. She was the quietest of them all, and less communicative than her sisters, so that her engagement to the Earl of Fife, eighteen years her senior, came as something of a surprise. Her mother had not encouraged the match; indeed, when Queen Victoria wrote to the Prince of Wales about the lack of enterprise shown in searching for eligible suitors for his daughters, the Prince replied that, 'Alix found them such good companions that she would not encourage their marrying, and that they themselves had little inclination for it.'[123] This was utter selfishness on the Princess' part, and forms an interesting paradox since, when her own happiness was not at stake, her generosity and consideration were legendary. Princess Louise, then, had been brought up without too much education and had led a largely sheltered life, and her engagement caught her parents unawares.

In 1889, the Earl of Fife had taken Castle Rising, a nearby estate, for the shooting, but it soon became evident that he had his eye on Princess Louise, eighteen years younger than himself, and in due course they became engaged, despite her mother's opposition. The match did not please everyone; the Queen would have been less pleased had she known that Fife was the subject of a good deal of scandal in Paris – but she did not know this, and approved the plan. 'It is a vy brilliant Marriage in a wordly point of view as he is immensely rich,'[124] she wrote happily to her daughter, Vicky, in Berlin. The Queen liked her descendants to marry outside the narrow family circle, and she was not deterred by the experience of her own daughter, Louise, who had married thus, and to another Scot, but whose marriage had not been a success.

The news of the betrothal was the occasion for another visit by the Queen to Sandringham, her first since the Prince of Wales had been struck down by typhoid. This time there was no sense of urgency and impending doom. The Prince's preparations for the Royal visit were elaborate, and are best learned from the Queen's journal:

Sandringham, 23rd April, 1889. – At two left Windsor, with Louise, the Duchess of Roxburghe, Sir H(enry) Ponsonby, Sir H. Ewart, and Dr Reid... At Lynn, Bertie and Eddy came in, and the Mayor handed an Address and his daughter a bouquet. A few minutes brought us to Wolferton Station... Here were great crowds. Alix, the dear girls, Lady Moreton, Charlotte Knollys, and Sir Dighton Probyn met us. The station was very prettily decorated, and just beyond it there was a triumphal arch. The sun came out, and all looked very bright. I got into Bertie's landau, open, with four horses and postillions, and dear Alix insisted on sitting backwards with Louise, in order that I might be better seen. Bertie and Eddy rode on either side, Sir D. Probyn in front, preceded by the Hunt, sixty in number, forty of whom were in their red coats. The road was lined with people, and numbers drove and rode. Great enthusiasm. We passed two more arches, and from the last, almost to the gates, there were Venetian masts. It was a very pretty sight. All Bertie's neighbours came out.

Everything came back to my mind, as we drove in at the gates and I saw again the house and stepped out and entered the hall. All was the same as at that terrible time and yet all is so different! A happy contrast. Bertie asked me to stand at the door to see the gentlemen of the Hunt, who had escorted me, pass by. There was a Guard of Honour of the Norfolk Artillery with their band, who afterwards marched past. Bertie and Alix then took me upstairs to the well-known old rooms, which have been freshly done up. I had some tea in my room and rested. We dined at a quarter to nine, Bertie leading me in, and Eddy sitting on my other side.

26 April.– We went down into the Ballroom, which was converted into a theatre, after talking till ten. There were nearly 300 people in the room, including all the neighbours, tenants and servants. We sat in the front row, I between Bertie and Alix. The stage was beautifully arranged and with great scenic effects, and the pieces were splendidly mounted and with numbers of people taking part. The piece, *The Bells*, is a melodrama... and is very thrilling... (It) was followed by the trial scene from *The Merchant of Venice* in which Irving played the part of Shylock, and that of Miss Ellen Terry that of Portia beautifully... It was a most successful performance. I waited in the Drawing-room a moment to speak to Irving and Ellen Terry. He is very gentleman-like, and she, very pleasing and handsome. It was one when I got upstairs.

Windsor Castle, 27th April.– We left Sandringham at half past ten, having spent a very pleasant time under dear Bertie and Alix's hospitable roof, and I was greatly touched by all their kindness and affection.

The weather was very favourable. They and their children accompanied us to Wolferton Station, and here they took a most affectionate leave of us. Reached Windsor at 2.25.[125]

Every care had been taken; even Sandringham time had been set back to conform to Greenwich. Nor could she have known of the confusion caused by her wish to see Irving and Ellen Terry after the performance – the actors were changing and removing their make-up when the summons came, and there was a frantic scramble to avoid keeping the Queen waiting; nor that the house was so full of visitors and her own large personal staff and servants that Irving and Terry had to return to London that night. Nevertheless, the Queen's visit, though she was never again to come to Sandringham, gave public approval to Princess Louise's engagement. The couple were married later that year in the Chapel Royal, and spent some weekends at their house in Richmond Park. The groom had been created a Duke, with some reluctance on the Queen's part, and his Duchess thereafter largely retired from public life and spent much of her time salmon fishing, with great expertise, in Scotland. An early report of their marriage was encouraging:

> Princess May and I prolonged our walk (after church) after Pcess Mary Adelaide had gone in. Coming home near the house we saw a little pony carriage, in the shape of a low dog cart coming along – a lady driving herself – a little groom behind. The lady stopped, it was Princess Louise, Duchess of Fife – She looked so pretty – almost as pretty as her mother – with a bright colour – pretty blue eyes – lovely teeth… Pss May says Pss Louise is so happy.[126]

Those who had known the Princess as a shy, tongue-tied girl were delighted that marriage had brought out a vivacity that they had never seen before. 'It does one's heart good to see them,' wrote the Duchess of Teck. With their immense wealth, the Fifes had two homes in Scotland and, when in England, they could choose between Sheen Lodge, near Richmond, which was their favourite residence, London and Brighton. Having escaped from the nursery world of Sandringham she had contrived to do so very thoroughly.

At this stage in the life of the family, Prince George was often at sea as a serving naval officer, and Prince Eddy was falling in and out of love with distressing frequency. The question remained how he could usefully spend his time. In 1889, Prince Eddy had embarked on a tour of India, where his choice of companions and entertainments caused scandal and from which he had returned worn out with dissipation – nothing had been accomplished except the further weakening of a constitution which was not naturally robust.

In May 1890, Prince Eddy was created Duke of Clarence and Avondale, and it was becoming increasingly clear that he must marry and settle down. His first essay in serious courtship was with Princess Alix of Hesse, one of the Queen's granddaughters by Princess Alice. But she would have none of him. Then, in 1891, he fell deeply in love with Princess Hélène of Orleans, daughter of the Pretender to the French throne. He would have to persuade her to change her religion, for a Catholic could never become Consort to the future King of England, neither constitutionally could the heir-presumptive become a Catholic. The Queen saw the impossibility of the match – though, when she met the two lovers at Balmoral, she was, somewhat surprisingly, won over, and promised to see what might be done. But the Prince's hopes were dashed by the refusal of the Princess' father, and the Pope, to allow Princess Hélène to renounce her faith. She was, perhaps, the one and only true love of the Prince's life, and it seems that she was genuinely in love with him – she had not known him long. During his last illness he was heard to murmur her name. The Princess of Wales, who had been delighted by the engagement and who would never have wished her son to marry a German, was as disappointed as Prince Eddy by the abandonment of the plan. 'This brings everything to a deadlock,' the Prince of Wales wrote to Prince George; 'and it is a sad state of things and makes poor Eddy quite wretched.'[127] The story of this romance loses some of its tragic appeal when it is recalled that Prince Eddy was already casting his eyes elsewhere. Although to most people this would seem impossible, yet the Prince could write that 'exceptions will happen at times.'[128]

The question of the young Prince's future now became urgent as his prospects with Princess Hélène faded and his conduct gave rise to further scandal. The Prince of Wales was fast becoming exasperated with his son, having removed him abruptly from Cambridge. On 5 August 1891, he wrote to the Queen: 'His remaining in the Army is simply a waste of time… His education and future have been a matter of some considerable anxiety to us & the difficulty of rousing him is very great. A good sensible wife with some considerable character is what he needs most, but where is she to be found?'[129] It was a question which the Queen herself had asked some thirty years earlier, when the Courts of Europe were searched for a suitable bride for the young Prince of Wales. There were a number of options open to Prince Eddy's parents; the Queen had recommended a tour of the European capitals, which would widen his outlook on the Continental scene, but, as Sir Francis Knollys wrote:

> Unfortunately, her views on certain social subjects are so strong, that the Prince of Wales does not like to tell her his real reason for sending Prince Eddy away, which is intended as a punishment, and as a means of keeping him out of harm's way; and I am afraid that neither of those objects would be attained by his simply travelling about Europe. She is therefore giving her advice in the dark.[130]

She had kept herself surprisingly well-informed, however, of the young Prince's activities, and was well aware of his instability: 'You speak of his apathy and want of application,' she wrote to her eldest son. 'You disliked your lessons very much, and it was very difficult to make you apply. But you travelled a great deal, and with good people, and you profited immensely by what you saw... No doubt you were much more lively than Eddy.'[131]

What is less clear is the Queen's awareness of Prince Eddy's reputed tendencies. They had been broadly hinted at while the Prince was at Cambridge where scurrilous verses debating his sexual orientation had been published, and his parents were anxious to distance him from sources of temptation. His mentors were exercised to provide him with appropriate attractions and diversions. He had a certain charm and was good-natured in an indolent way; too idle to be bothered to practice at polo, but enjoyed whist.

The Prince of Wales was in favour of a tour of the colonies; it was not expected that any benefit would be derived from this but the real reason was, as the Prince of Wales told the Queen, that 'the voyages would be longer.' The Princess of Wales herself hoped that her son might remain in the Army – there he would be more accessible to her, and she could keep an eye on him. But it was too late to reconsider that as a viable alternative, and she turned her thoughts towards the final option, and the one ultimately favoured by all parties: marriage to Princess Victoria Mary of Teck ('May'). The Prince of Wales, out of patience with his son, and humiliated both by the unpopularity he himself had incurred, and his wife's disfavour as a result of his indiscretions in the Tranby Croft affair and with Frances Brooke, escaped to the pleasures of Homburg, leaving the Princess of Wales to make the final decision.

Princess May, as she was popularly called, would prove an unexceptionable bride for Prince Eddy, the Princess of Wales reflected, and he would, as likely as not, fall head over heels in love with her. It would be an ideal match – ideal from the viewpoint of the Prince's parents and, indeed, the Queen, and there was no difficulty in persuading Prince Eddy that she was a capital girl. He was carefully drilled and obediently proposed to her at Luton Hoo in December 1891, and was accepted, to his parents' extreme satisfaction and relief. It seemed at last as though the whole worrying situation might be brought to a happy conclusion. But who was this Princess May; who had been selected as Prince Eddy's bride, and what might have been her thoughts on the matter?

The Princess, born in May 1867, was the eldest of the four children of the Duke and Duchess of Teck. Her father was descended, by a morganatic marriage, from the Duke of Wurttemberg. When he came to England in search of a bride, in 1866, he was a fine-looking man of twenty-nine, though somewhat sensitive about his ancestry. His courtship of Princess Mary Adelaide, a granddaughter of George III through Adolphus, Duke of Cambridge, was brief and entirely successful. There was no competition – the Princess was said to turn the scales at 17 stone, which had effectively repelled a number of suitors who, having paid court, departed shaking their heads. 'Her size is fearful,' commented the Queen.[133] At thirty-three, it had seemed unlikely that anyone could be found who might offer for her.

Princess Mary Adelaide and her mother, 'the stout parties from Kew' as Lord Clarendon dubbed them, lived at Cambridge Cottage on Kew Green. The Princess was genial, gregarious, extrovert, ruthless in achieving her ambitions, unpunctual – and utterly incapable of understanding the meaning of money. The public loved her and she cheerfully acknowledged their warmth. 'There goes fat Mary!' they shouted as she drove, beaming, in her carriage. Though not always punctilious in her duty to the Queen, her cousin, she was able through sheer persistence to persuade her to grant White Lodge in Richmond Park to the Teck family, despite the Queen's awareness of the financial problems which could, and later did, overtake her – in addition to a fine suite of rooms in Kensington Palace. She possessed a large capacity for company and entertainment and was oblivious of the expense which was a necessity to these indulgences. Her marriage to Prince Teck surprised everyone; the wedding took place after barely four months' acquaintance with each other. Her husband, now created a Duke, had little enough to occupy himself with, but he had excellent taste and planned the garden at White Lodge and refurbished its rooms. Even so, for a man who had spent much of his active life in the army, such inactivity was bound to lead to restlessness and irritability and, eventually, proneness to attacks of 'nerves'.

Princess May was a central figure at Sandringham and in the life of the nation for more than forty years. For much of this time her shyness and reserve attracted comment and the early causes of what the Countess of Airlie described as 'the hard crust of inhibition' are to be found in her parents. Princess Mary Adelaide educated her children on sound principles, giving them a dimension in their lives never contemplated for the children of the Prince and Princess of Wales. The jovial exuberance and vitality of her mother gave the young Princess May scope only to listen and watch. It was not long before she became aware that her mother's size was not only unusual but provoked amusement among children of her own age. She could not fail to observe that where one chair was sufficient for other grown-ups, the Princess needed two, causing indiscreet comment and hilarity. In conversation, Princess Mary Adelaide was apt to remark on her daughter's shyness, which could only aggravate such sensitivity in any child. Furthermore, she must have seen, and wondered at, the contrast between her parents. Later, her father's unpredictable behaviour (he had suffered a stroke in 1884) would have increased her reserve; neither could she have failed as an intelligent, adolescent girl, to be aware of her mother's disregard of the family's acute financial difficulties which, following the increasing insistence of her creditors and the exasperation of her relatives, were to lead to their two-year exile in Florence. Although as children they had played together, Princess May knew that a gulf created out of differing cultures and interests separated her from her in-laws; she was truly 'the poor relation'.

It was not to be expected that this marriage to Prince Albert Victor would be, at any rate initially, a love match. Princess May was well aware that Royal marriages were arranged, often for political purposes. She had been brought up to recognise that service to the throne was the highest and most honourable occupation she could envisage. Further, she knew and liked Prince Eddy; they had known each other for years but – and this was important – only intermittently. To what extent she was aware of his indiscretions and dissipations can only be guessed at, but she did know about Princess Hélène and sympathised with him. Later, in London, she began to have doubts and wondered whether she could 'really take this on',[134] but the Duchess, who was not easily to be deflected from a project which would not only have brought honour to her family but, in all likelihood, respite from her chronic financial difficulties, had reassured her. 'Of course you can,' she replied buoyantly. Though the Princess had faltered, she nevertheless began to prepare her trousseau and to make arrangements for the visit to Sandringham to celebrate her fiancé's birthday. Meanwhile, as a purely temporary measure, Prince Eddy was to remain with his Regiment until the spring. It was hoped that this would ensure that he kept out of trouble until he was safely married.

Of the other Wales children, Princess Maud and Princess Victoria remained close to the family circle. Their mother's claim that they 'had no inclination' for marriage must be discounted as the wishful thinking of a selfish and increasingly lonely woman who would resist any weakening of the bonds of a close family life. The Princess of Wales was not imaginative, and never less so than when her own comfort and convenience were threatened. The then Prime Minister, Lord Rosebery, tentatively considered offering for Princess Victoria but the idea was not pursued, and any notions she may have had of marrying a commoner were firmly rejected by her parents. The close bonds linking her to her mother effectively prevented the kind of freedom which might had led to more realistic opportunities.

During the First World War, Princess Victoria remained generally with her mother at Sandringham, visiting families on the estate whose menfolk had joined the Services. She visited camps in France and hospitals in England, where her visits were awaited with some trepidation, since she had an uncanny knack of sympathising with the sick and wounded in a well-meaning but tactless way which seemed to draw attention to their condition. 'Poor man!' she would say; 'I can see you are very ill.' When King George was seriously ill in 1928, the Princess was kept out of his room for precisely this reason, but she contrived to slip in and very soon convinced her brother that he was dying, leaving him depressed and exhausted.

Princess Maud was more fortunate than her older sister; she was able to attract the notice of her first cousin, Prince Charles of Denmark, and they were married in the Chapel at Buckingham Palace in July 1896. The Queen signified her approval of the match by attending not only the service but the luncheon in the Ballroom afterwards. The couple planned to spend a short honeymoon at Appleton, the former home at Sandringham of Louise Cresswell, which had been given to Princess Maud by her father as a wedding present. But the pull of family ties was powerful: Princess Maud was reluctant to leave the Sandringham estate and her family; moreover, she was well aware that 'Toria' would be left single-handed to be her mother's companion and had few illusions about the kind of life her sister would lead. In the event, the honeymoon lasted five months and caused considerable embarrassment to the Prince's family who, three weeks after the wedding, had gathered to welcome her to Denmark. More relations arrived but Prince Charles and Princess Maud tarried at Sandringham, following the traditional pattern of her own family life with scant regard for the inconvenience they were causing their relations in Denmark. Eventually, the welcoming committee dispersed without having glimpsed the young couple. It was not until shortly before Christmas that they finally reached Denmark where they received a belated, but nevertheless warm, welcome. Their married life was not uniformly easy; Prince Charles, as a serving naval officer, was frequently absent for long periods, and the Princess yearned for her own home at Appleton where she would frequently return to rejoin the family circle.

In 1905 their lives, which had been unremarkable in its domesticity, underwent an abrupt change. The Act of Union between Norway and Sweden was dissolved by the Norwegians who then found themselves without a monarch, whilst Sweden refused to recognise the dissolution. Anglo-German relations were strained, each viewing the other with suspicion, and Denmark was therefore invited to find an occupant for the throne. Every eye was turned towards Prince Charles, who accepted the invitation, though with a reluctance shared by Princess Maud. King Haakon VII, as he was now known, and Queen Maud were duly crowned at Oslo in the following year. Queen Maud's health was precarious and it had long been agreed that she would continue to spend part of every year in England, where she remained a familiar figure on the Sandringham estate, supporting her mother and sister and happy within the close family circle.

Shy as children and retiring in their maturity, the daughters of King Edward VII and Queen Alexandra never sought the limelight and they were not widely known among the British public during their lifetime. But they were an inseparable part of the Sandringham scene for nearly sixty years. Louise and Maud achieved their freedom but 'Toria', in her lifetime of service to her mother, deserves our sympathy. Though she enjoyed an affectionate relationship with her brother, Prince George, the deadly sameness of the Sandringham routine must have weighed upon her. When she was finally liberated in 1925, it was too late – she felt lost in a world that had largely passed her by and all that was left for her was another ten years of loneliness in her apartments in Kensington Palace and at Coppins, her Buckinghamshire home.

CHAPTER SEVEN

TROUBLED YEARS

The years 1890-91 were among the most troubled of the Prince's maturity. Not only were the Royal couple worried about Prince Eddy's future, which looked more and more unpromising, but the Prince of Wales himself was drawn, albeit unwillingly, into situations which were heavy with scandal.

Early in September 1891, the Prince was staying, with some reluctance, at Tranby Croft, near Doncaster, the home of a Mr Wilson, a shipping magnate. Another time he might have accepted the hospitality of Christopher Sykes who by now had ruined himself in trying to match the Prince's standards. Among the guests was Sir William Gordon-Cumming, a colonel in the Scots Guards, who was immensely wealthy and a close friend of the Prince. After dinner the gentlemen sat down to play baccarat, but it was not long before it was observed that Sir William appeared to be cheating. Similar instances were again noticed on the following evening. On the next day, Sir William was accused of cheating but, in view of the presence of the Prince of Wales, a promise of secrecy would be given in exchange for an undertaking by him that he would give up playing cards. Sir William denied the charges but agreed to sign the document since the evidence against him seemed overwhelming.

The matter might have ended there but, almost inevitably, the secret leaked out, though by whom has never been satisfactorily established. Sir William, greatly angered by the unwelcome publicity, issued a writ for slander against the five signatories to the document. The action excited wide interest, which quickened when it was learned that the Prince of Wales himself had been involved in a game which at that time was illegal. Furthermore, as a Field Marshall, he had disobeyed Queen's Regulations by not reporting Sir William, if he had really believed that cheating had occurred. Either way, the Prince showed up badly. Sir William lost his case, but the publicity surrounding the Prince's appearance in court made it seem almost as if he himself were the guilty party. The opinion of Society was divided, creating lasting bitterness; the Queen criticised him openly and the Press condemned his participation in the game. The repercussions continued for some time and, indeed, overlapped with another crisis.

One of the Prince's closest friends was a Lord Charles Beresford, whose brother Marcus was the manager of the Stud at Sandringham. Lord Charles was a naval officer who by his courage and good nature won the loyalty of those serving under him. He was also wealthy, energetic and amusing – in short, exactly the kind of man whom the Prince found congenial company – and a founder member of the 'fast' Marlborough House Club. His practical jokes were elaborate and entertaining. On one occasion he donned navvy's clothes and, with a group of friends, dug up a section of Piccadilly, which rendered the road useless for three days. He was, of course, often to be seen at the house parties among the Prince's closest friends. The Prince used his influence on his friend's behalf, so that in 1884 he was appointed 4th Lord of the Admiralty. It was at this point that Lord Charles, himself married to a woman ten years older than himself, fell in love with the wife of Lord Brooke, who was inclined to take a tolerant view of his wife's infidelities. There was no attempt at concealment; Lady Brooke even told Lord Charles' wife that she would elope with her husband, which seemed to imply that the Brooke's marriage was to all intents and purposes at an end. Then, in 1889, she heard that Lady Charles was expecting a baby and, instead of accepting the situation with dignity and withdrawing from the liaison, wrote a letter to Lord Charles which suggested that she was the injured party and that in returning to his wife, he had been unfaithful to herself. It was, perhaps, unfortunate that the letter fell into the hands of Lord Charles' wife, Mina, who had been authorised to open her husband's post in his absence. Lady Charles left this letter with her solicitor, George Lewis, together with instructions to sue Lady Brooke for libel if she caused further trouble. 'Daisy' Brooke, however, called on Lewis claiming the letter since she had written it. Lewis told her that it was Lady Charles' property, and he had no authority to hand it over. At this point Lady Brooke called on the Prince of Wales for assistance, for she had long been one of his favourites. With a singular lack of judgment he tried to persuade Lewis to burn the letter; when he failed, he ensured that Lady Charles would be socially ostracised, which caused her husband to visit the Prince to tell him that he had behaved like a blackguard and had had no right to interfere.

For years the row simmered, Lord Charles behaving in a slighting manner when in the presence of the Prince, and it was not until 1897 – and at the races – that the Beresfords dared to seek reconciliation.

The Prince explained to Lady Brooke in terms warmer than mere friendship the circumstances which had led to this encounter:

> Shortly before leaving Ascot today, Marcus B. came to me & said he had a great favour to ask me... He then became much affected, & actually cried, & said might he bring his brother C. up to me to offer his congratulations on Persimmon's success. I had no alternative but to say yes. He came up with his hat off, & would not put it on till I told him, & shook hands. We talked a little about racing, then I turned and we parted. My loved one, I hope you won't be annoyed at what has happened, and exonerate me from blame, as that is all I care about.[135]

The affair had even involved the Queen, to whom Lady Charles had also appealed. She was well aware of the disrepute brought upon the Monarchy by this latest of her son's indiscretions. She deeply distrusted the aristocracy in general, and the 'Marlborough House Set' in particular, denouncing them as frivolous, selfish and immoral: 'wretched ignorant Highborn beings, who live only to kill time.'[136]

As for the Prince, he had much to make up: the unwelcome publicity had shed a harsh light on his habits; it was not the first time that he been booed at race meetings; he had transgressed the unwritten code of Society and, what was perhaps worse, offended the increasingly influential middle class. The aristocracy understood, and forgave, infidelity – provided absolute discretion was maintained. Everyone who was anyone knew the rules; every country house party had its own code of practice and this was expected to be observed – a plate of sandwiches left outside a bedroom door might, or might not, have its own significance, but this revelation of sexual intrigues was unforgivable, even though 'Daisy' Brooke was notorious for her indiscretions. The middle classes reacted strongly: Royalty was expected to set an example to the nation, and the repercussions of this affair sent a shock through the country of which the Prince could not but be aware. The Princess of Wales, who had suffered much in silence, evoked admiration for her tact and loyalty to her husband, but she never accepted 'Daisy', the 'Babbling Brooke', and never invited her to Sandringham.

The Princess of Wales might be forgiven if she had expressed resentment at her husband's unfaithfulness, but she never allowed her actions to express displeasure until 'the Beresford affair', when she deliberately missed the Prince's fiftieth birthday celebrations at Sandringham. She might refer to him in private as her 'naughty little man' but she remained intensely loyal to him. Was there, perhaps, a certain chilliness about her beauty, or had her ardour abated after bearing him six children? Her almost suffocating affection for them and the simplicity of her mind might provoke the suspicion that there was an element of immaturity in her love for the Prince, whose restlessness and susceptibility for beautiful women led him to stray. Yet he always returned to the Princess and her own wisdom allowed her to accept the inevitable. What seems certain is that she never gave cause for suspicion that she was unfaithful to him. One friendship, however, deserves consideration.

Oliver Montagu, whose brother Edward was a friend of the Prince's, formed a bond with the Princess which was to last for a quarter of a century. A younger son of the Earl of Sandwich, Montagu was appointed an Equerry to the Prince in 1868 and frequently attended the Princess on social occasions; away from Royal circles he had a reputation for wildness. Certainly, in an idealised way, he adored her, nor can there be any doubt that she valued his company. But the relationship remained platonic and caused scarcely any gossip. They were both religious, and the Princess had been carefully brought up. Though she could indulge in practical jokes and badinage, she knew at once when things had gone far enough and would kindly, but firmly, check any attempt at familiarity. If this may appear inconclusive, it must be remembered that a wife's infidelity was regarded as a much more serious matter than a husband's. The Princess was aware of public opinion and would not have risked forfeiting her husband's love for her, which remained steadfast throughout his inconstancy.

In August of this ill-fated year, 1891, the Prince and Princess were together for Cowes Week. At this time they were faced with the necessity of grappling with the problem of Prince Eddy's future, which had become a matter of some urgency. But the Prince, hard-pressed by other difficulties, dodged the issue and left for Homburg. The Princess thus had to consider the options before her: various permutations of foreign tours for Prince Eddy were suggested, which would keep him out of at least some of the influences to which he was unfortunately so prone, or marriage to Princess May. The Princess settled for the latter and almost at once left England for Denmark. It was while she was abroad that news of the Beresford affair reached her and, since such publicity was unendurable to her, she postponed her return and elected to visit the Czar and Czarina, who were celebrating their silver wedding in the Crimea. It was particularly significant that her absence at this time meant that she would miss the Prince's fiftieth birthday festivities at Sandringham, an event not lightly to be passed over. She missed a good deal more, for on the night of 31 October fire broke out on the top floor of the house. It seems that fires had been lighted to air the rooms before the Prince's arrival, the weather having been unseasonably wet. Early the following morning, smoke was observed to be issuing from the upper windows and the alarm was raised. Local fire brigades were summoned, and the Prince, who was staying with Lord and Lady Brooke in Essex, was telegraphed. Despite his concern, he remained calm and simply awaited further news. This must have called for some self-command on his part, for he had long been interested in conflagrations and, having assisted at a number of fires in London, had taken elaborate precautions to ensure that there was an effective fire service on the estate, and he would have wished to see, now that it had been called into action, how effective his measures had been. By the time the fire engines had arrived the top floor was well alight and soon afterwards the roof collapsed in a burst of flame and sparks, while the men below ran for safety. On the lawn, all those not engaged in fighting the fire laboured to rescue the treasures of the house. Pictures, ornaments and furnishings from the over-crowded rooms were carried to safety, whilst on all sides firemen swung the handles of the fire-pumps. It was some time before the fire could be brought under control, but it was fortunately largely confined to the top floor.

The Prince arrived at Sandringham the next day, to gaze at the charred rafters and the runnels of sooty water from ceilings and walls. It was scarcely an auspicious start to his birthday festivities. The dining room, which was immediately below the area most affected, had sustained much of the damage, most of it by water, which had badly stained the valuable Goya tapestries given to the Prince by King Alfonso of Spain. Happily, it was found that the stains could be removed and the damage repaired for less than £10,000. These tapestries had been much admired by the Prince on a visit to Spain. King Alfonso had promised to have copies made but somehow the order had never been executed and the King had generously sent the originals. Considerably heartened by his review of the situation, the Prince departed for London as soon as the restoration work commenced, announcing that he would, as usual, celebrate his birthday at Sandringham. His plans were ruined, of course, both by the fire and by his wife's absence; there was a week, however, in which to put the house to rights so that he could still hold some kind of a celebration there. Any measure of enjoyment achieved was a triumph over the odds, with parts of the house still damp and smelling of smoke, the roof under tarpaulins and the Princess conspicuous by her absence.

Yet it seemed that there was no end to their worries for, on the day after his father's birthday, Prince George complained of a bad headache

followed by a high temperature. The symptoms were serious enough for
his doctor to advise a move to London, where typhoid was diagnosed.
'I had a pretty bad attack,' Prince George wrote afterwards,

> ...and never moved out of my bed until Dec. 21st... Motherdear and
> sisters returned from Russia on Nov. 22nd. I was very glad to have her
> back... On Dec. 30th I came down to dear Sandringham with Papa,
> Motherdear, Eddy, Toria, Harry, Charlotte, Ellis and Holford; the
> journey did me no harm, although of course I am very weak.[137]

Prince George fortunately possessed a strong constitution; even so, he was
laid up for six weeks and left much debilitated. The fever had been serious
enough to cause real public concern: had not Prince Albert died from it
and, so nearly, the Prince of Wales himself? Had Prince George also died,
the line of succession after Prince Albert Victor would have devolved on
Princess Louise. This would have been unfortunate, for though Queen
Victoria had shown beyond question that a woman could rule effectively,
her granddaughter was shy and retiring. The Princess of Wales cut short
her visit to the Crimea and returned to nurse her son. No wonder the
Prince wrote to his sister, the Empress Frederick: 'I cannot regret that the
year '91 is about to close as, during it, I have experienced many worries
and annoyances which ought to last me for a long time. My only happiness
has been Eddy's engagement and Georgy's recovery.'

Such was the situation when the family were struck by a new and
most grievous blow. The new year of 1892 arrived bringing with it a
continuation of the cold spell which had frozen the lake at Sandringham.
Indoors, influenza had laid low members of the Royal family and the
Household with equal impartiality, from Princess Victoria to Captain
Holford, equerry to Prince Eddy, while the Princess of Wales and Princess
May both suffered heavy colds. Prince George was still convalescent and
feeling very weak. This was the state of affairs on 4 January when the Tecks,
with Princess May herself who, we recall, had barely a month previously
become engaged to Prince Eddy, arrived to celebrate his birthday.

On the 7th, Prince Eddy was one of the guns of a shooting party. He
felt unwell during the course of the morning, but set out with the others,
turning to wave his hat to his mother. It was a gesture she was to remember
for the rest of her life. He felt increasingly unwell during the course of the

morning and, after meeting the ladies for lunch at Sir Dighton Probyn's house, was persuaded by Princess May to return to the house. Once he was comfortably installed in bed, the Princess went to sit by her fiancé in his cramped, narrow little room overlooking the great *porte-cochère*.

On the morning of his birthday it became clear that the Prince had caught the prevailing influenza. He came downstairs to look at his presents, but felt too unwell to remain long and soon returned to bed. Outside, the weather remained as cold as ever. 'Froze hard in the night and a little snow fell,' ran Prince George's diary entry. 'Answering telegrams for Eddy and writing all day.'[138] The evening celebrations continued according to plan, but something was lacking in the festive spirit. The birthday dinner, at which the Duke of Teck proposed Prince Eddy's health, was followed by an entertainment with a ventriloquist and a banjo-player, which might at any other time have appealed strongly to the absent Prince. At this stage, only twenty-four hours after the onset of the illness, there was no sense of anxiety. Influenza was almost commonplace among one's acquaintance at this time of year, and in a telegram to the Queen at Osborne, the Princess wrote philosophically: 'Poor Eddy got influenza, cannot dine, so tiresome.'[139]

By the following day it was apparent that the Prince's condition had deteriorated, and Dr Laking, Physician-in-Ordinary to the Prince of Wales, who had been sent for to assist the local physician, diagnosed incipient pneumonia and sent for Dr Broadbent, who had attended Prince George when he had contracted typhoid. On the 11th, the patient's condition was somewhat improved, but on the 12th there was a relapse, and by the 13th he was delirious, shouting about his Regiment and brother-officers, his love for the Queen, and frequently uttering the name 'Hélène,' the Princess of Orleans, with whom he had been ardently in love the previous year. His lips were livid, and his finger-nails had turned blue; the physicians who had gathered around his bedside, in those days long before the miracles of penicillin and antibiotics, could not but form a pessimistic prognosis: pneumonia was a killer. The Prince's family, with the Tecks and Princess May, were waiting for news in the small sitting-room next door. Often the Princess of Wales went to sit quietly by her son, wiping the sweat from his forehead and trying to calm him, while the nurses put ice on his head to cool the fever. His father, unhelpful in the sickroom, wandered about the house restlessly, feeling himself useless and borne down by anxiety.

The day wore on, and it was not until after midnight that the Princess was induced to take some rest, but she was soon recalled with the report that Prince Eddy was dying. 'I had to master my deep, deep despair, and be calm,' the Princess wrote. 'Although the tears were running down I spoke to him, but Oh, he no longer heard me, and yet he was still talking, but only with great difficulty and effort and with that terrible rattle in his throat.'[140]

With the Prince's final struggle for life, the family congregated in the small room until it was crammed. Injections of ether and strychnine were administered, which appeared to revive the dying man. Once he cried out: 'Something too awful has happened. My darling brother George is dead.' Whether this was a confused reference to his brother's typhoid will never be known. As hopes faded, the prayers for the dying were read by Mr Harvey, domestic chaplain to the Prince of Wales. The Princess sat at the head of the bed, holding her son's hand. At one side knelt Dr Laking, feeling the weakening pulse; at the other, Prince George, too, knelt, with a nurse and Dr Manby beside him; but all were powerless to prevent him slipping away. He repeated 'Who was that?' as he sank into a coma, and at 9.35 a.m. on the morning of the 14th, Prince Albert Victor, heir-presumptive to the throne of England, died.

'Never shall I forget that dreadful night of agony and suspense as we sat round his bed,' Princess May wrote to Queen Victoria. 'Darling Aunt Alix never left him for a moment and when a few minutes before the end she turned to Dr Laking and said "Can you do nothing more to save him?" and he shook his head, the despairing look on her face was the most heart-rending thing I have ever seen.'[141]

For his parents, Prince Eddy's death was a shattering blow. After years of anxiety about him and his weak, unstable character, his engagement to Princess May of Teck, an intelligent, steady and in every way desirable bride, had been a source of the deepest satisfaction and, let it be admitted, relief to them. And now, suddenly, in a few days, all this had vanished. That he had seemed in all likelihood totally unsuited for the throne no longer mattered. On this day, the hopes they had nourished for the future were utterly destroyed.

Yet all was not over. The distraught parents felt all the force of the Victorian fascination with death. Again and again they visited the room where Prince Eddy's body lay, as in a chapel of rest. When the Princess's old and trusted friend, Oliver Montagu, hastened to Sandringham to pay his respects, he was taken several times upstairs to that small room. Nothing was to be changed there for many years. As at Windsor, where the Prince Consort's shaving water and fresh clothes were still put out daily, as if he were still alive, so in Prince Eddy's room the water in his jug was kept fresh, the soap was changed whenever it lost its pristine appearance. On the bed, the Union Jack was spread. Even the hat he had last worn on that fateful shooting expedition was carefully preserved. Today, this preoccupation with the trappings of the dead may seem morbid: to the Victorian mind it perpetuated the memory of the beloved and, though perhaps carried to the extreme by the Royal family, was only an extension of preserving the relics of the dead.

The Prince and Princess were brought closer together than for some time by the death of their eldest son. They both broke down when Oliver Montagu arrived to comfort them. When Prince Eddy's coffin was borne to the church on the edge of the gardens, the Princess wrote: 'Bertie and I followed him on foot Friday night at eleven o'clock to our own little church'. She had wished that the Prince could be buried beside their infant son Alexander John at Sandringham, but the Prince felt that he should take his place as a one-time heir-presumptive among the Kings and Queens at Windsor. Copies of the sermon preached at Sandringham the Sunday after the Prince's death were printed. The bereaved father gave a copy to his wife, signed, 'From her devoted but broken-hearted husband, Bertie.' Though the Princess watched the funeral service in St George's Chapel, Windsor from a gallery known as the Queen's Closet; she had said farewell to her son, in her heart, as she watched from the Big House as his coffin was carried from the little church across the lawns to Wolferton Station. On the pew where he had sat with his parents ever since he was a small boy a brass plate recorded: 'This place was occupied for twenty-eight years by my darling Eddy next to his ever sorrowing and loving Motherdear, January 14th, 1892.'

The Queen, who had wished to visit the family at Sandringham but had been dissuaded by the Prince of Wales, wrote in her letter of sympathy of the 'overwhelming misfortune' of Prince Eddy's death – it was a time for conventional expressions of grief. His sisters replied and Princess Victoria wrote: '...It is almost impossible to believe that our beloved Eddy has really been taken from us – Just now when all his future seemed bright, it seems cruel he should have had to go...' Princess Louise noted that, 'His was such a gentle, kind and affectionate nature that everyone was devoted to him.' The Prince's compliant and affectionate gentleness was what the family would remember – and the appalling suddenness of his death.

The Press was more guarded. The Prince had never been a public figure and his obituary notices were as near neutral as it was possible to be. The *St James Gazette* wrote that 'he may be said to have lived under the shadow of the shadow of the throne.'

The funeral ceremonies ended on a wry note. The Princess had expressed the wish that women should not attend her son's funeral, but the 'Aunts' from Osborne were unwilling to miss such a family occasion. Somehow, at the end of the service, they found their pew door stuck, and had to be released, and they came to the conclusion that they had been locked in, which brought a strongly-worded protest. Sir Arthur Ellis, an Equerry to the Prince of Wales, replied to the Queen's Private Secretary:

> The Prince of Wales desires me to say that the harem of Princesses was not locked into the further Zenana pew closet but the door got jammed, and adds that they were none of them wanted at all. No ladies were to attend, and the Princess of Wales especially requested privacy – and to avoid meeting her Osborne relations. So they all came. If Princess Beatrice was annoyed it cannot be helped and she must get over it – as she likes.[142]

The same writer estimated the bill for answering the thousands of telegrams which poured in to Sandringham at £2,000. But not all the eulogies from monarchs and statesmen that flowed around them like a sea could brighten the gloom as the grieving parents returned to their silent house in the Norfolk countryside. Yet, even while the Prince of Wales grieved, he knew in his heart that his eldest son had been entirely unfit for the high position to which the circumstances of his birth directed him. He could find solace in the fact that his new heir, Prince George, possessed sterling qualities that would one day stand him in good stead.

Later, the parents paid a visit to the Queen at Osborne to recount the manner of Prince Eddy's death. 'Poor darling Alix looks the picture of grief and misery,' wrote the Queen, ' and he very ill; dear Alix looked lovelier than ever in her mourning and a long black veil, with a point, on her head.'[143]

The death of her eldest son was a blow from which the Princess never fully recovered. Not only was it the grief of a deeply affectionate mother but also, perhaps, the special love that a mother has for the weakest and most wayward of her brood. Prince Eddy, for all his charm, his dreaminess and his susceptibility to women, was lethargic, dissipated, allergic to nearly every form of education and a source of constant worry to his parents, but all this was discounted by his premature death. Two years later, the Princess was to write in a letter of sympathy to the Marchioness of Granby: 'I was so touched that you should have turned to me who have had to bear the same despairing sorrow which nothing on earth can ever lessen or change, which must be borne with patience and submission to the will of God.'

It was for later historians to assess the effect of the Prince's death, which must be seen in the context of the comparatively secluded life of the Queen and the prevailing unpopularity of the Prince of Wales. Indeed, the Monarchy might not have survived the reign of a weak, vacillating successor to Edward VII in whom every quality required of a sovereign was lacking. No wonder Prince George's succession has been described as a 'merciful act of providence.'

There was, thankfully, much to be done during that sad summer of 1892. The damage to the house had to be made good and the Prince took the opportunity to engage Colonel Edis again to construct a range of rooms above Teulon's conservatory, whose style was to be preserved in the extensions. The effect is especially noticeable from the west, where the later work, with its lower roof-line and contrasting brickwork, joins Humbert's house at an octagonal turret. Only a sentimental attachment could have accepted such a strangely incongruent effect: each half of the house seems to be competing for supremacy but there is little architectural merit in either. To all intents and purposes the Big House, now containing some 365 rooms, was complete. Of greater importance, Prince George had now become, through default, the heir-presumptive, and it was necessary to prepare him for his future role. This, and other related considerations, would occupy the parents in the ensuing months.

CHAPTER EIGHT

PRINCESS MAY

Queen Mary, who had been born Princess Victoria Mary of Teck – Princess May – was to become a central character in the story of Sandringham, her home for half a century, and her developing role deserves study. She was appalled by the suddenness of her fiancé's death and, shocked into numbness by the tragedy and not in the best of health herself, she remained at Sandringham with her family until Prince Eddy's funeral at Windsor, comforted by the kindness shown by the Prince and Princess of Wales. 'Bertie and Alix kindly wished to keep us on,' the Duchess of Teck wrote to Queen Victoria, after the Prince's body had been taken to the church, 'united as we are by a common sorrow... Of their kindness to our May, I cannot say enough. They have quite adopted her as their daughter & she calls Alix 'Motherdear' & hopes you will allow her to call you 'Grandmamma?' [144] Was Princess Mary Adelaide's agile mind already at work planning another marriage for her daughter?

After the funeral the Tecks returned to their home at White Lodge and then, having endured three weeks of misery, travelled down to Osborne. The Queen was quick to observe the change in Princess May: 'The dear girl looks like a crushed flower,' she wrote, 'but is resigned & quiet & gentle, – it does make one so sad for her. She is grown thinner, but otherwise is not looking ill.' [145] At the end of February the Princess visited the Prince and Princess of Wales at Eastbourne. It was a muted gathering, for the visit coincided with the date of Prince Eddy's intended marriage and the bereaved family felt all the poignancy of the cancelled occasion; yet the Princess was received with the utmost kindness. 'May has become the child of the Waleses,' her father wrote. 'I foresee that she will be very much taken up with them.' [146] Not long afterwards the Tecks took a villa in Cannes; curiously enough, the Waleses were staying at Cap Martin, a little further along the coast. Was it not strange that the two families found themselves in such proximity? Not in the least; Princess Mary Adelaide had already contrived just such a situation, developing an idea which had already occurred to the Prince and Princess of Wales: May must marry George! The Prince of Wales, however, was not quite happy at the prospect of the Tecks' proximity; it lacked subtlety and might very easily cause ill-natured gossip.

The question looming in everyone's mind after Prince Eddie's death was that of the succession. In the fullness of time Prince George would succeed his father to the throne, and the future of the monarchy must be considered. As yet, there were no male children of the marriage of Princess Louise and the Duke of Fife, and the finding of a wife for Prince George had become a matter of importance. There was no Princess in Europe so eligible and so accessible as Princess May; the cousins had enjoyed an easy family relationship for many years but recently, of course, she had been engaged to Prince Eddy. Now fate had thrown them together, and the way forward towards matrimony, though by no means straightforward, was being prepared. Prince George himself at one time had been attracted to his cousin, Princess Marie of Edinburgh – 'Missy' – and her parents were asked to sound out her views. Influenced no doubt by her mother, the daughter of the Czar of Russia, she rejected this proposition. The Princess of Wales, fearful that 'the bond of love… that of Mother & child' might be severed, did nothing to urge the match. 'Nothing & nobody can or shall ever come between me & my darling Georgie boy.'[147] Soon after Prince Eddy's death she had written that George 'must give us double affection for the one that has gone before.' Thus, in this bleakest of years in all her marriage, did the bereaved Princess try to cling to the nursery days which seemed to her to represent happiness. Yet it was a fast-vanishing world: Eddy and the baby Alexander were dead; Louise was married; only three of the family were left – and Prince George, though often at sea, had his own life and amusements ashore; at this time he was giving his attention to Julie Stonor; alas, she was a Roman Catholic and a commoner and would never do, though they remained life-long friends. He had written, at the age of twenty-one, to his mother, when missing a family reunion at Sandringham: 'How I wish I was going to be there too, it almost makes me cry when I think of it. I wonder who will have that sweet little room of mine, you must go and see it sometimes and imagine that your little Georgie dear is living in it.'[148]

Such immoderate language immediately engages our attention: was this 'family talk' used by the Prince to humour his mother who wished to retreat into the nursery world which had already receded, a humorous turning aside perhaps of his real regret, or even a private joke between mother and son? Certainly there were echoes of the Princess of Wales's own language in her letters to him and reflections of the child-world to which she clung. We should not assume that this is an example of immaturity in the Prince. He was at this time a young Naval officer afloat; when ashore at Sandringham, he was a country gentleman, comfortably well-off and expecting the best as a matter of course, yet with simple tastes, enjoying nothing so much as a shoot on the family estate, or those of his friends. In 1892, he had been promoted and been put on half-pay, which enabled him not only to enjoy deer-stalking at Mar Lodge but also, with his future responsibilities clearly in mind, to spend two months in Germany to improve his command of the language and further his relationship with his German cousins. Before his brother's death, in between sea-going commissions, his leisure pursuits had indicated a lifestyle largely independent of domestic considerations.

By the beginning of 1893 rumours were flying: the young couple were seen walking arm in arm in Richmond Park; the newspapers were hinting broadly at an imminent engagement. Though the Queen had set her heart on it, the Prince's parents were not over-enthusiastic: that Prince Eddy's betrothed could bestow her affections on his brother scarcely a year after his death suggested to them that her heart had not been in her previous engagement – which was true. The Waleses had been very kind to her after Prince Eddy's death, but they had already noted her shyness and reserve. She was, after all, so very different from themselves. Prince George was hesitant. He had been hurt by 'Missy's' refusal of his advances and was uncertain of Princess May's feelings towards him. Those early months of 1893, full of gossip and uncertainty, must have been distinctly uncomfortable for both the protagonists in this drama, but all was happily resolved on 3 May when he met the princess at the home of the Duke and Duchess of Fife at Sheen. 'We walked together afterwards in the garden and he proposed to me, & I accepted him,' Princess May recorded in her diary.[149]

There were but eight weeks in that torrid summer of 1893 before the wedding was to take place. There was much to arrange, not least the question of where the young couple would live. For their London home the Prince was granted a suite of apartments in St James' Palace, to be known as York House. At Sandringham, which was of course a private property, the Prince of Wales gave his son the Bachelor's Cottage originally intended for Prince Eddy and his bride, but always called, from that time, York Cottage. It was here that Prince George, recently created

Duke of York, brought his bride on their wedding day, the 6 July. Both of them were half-dead with exhaustion from the blistering heat and the strain of the ceremony in the Chapel Royal, St James's Palace, and the reception at Buckingham Palace, and covered with a film of dust from the carriage drive from Wolferton Station. That the Duke had selected their future home for his honeymoon did not seem to him in the least strange; here, he felt, he could find peace and contentment with the woman he loved, amid surroundings in which he had grown up. Queen Victoria regretted his decision, thinking it 'rather unlucky and sad.'

York Cottage was to be the home of the Duke and Duchess – or, as they became, King George V and Queen Mary – for thirty-three years, and must be described. King George V's biographer, Harold Nicholson, was told by King Edward VIII: 'Until you have seen York Cottage you will never understand my father.' It had been built for the Prince of Wales by his architect, Humbert, for bachelor guests who could not be accommodated in the often crammed Big House, from which it was separated by a couple of hundred yards of gently sloping lawn. It has been described variously as 'a glum little villa', 'an ornate hutch' and 'irredeemably hideous'. Never handsome, it attempted to combine some incongruous styles of architecture and construction: Mock Tudor, local stone, roughcast and pebbledash. Even before additions were made, it might have been a boarding house transported complete from the sea front at Cromer. Its appearance was not improved by the addition of a wing, designed by Colonel Edis to increase the facilities for the Yorks, and the slate-roofed turret which served to join this to the main building; the south-east aspect, of grey stucco, is decidedly bleak. The larger drawing-room, dining-room and billiard-room were still of only moderate size; the remainder of the accommodation tended to be small and dark. A certain cosiness was achieved, for Princess May was nothing if not a home-maker, but it was impossible to avoid a feeling of overcrowding. 'One should really have in mind a doll's house,' she told Lady Airlie, when they were choosing patterns for curtains.[150] Around meal-times smells of cooking pervaded the house, the corridors were narrow and one had to squeeze past the waiting footmen. Secretaries worked in the bathrooms, where boards were placed across the baths to make do as desks. Yet, despite all its inconveniences and eccentricities, it was 'home', where the Duke and Duchess could find a degree of privacy and bring up their family away the limelight.

For years the Duke had been accustomed to the Spartan, confined quarters allotted to junior naval officers, and his affection for York Cottage affords a clue to his character. He was a plain, simple man, who greatly preferred the homeliness of the rooms to the splendours of a stately mansion. It was not of the smallest concern to him that the view from the windows of his study was largely obscured by laurels, or that the floors were so thinly boarded that a lady-in-waiting upstairs once sent word to the servants that she did not mind overhearing their conversation if they themselves had no objection. Into this somewhat confined space, then, crowded a growing family of six children and their attendants, and the Royal couple with their Household. The Duke was aware of the difficulties and more than once remarked lightly that he 'supposed the servants slept in the trees'. For him, at least, there was one supreme advantage: the rooms were too small to allow the kind of large-scale entertaining which he so cordially disliked. The Duke's study was on the ground floor; its walls were covered with a red fabric once used for the trousers of the French army which had been found nobody knew where, and adorned with photos of the ships in which he had served, and other naval memorabilia. There still exists in this room the mirror on a wall near the window by which the Duke, sitting in his chair, could see who was approaching the house. He could thus send word to the servants if he did not wish to be disturbed.

The Duchess's rooms were on the first floor: bedroom, dressing-room (with cupboards for her extensive wardrobe and a large safe for her jewellery), and boudoir – and immediately on her arrival her heart sank as she saw the need for tact and self-control. They had been 'done up' by the Duke and his sister, the Duchess of Fife: they had chosen the patterns for the carpets and curtains, and had bought furniture from Maples. The Duke's well-meaning action thus effectively prevented the Duchess from doing the very things which any newly-married woman must look forward to and undertake with real delight. In all her subsequent moves one of her chief joys was to be found in 'arranging her things'. In these early days she was to become more aware of the nature of the family into which she had married. After 1893, her reserve deepened in the face of criticism from the artless and childish 'Wales' sisters. Prince George was not insensitive to the difficulties inherent in the close proximity of his relations to York Cottage and admired his wife for her quiet common-sense, which enabled her to avoid the minefields so frequently encountered when a newcomer lives in close proximity to her in-laws.

For the Duke, too, there were conflicts which only time and patience could resolve: loyalty to his wife, whom he really loved and admired, and to his mother, whose affectionate endearments sometimes cloyed; in the new domestic life at the Cottage, with its quiet, simple ways and the joys of an increasing family, and the style of life at the Big House, which he had known since his boyhood and which resisted change. That he could resolve them successfully was due to his love for the Duchess and to their joint good sense. The Duchess's situation cannot be summarised better than in the words of King George V's biographer Harold Nicholson:

> The Duchess had married into a family which for years had been self-sufficient, a family which the Princess's genius for affection had turned into something that was certainly a closely-guarded clique and was not far short of a mutual admiration society. It was a family little given to intellectual pursuits, without much in the way of artistic tastes or taste, a family not easily to be converted to any other manner of life than that which they had found all-sufficing in an age wherein privilege vigorously survived.
>
> The Duchess was intellectually on a higher plane; she was already well educated – well read and interested in the arts, and was constantly seeking to increase her store of knowledge in many fields beyond the range of the Princess of Wales and the family in the Big House. She was full of initiative, of intellectual curiosity, of energy, which needed outlets and wider horizons.
>
> Their recreations were not hers. Their manner of life could not satisfy her notions of the ideal in the intellectual life of those days. And she was living in a small house on an estate which drew its inspiration wholly from the Prince and Princess, whereon every smallest happening or alteration was ordered and taken note of by the Prince. The very arrangement of her rooms, the planting of her small garden, were matters which required reference to Sandringham House, and the smallest innovation would be regarded with distrust...
>
> Sometimes the Duchess's intellectual life there may have been starved and her energies atrophied in those early years... For many women, then as now, the daily call to follow the shooters, to watch the killing, however faultless, to take always a cheerful appreciative part in man-made, man-valued amusements, must have been answered at the sacrifice of many cherished, many constructive and liberal ambitions. It is fair to assume that the self-effacement which conditions at Sandringham in those days demanded of a fine and energetic character must have fallen hardly on the Duchess; and fair also to suggest that the Prince and Princess (of Wales) might have done more to encourage her initiative and fill her days.[151]

Though all this lay in the future, we may wonder whether these difficulties were not entirely unperceived by the Duchess. She knew her Wales cousins well enough to have gained some insight into their lifestyle; but she was intelligent and optimistic. As for the Duke, he wrote to an old friend in the Navy a few days after the wedding:

> I can hardly yet realise that I am a married man, although I have been so for the last 10 days. All I can say is that I am intensely happy, far happier than I ever thought I could be with anyone. I can't say more than that. We are spending our honeymoon here in this charming little cottage which my father has given me & it is most comfortable & the peace and rest after all we went through in London is indeed heavenly... [152]

Yet already there had been difficulties; the newly married couple had not been installed twenty-four hours when there was a violent thunderstorm, which left the Duchess with a severe headache, followed by a period of heavy rain, keeping them indoors, with as yet few resources or much to say to each other. The Duchess must have regretted that there was nothing left for her to arrange in the house, since it had all been done. Within a fortnight, the Waleses arrived at the Big House, with their daughters, the Princesses Maud and Victoria, and members of the Danish Royal family, which seriously disturbed the peace and quiet of York Cottage. Their privacy was constantly interrupted by invasions from the family, even to the extent of their arriving early and sitting with the couple while they ate their breakfast. The Duchess found herself within the family circle, yet not entirely of it: it was not in her nature to participate in the airy badinage and the feeling of spontaneous gaiety and frivolity. Her enjoyment of reading tended to alienate her, and her wide interests and curiosity about the outside world were unfathomable to the Wales family. Even in those early days, the Princess of Wales began to realise that her son now had twin loyalties, and it was with some difficulty that she could relax her possessive hold on the Duke; but she no longer wrote to him as her 'dear little Georgie'.

The Princess was intellectually incapable of understanding her new daughter-in-law and, taking their cue from their mother, the Wales sisters voted her dull and uninteresting. Princess May, whose virtues had been so widely extolled at the Big House, was no longer spoken of as 'sweet May', but 'poor May'. At Windsor, Princess Victoria was heard to say to a dinner guest: 'Now do try to talk to May at dinner, though one knows she is so deadly dull.' [153] Princess May's reserve was unlikely to be broken down

The Royal family at the Christening of Princess Elizabeth.

King George V and Queen Mary with the Duke and Duchess of York (holding Princess Elizabeth), Buckingham Palace, 1927.

'Forty wonderful years': the regents Queen Victoria, Edward VII, George V, Edward VIII and George VI.

Lord Kitchener, who stayed at Sandringham: 'If you are frightened in the night,' he was told by his thoughtful hosts, 'dear Lady Salisbury is just next door.'

Winston Churchill, whose warm friendship with George VI was cemented over a weekly informal lunch where they could discuss the war situation without risk of interruption.

The Prince of Wales in 1929, visiting miners at Durham. His rocky relationship with his father, George V, was briefly healed during this year as ill-health took its toll upon the King.

Sandringham today, with views of the lawn and the lake.

Sandringham, north front. These were the rooms of King George VI before he died.

Prince Albert Victor, on the left, and the Prince George of Wales in around 1873.

Albert Edward and Alexandra, Prince and Princess of Wales, at Sandringham in 1863.

The drawing room, looking into the bowling alley, 1871.

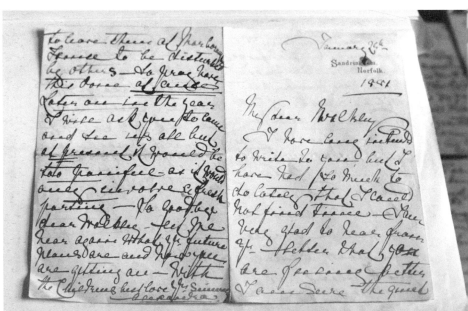

Letter from Alexandra, Princess of Wales to Mrs Walkley on 25 January 1881.

King Edward playing ice hockey in 1908.

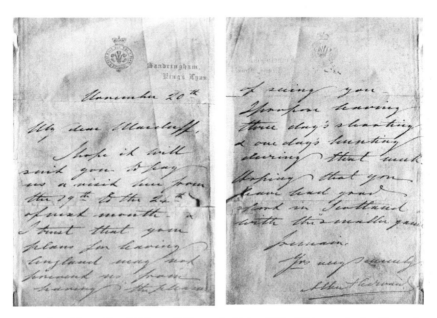

Letters from Albert Edward, Prince of Wales to the Duke of Fife. (Wolverton Station Museum)

Shooting Party, 1908. Queen Alexandra and King Edward VII are either side of the horse.

Shooting at Sandringham: Kind Edward VII and George, Prince of Wales, in 1908.

Maud, Princess Charles of Denmark, at Appleton on 30 June 1903.

York Cottage, original building on the right.

The Duchess of York's boudoir, 1897.

The Duke of York's study, York Cottage.

away so long. I
hope you will put
your son in the
Navy, it is the
best school going
& we want as many
as we can get.
I am just off to
Portsmouth to pay
the "Melampus" off
& then I am going
to Germany for a
couple of months to
study German. I
hope Mr Verner is
very well

Believe me
sincerely yours

George.

Letter from King George on his trip abroad to study German, sent from Marlborough House in August 1892.

Prince Edward, Prince Albert, Prince Henry and Princess Mary, with Forsyth and Cameron, 1903.

Skating at Sandringham, 5 January 1908. From left to right: Mr H.P. Hansell with Prince Henry; Prince Edward; Victoria Mary, Princess of Wales; unknown; Prince Albert; Princess Mary; George, Prince of Wales.

Mrs Wigram, wife of the King's private secretary, in a portrait by Oswald Birley. She dubbed Park House, Sandringham, a 'charming little house'.

The children of King George V and Queen Mary, in around 1914 or 1915. Left to right: Prince Albert, Prince John, Edward, Prince of Wales, Princess Mary, Prince Henry, Prince George.

King George V and Queen Mary with Walter Jones at York Cottage in 1920.

Luncheon at Sandringham in 1920; Queen Alexandra is fourth from the left.

*Dear Bertie joins you
today. I fear this will
be my last letter to
you from our dear
little old home where
we have been for
33 years — I am sad at
leaving it with its
many memories + old
associations.*

An extract from one of Queen Mary's letters to King George V, this from 24 August 1926.

Queen Mary, Princess Mary, and Lady Cynthia Colville at a bazaar at Sandringham Rectory in August 1951.

Queen Mary and the Duke of Windsor,
Marlborough House, October 1945.

The Royal family at Sandringham in Christmas 1951. From left to right: on the back row, Duke of Kent, Princess Margaret, Princess Alexandra of Kent, Duchess of Kent, Duke of Gloucester, Princess Elizabeth, Duke of Edinburgh, Duchess of Gloucester; seated, Queen Mary, King George VI with Princess Anne, Queen Elizabeth with Prince Charles. Foreground: Prince Richard of Gloucester, Prince Michael of Kent, Prince William of Gloucester.

by the superficiality of the Wales family and their habitual chaff must have been trying to the newcomer during the settling-in period of her marriage.

Part of the problem was, of course, the proximity of York Cottage to the Big House. The Duchess's Aunt Augusta, the Grand Duchess of Mecklenburg-Strelitz, with a sharp eye and sometimes acid tongue, wrote: 'I am sorry their Country Quarters are so near Sandringham, it mixes them up so entirely with the present Wales surroundings.' [154] Yet there were many bright times: some re-arrangement of furniture and family photographs to be hung; and the Duchess made the happy discovery that her husband enjoyed reading aloud, a practice that he had learned in his childhood and was to continue until his accession. Despite these inauspicious beginnings and much that they found contrary in each other's nature, Princess May's intelligence, restraint and sense of duty, and Prince George's affection and charm came to their rescue. He was to write some months after their marriage: '...I have tried to understand and know you, & with the happy result that I know now that I do love you darling girl with all my heart...' [154a] The problems were acknowledged by Princess May in a letter to her husband written a year after their honeymoon:

> I sometimes think that just after we were married we were not left alone enough & had not the opportunity of learning to understand each other as quickly as we might otherwise have done, & this led to many little rubs which might have been avoided. You see we are both terribly sensitive & the slightest sharp word said by one to the other gave offence & I fear neither you nor I forget these things in a hurry.

Princess May's parents first visited the Yorks four months after their wedding, after the Duke and Duchess had gone to Osborne for Cowes week and thence to Balmoral. Princess Mary Adelaide, that lady of vast proportions, large ideas and an income wholly inadequate for her needs, saw at once that York Cottage was far too small for the couple, and spoke to the Princess of Wales: 'She was most sensible about the adding on to York Cottage,' she wrote. The end product, designed by the Norwich firm of Beck, was the three-storied wing. Of course, more furniture was required and some re-arrangement would be necessary, in which the Princess of Wales determinedly took a hand. 'Motherdear, sisters and Charlotte (Knollys) lunched with me today... Mama afterwards moved the furniture in the drawing-room,' wrote Prince George, 'which gives ever so much more room, & I think looks much prettier, of course if you don't like it... we can move it all back again in a minute.'

To this charmingly naïve appeal the Duchess replied with much tact and perhaps just a tinge of irony:'I am so glad Motherdear tried to arrange our drawing-room she has so much taste, & it certainly looked much too stiff, only I thought that as the Scotch furniture has not come, it was scarcely worth while to waste a lot of time arranging it when it will have to be moved.'[155]

Despite such early setbacks it is clear that the Duchess had already thoroughly justified Queen Victoria's high opinion of her. Even at the time of her engagement the Queen wrote:'Let me say how much I rejoice at your becoming my Grandchild & how much confidence I have in you, to fill worthily the important position to which you are called.'[156]

It is evident, then, that the marriage of this very dissimilar couple, which the public had followed with such rapt interest and enthusiasm, was attended by considerable difficulties. Until she married into the Wales family she could only guess at the problems most likely to beset her, and it is to her great credit that she was able to inspire love and devotion in a man who all his life had been accustomed to the uncritical praise and artless frivolity of his family, or to the bluff heartiness of a Naval wardroom. In this, the veneration in which she held the monarchy and her own assessment of her high calling came to her aid, enabling her to overcome a certain diffidence in her nature, though there remained a reserve, even a shyness, which persisted even in old age. Indeed, her whole life was spent under constraint: if she was not wilting from the embarrassment of her mother's heartiness and awful size, she had to endure the lightweight amusements and artlessness of the Waleses. If she was never wholly at ease indulging in the revelry at the Big House, she remained true to her training and inclinations, inspiring in her husband an enduring love, admiration and loyalty.

NINE

FALLOW YEARS

I n the first year of his marriage the Duke of York contrived to
reconcile the diverse charms of Sandringham and all it stood for
and his new life of domesticity. His days were carefully regulated
and ordered; his responsibilities outside the Cottage were only such as
were designated to him by his father, and he was as much a gentleman of
leisure as any wealthy landowner. When he succeeded Prince Eddy as heir
presumptive to the Throne, he understood that he would ultimately have
to relinquish his commission in the Navy. He had been conscientious in
his training and an affable and gregarious shipmate, and he might, in other
circumstances, have risen to high rank through his own merits. His career
in the Royal Navy was interrupted by official duties, although it did not
effectively terminate until 1898, following a brief period in command of
H.M.S. *Crescent*. There must have been times when he wished he could
have remained at sea despite a tendency to sea-sickness. His loyalty to
the Service was undiminished; while still a bachelor he wrote to a friend:
'I hope you will put your son in the Navy, it is the best school going &
we want as many as we can get. I am just off to Portsmouth to pay the
"Melampus" off and then I am going to Germany for a couple of months
to study German...'

The period following his marriage to Princess May has been described
as 'years of inanition' but, although as Duke and Duchess of York they
lacked a clear occupation and had few official commitments, they were
not entirely idle. His was the life of a country gentleman, taking a keen
interest in every aspect of the Sandringham estate and with responsibilty
for one of the small outlying farms. His special care, with his father, was the
management of the game preserves in preparation for the all-important
shooting season. He also began at about this time to pay more attention
to politics and to study the constitution as one who, in all likelihood,
was destined to become King. Meanwhile, the Prince of Wales pursued
his accustomed round of Royal duties and personal pleasure, deputising
more frequently for the Queen who, lame and with diminishing eyesight,

was quietly withdrawing from public life. Her Diamond Jubilee in 1897 brought widespread loyalty and enthusiasm, but it was noticed that on arriving at St Paul's Cathedral for the commemoration service, she did not leave her carriage

At the Cottage he would give the Duchess her breakfast, when she was laid up after her confinements, at 9 a.m., have his own at half past and be away by 10 a.m., for he hated to miss a day during the shooting season. In the evening he saw to any business matters which required his attention, visited the nursery, and returned to the Duchess. Later he would look over his stamps or play billiards with a member of his Household, and retire early to bed. During the summer months the Duke, always deferring to his father's wishes, occupied himself by visiting the plantations and outlying areas of the estate and interesting himself in the rearing of the game birds. On Sundays he joined the party from the Big House on a tour of inspection taking in the stables, kennels and dairy. If the Duchess were visiting relatives, or absent abroad with her mother, the couple corresponded regularly.

There were, as might be expected, some difficulties with the in-laws on both sides. The Waleses' proximity was a disadvantage from which there could be no escape. On the other hand, the visits of the Duchess's mother, Princess Mary Adelaide, sorely taxed the Duke's good nature. She was for ever 'running in and out' of York House in St James's Palace and showed considerable lack of tact when visiting the family by not giving the couple time to themselves. The Duchess could only concur with the justice of her husband's criticism: 'We could hardly ever be alone without being interrupted,' she agreed, and would see what she could do when he asked her in a letter to 'try and mention it in a casual sort of way'.[157]

The truth was that the Tecks missed their daughter greatly – her father himself was becoming more difficult and eccentric, and there was little sense of direction in her mother's life without 'our May's companionship'. By Princess Mary Adelaide's own account, it seems that something was said by the time the Duchess' second child, Prince Albert (later King George VI) was born on 14 December 1895. She was not invited until the baby was three weeks old. On this visit to York Cottage she wrote: 'In the afternoon I walked or wrote till tea-time, which I took with May in the boudoir remaining with her until George came up from his tea, when I *discreetly retired* and wrote in the sitting-room downstairs till dressing time.'[158] There was nothing to be done about the Waleses, though; they, and Prince George, were on their own territory and it would have been inconceivable to try to alter the Princess's ways – and impossible to achieve any kind of success. Princess May had to endure these 'little rubs', which she did with all her customary good sense. As we shall shortly see, the effect of these boisterous incursions into their privacy was to make her withdraw further into herself, creating an air of reserve which her in-laws entirely failed to understand or alleviate.

The Duke and Duchess of York's first child, Prince Edward (later King Edward VIII) was born at White Lodge, Richmond, the home of the Duchess' parents, on 23 June 1894. But this was not an ideal arrangement, and the Duchess' subsequent confinements all took place at York Cottage. Prince Albert himself chose to arrive on a date that seemed startlingly inauspicious — precisely thirty-four years after the death of the Prince Consort, and sixteen years after that of Princess Alice. 'I am afraid dear Grandmamma,' the Duke wrote apologetically, 'that you were rather distressed that he was born on the 14th that doubly sad day to you and all the family, but we hope that his having been born on that day may be the means of making it a little less sad to you.' [159] The aging Queen did not visit Sandringham but remained at Osborne to comfort her bereaved youngest daughter Beatrice (Princess Henry of Battenburg), whose husband had recently died abroad, but replied graciously, hoping that: 'it may be a blessing for the dear little boy, and may be looked upon as a gift from God.' She welcomed her grandson's invitation to be a godmother. 'Most gladly do I accept being Godmother to this dear little boy, born on the day his beloved Great Grandfather entered on an even greater life. He will be specially dear to me. I thank you lovingly for your kind letter & will write again soon but I must end now to save the post. V.R.I.' [159a]

The new Prince joined his brother, Prince Edward, in the Night Nursery, one of two rooms on the first floor set aside for the children. A swing-door in the passage separated them from their parents' rooms: it was an age when, in general, it was recommended that children should be seen but not heard, and often were not even seen for much of the day, being in the care of a nurse. The Duke of Windsor wrote:

When there were only three of us children, Bertie, Mary and myself, we all slept in this one room with a nurse. There we were bathed in round tin tubs filled from cans of water, brought upstairs by servants from a distant part of the house. Our windows looked out over the pond, and the quacking of wild duck that lived there supplied a pleasant pastoral note at dawn and dusk. [160]

As the family increased, additions were made to the Cottage which was already notable for its eccentric architecture. The Duchess had nevertheless contrived to give an air of 'cosiness', which must have been very welcome to the young children.

During these seemingly empty years spent, not unprofitably, in raising a young family, the Duke and Duchess of York were often apart on their respective commitments. Princess May's mother was failing: she needed her much-loved daughter's attendance when she made the last round of visits to her haunts in Europe; the Duke of York was summoned in haste to St Petersburg by the Prince and Princess of Wales to attend the funeral of Czar Alexander III of Russia, but the couple disliked being separated. Princess May accompanied her husband to Wolferton station. Goodbyes at railway stations are never easy, and this parting was no exception. 'That saying "good-bye" this morning was awful,' she wrote, '& I did it so badly too, for I felt so miserable. Anyhow I know you understood what I felt & what agony it was having to take leave. It poured so heavily that we had to return in the closed carriage...' The scene can easily be imagined: the rain sheeting down, and dripping heavily from the pine trees lining the road; the coachman muffled, the horses splashing through the mud, swinging into the grounds of the 'Big House' and drawing up at the Cottage at the end of the drive. 'After lunch it rained so... that we gave up going out,' continued Princess May's letter, '& sat all together in the little sitting-room & Victoria stuck in photos in your book and mine, while Harry (Princess Maud) read & I wrote and read etc. We all felt very chippy and wretched.'[161]

On 22 January 1901, Queen Victoria died at Osborne, her Isle of Wight home. In her eighty-second year her death could not come as a surprise: her health had been failing over the past year; but she had become an institution – to the family as much as to the nation. The children of the Duke and Duchess of York were not greatly affected: 'Great-Grandmamma' inspired awe and respect but, despite their occasional visits to her at Windsor, Osborne and Balmoral, she had remained for them a somewhat remote figure. Now the change in their situation was considerable. The Prince of Wales succeeded his mother as King Edward VII and, in November of the same year, the Duke and Duchess of York became the new Prince and Princess of Wales, and as such they must now be called. It was not, however, necessary that the pattern of life at York Cottage should be much altered. The Prince, now heir apparent, studied the constitution with rather more zeal, but the family followed the King and Queen on their annual round; Frogmore when they were at Windsor; Abergeldie at Balmoral; York Cottage at Sandringham; Marlborough House when they were at Buckingham Palace, and with them on board the Royal yacht at Cowes. There were times when the Royal children remained behind at York Cottage when their parents were elsewhere. Such an occasion was the State visit to India of the new Prince and Princess of Wales; during their absence work suffered, as the children were happily indulged by the grandparents. 'It was quite impossible for me to hold an examination as they returned so late from Sandringham,' Mr Hansell complained. Surely we can hear echoes of Mr Dalton in a previous generation. Visiting their grandparents in the Big House was one of their recurring delights, and in the evenings they would survey the glittering scene: dukes and duchesses, bankers and lords of the turf mingled in evening dress, the men wearing their Orders and decorations, the ladies their tiaras and jewels. There was the hum of conversation, the strains of Gottlieb's orchestra and the aroma of cigars – a world away from the cramped confines of York Cottage, and the austere atmosphere of the schoolroom.

With the inevitable increase in their public commitments, the new Prince and Princess of Wales were obliged to enlarge their household. King Edward and Queen Alexandra were, of course, obliged to move from Marlborough House to Buckingham Palace. The Queen held out desperately for her old home which had been their London residence for forty-eight years; no wonder she was reluctant to move – she felt 'she was being torn away' from it. In the course of the re-arrangements to her household, the Princess of Wales invited the Countess of Airlie, whom she had known since childhood, to become one of her additional ladies-in-waiting. When Lady Airlie hesitated, for her husband had recently been killed in the Boer War and she was still in mourning, the Princess kindly encouraged her by outlining her duties:

> I propose having four ladies who will each do duty for three months in the year, say a month at a time, and I propose that the ladies should arrange the dates of their waiting among themselves. The principal part of the writing would be done by my private secretary, the ladies only doing my private charities and so forth.[162]

Lady Airlie had been worried lest her duties with the Princess should coincide with her sons' school holidays. The Earl's death had left her with a considerable Scottish estate to manage but the Princess' thoughfulness dispelled her doubts and made it possible for her to accept. She was to remain a lady-in-waiting and companion to Queen Mary for over fifty years. Her arrival at York House in St James' Palace is revealing:

> The Princess received me in her sitting-room... formally – almost coldly, I thought – but when we were alone together she put her arms round me and kissed me on both cheeks. Her eyes were full of tears... 'Dearest, dearest Mabell, I can't tell you how much I have felt for you, and how glad I am that you have come to me.'... As the Princess had no afternoon engagements we had tea together and talked of old times. It was then that I began to understand the subtle change in her. Even as a girl she had been shy and reserved, but now her shyness had so crystallised that only in such moments of intimacy could she be herself. The hard crust of inhibition which gradually closed over her, hiding the warmth and tenderness of her own personality, had already begun to form.
>
> She had grown very vulnerable to criticism, and always sensed it even when unspoken. It was not wanting, especially from Queen Alexandra and Princess Victoria. In spite of their cordial relationship the Queen had succeeded in creating in her daughter-in-law a lack of self-confidence. Although it was screened behind an air of great dignity and reserve, Princess May in reality longed for approbation.
>
> Prince George, ordinarily not an imaginative man, understood this, and always showed his admiration for her...[163]

Yet in more than one sense, devoted and anxious for their children's well-being though they were, something was missing. Prince George inspired a deep respect in his children, bordering on fear: the chaffing and banter that was part and parcel of life at the 'Big House' and the critical interrogations about their activities did not encourage an easy response and 'added to the shyness and tied the tongues of those by nature the most diffident'. Less tolerant than his own father, the Prince gave vent to his feelings in no uncertain manner and, though he enjoyed bathing them and playing with them – 'I am a good lap,' he once said – there lacked a closeness in their relationship. A gruff manner and an uninhibited tendency to shout when annoyed was unlikely to promote much more than awe: it was said that the Duke trusted his servants so greatly that he could always express his feelings 'instantly and without reserve'[164] to any member of his household; a freedom he seldom failed to exercise. When Prince Albert was five his father wrote: 'Now that you are five years old, I hope you will always try and be obedient & do at once what you are told, as you will find it will come much easier to you the sooner you begin...' [165] As a father he was proud of his children, but he was a more anxious parent than he ever realised and, lacking in imagination to an astonishing degree, felt that it was never too soon to commence their training for public life.

The Princess enjoyed the company of her children and transmitted to them what little culture they possessed in later life, but they saw her as one with their father, and never knew until much later in life that she had frequently interceded for them with her husband. The Duke of Windsor told James Pope-Hennessy:

> My father was a very repressive influence. When he used to go banging away for a week or two at some shoot in the Midlands, and my mother would never go to those things, we used to have the most lovely time with her alone – always laughing and joking... she was a different human being away from him. [166]

They were unlucky in their nursemaids, too. The first, engaged on the birth of Prince Edward, had been dismissed for being insolent to the Duchess of Teck; the second, jealous of the parents' affection for her charges, used to pinch them as they were brought in for the evening visit, so that they were often in tears. The parents, helpless and frustrated, and lacking in experience, sent for the nurse to have them taken away. After three years, this distressing business was uncovered, and the nurse dismissed. It then came to light that the poor woman had not had a single day's holiday in three years. After this, the under nurse, Mrs 'Lalla' Bill, took charge of the nursery and the children flourished in a happier environment. Nevertheless, it has to be said that the Royal children had a strange upbringing. Mrs Bill was joined by the Princess' former governess, Mme Bricka – proficiency in French was strongly encouraged. When Prince Edward was seven, he and Prince Albert were placed in the care of a valet, Frederick Finch, who looked after them with great devotion, supervising their clothes and their cleanliness, and chastising them when necessary. He must have earned their respect, for he remained in Royal service until his retirement in 1935.

With the transition to the schoolroom came another change. Mr Henry Hansell was appointed tutor to the Princes. He was thirty-nine years of age, tall, a bachelor and a keen golfer. He had already been tutor to Prince Arthur of Connaught and so could in a sense be considered well qualified. Preferring private tutoring, he had little experience as a schoolmaster. Subject to fits of abstraction, when he would stare into space, and without much sense of humour, he nevertheless succeeded in gaining the affection of the boys. From his limited experience as a preparatory schoolmaster, he was privately of the opinion that a school would be the environment best suited to the Princes but he set about the creation of an academic environment conscientiously: 'Mr Hansell organised a schoolroom on the second floor,' wrote the Duke of Windsor.

> He imported two standard school desks with hinged lids and attached chairs, with hard wooden seats and straight backs. A blackboard, a set of wall maps and, of course, an ample stock of arithmetic and history books, grammars and copy books with lined pages completed the equipment.
>
> Next he drew up a daily timetable of work designed to make us follow the regime of the ordinary schoolboy. Finch woke us at seven and saw to it that we were dressed and at our desks half an hour later for three-quarters of an hour's 'preparation' – homework – before breakfast. In the winter it would still be dark, and I dreaded entering that cold room to grapple with some unfamiliar problem on an empty stomach. At 8.15 Mr Hansell would appear to take us downstairs to breakfast, and by nine we were back at our desks to study until lunch, with an hour's break in the forenoon for play. After lunch he would take us out, perhaps for a walk in the woods or to kick a football on the lawn. Then we would go back to our lessons for another hour, always stopping at tea-time for muffins, jam and milk – our last meal of the day. [167]

After tea, the Princes were summoned downstairs to greet their parents. The Prince of Wales seldom stayed long, going off to the Library, but the Princess taught them songs and, during the precious hours before dinner, read and talked to them. It was then that they began to acquire the advantages of her cultured mind. As neither their father nor their grandparents claimed any pretensions to artistic tastes, it was not surprising that the Duke's children were brought up 'with their backs to one of the finest collections of pictures in the world.'[168] Mr Hansell lacked the inspiration to inspire small boys; outings were few and far between. It even began to seem that he was not an effective teacher and, as their lack of progress became more marked, additional tutors were engaged as specialists in their own subjects. Mlle Dussau was engaged as Princess Mary's French tutor: she disliked small boys and hostilities commenced when she insisted that French was to be spoken at meals. It was then that M. Hua, who years earlier had taught Prince George, was summoned back into Royal service to reconcile the opposing forces and to teach the language to the Princes. Meanwhile, Mr Hansell's own emphasis was on virtue as an end in itself and, with few other attributes, it is difficult to estimate the service he rendered to his Royal charges, though he remained with the Princes when they entered the Royal Navy. 'Both boys must give a readier obedience. I often describe them to myself as obedient boys at the second time of asking.' Describing the use of his Report Book, Mr Hansell wrote: 'With regard to my own work & the responsibility of surveillance, I propose only to make a direct report for special misbehaviour and idleness, such report only to be made after due consideration and with full conviction.' [169]

Such reports almost invariably meant a summons to the Library. That there was mischief and misbehaviour is indisputable: discipline in these unusual academic surroundings was shaky. Dr Oswald, the German tutor, complained: 'Your Royal Highness, it isn't only that Prince Albert is inattentive, but when I scold him he just pulls my beard.' [170] And Mr Hansell:

I must keep Princess Mary (aged six) apart from the others as much as possible, whenever it is a matter of work. Her disposition is mercurial; one can enforce discipline and order of a sort but the fact remains that, so long as she is in the room, her brothers cannot concentrate their attention on any serious work. [171]

The summons for the inevitable dressing-down that followed such reports was dreaded by the Royal children, but especially by Prince Albert, who was a highly sensitive boy at this time, developing a speech impediment which was to handicap him for much of his life. The cause is not fully known but may have been the result of a left-handed child being forced into right-handedness. When reprimanded by his father, he could only listen, unable to defend himself. His father's peremptory demand to 'get it out' only made matters worse. [172] His speech therapist, Lionel Logue, starting his work with the Duke in 1926, believed that the cause of the defect was physical rather than mental. Certainly Logue achieved considerable success.

When Prince Albert was eight he underwent remedial treatment for knock-knees, from which his father too had suffered. For a time he spent his nights and part of his days in splints: for a lively boy who was particularly well co-ordinated, the experience, though successful, must have been irksome and even humiliating, and distracted him from his lessons. 'Prince Albert's early morning work is rendered almost useless by the splints,' Mr Hansell wrote. 'Under the conditions however small results can only be obtained by very great and sustained efforts on the part of the teacher.'[173] In July the tutor wearily admitted defeat: 'Practically all Prince Albert's work with me has been combined with the splints. It is now quite certain that such a combination is impossible.'[174]

There were other difficulties; Mr Hansell was probably the only one in authority who understood the impossibility of his task. Within this wretched, ugly little house he had to create a preparatory school for two boys; he was bound to fail. There were perhaps other men better suited at least to try. Introspective and with a love of church architecture he must have chafed under this stultifying routine. Every morning he used to walk to the top of a small rise near the Cottage and stare out at the view. Prince Albert asked him what he found to look at. 'I don't think you will understand,' Hansell replied, 'but for me it is freedom.'[175]

Dutifully, he rounded up other boys in the neighbourhood to make up a football team: they met with some success, but the atmosphere was artificial. We are reminded of Prince Albert's futile attempts to provide companions for his own son, now King Edward VII, entertaining them with 'improving' conversation. After such dismal sessions it is scarcely surprising that in later life he chose his friends for their companionship and entertainment value. These Royal children lacked the wider horizons of other young people and, as Hansell was well aware, the companionship of contemporaries. Even contact with the children of members of the Household was limited; it was not surprising that, when they entered the Royal Naval College at Osborne, they seemed to stand out as 'different'. Yet they were neither lonely nor bored at Sandringham: they rode their bicycles at headlong speed down the hill to Wolferton, bought sweets at the village shop and learned to ride and shoot – but golf was not encouraged. 'If we let those boys on the fairway, they will only hack it up,' their father said, though he later relented. There were visits, too, when the Princes were in London to museums, exhibitions and the Tower.

It was at Sandringham especially that the young Prince Albert absorbed the sights and sounds of nature around him, so that he became a true countryman at heart. With Walter Jones, a local schoolmaster at West Newton, the Princes walked the bracken and heather and learned the haunts and habits of the wildlife. Mr Jones was a remarkable character: when Mr Hansell was on holiday, he replaced him in the schoolroom at York Cottage and earned the confidence of his charges and the respect of their father, who often included him among the guns of the shoot.

It was this relationship with nature that differentiated Prince Albert from his father. King George had grown up within the tradition of the formal shoot. One of the best game shots in the country (he shot with a straight left arm) and a greater enthusiast for the sport than even his own father, he accepted the challenge of high, fast birds, but it seems that he never considered reforming the established shooting customs at Sandringham. He himself was content to use hammer guns long after they were out of fashion. But he did engender a love of the sport in Prince Albert who, as we shall see, departed from these customs and developed his own interests and skills. On 23 December 1907, the twelve-year-old Prince made the first entry in his game book: 'Sandringham Wolferton Warren. Papa, David and myself. 1 pheasant, 47 rabbits. My first day's shooting. I used a single barrel muzzle-loader which Grandpa, Uncle Eddy and Papa all started shooting. I shot 3 rabbits.'[176]

In every aspect of his children's lives the Prince of Wales was demanding, critical and difficult to please. In 1911, the seventeen-year-old Prince Edward spent the winter at Sandringham with his young brother, Prince George, while his parents were on their tour of India. He wrote to his father:'I have had some splendid practice and feel that my shooting has very much improved. It is the small days that give one far more practice than the big ones. One can take one's time and shoot much better.'[177] The King's crushing reply indicated neither approval nor interest:

> Judging from your letters and the number of days you have been shooting, there can't be much game left at Sandringham, I should think. It also seems a mistake to shoot the coverts three times over, I never do that unless a few more cocks have to be killed. I can't understand Bland wishing you to do so. You seem to be having too much shooting and not enough riding or hunting... You must learn to ride and hunt properly and you have had such good chances this winter at Sandringham. I must say I am disappointed.[178]

Perhaps he had forgotten the easy and happy relationship he enjoyed with his own parents, though he had been in awe of his autocratic father. Small of stature – he was only 5ft 6ins tall – and lacking in self-confidence as a member of a family whose way of life was entirely subordinated to that of the parents, he appears consciously to have imposed an authoritarian, quarterdeck discipline on his children. A history of dyspepsia and, later, pain from his injury in Belgium, may have contributed to a tendency to irritability. As far as Prince Edward was concerned, the void existing between father and son was seldom bridged; chiefly during the war, and again when the King suffered from an abscess on his lung in 1929 (when the Prince realised that his father had suddenly aged and was seen to be vulnerable). The King, too, recognised the help that his eldest son had been to him during the war and for the tours of the Empire he had undertaken, and there was a real, if fleeting, warmth between them. In general, though, the further the King retreated into the past, the more the son advanced into the twentieth century. He recorded 'my father had a most horrible temper.'

The behaviour of the young Prince Edward, now Prince of Wales, spoilt by excessive adulation and affected by a change in his personality caused, in the opinion of those close to him, by a glandular illness at puberty, was giving his Household and others close to the throne a good deal of anxiety. He had few real interests; even those that he pursued, such as gardening, were principally alleviations from boredom. In those post-war years the accent was on change – even for the sake of change. It was Art Deco, innovative, unconventional and daring; it was the coming of jazz and the Charleston, of nightclubs and cocktails, all of which appealed strongly to the Prince's active mind. Behind the princely figure capturing the hearts of the Empire with his informality and charisma during those tours, there was a lonely young man longing for the freedom of the new age.

The accession of King Edward VII caused changes to the steady routine of Sandringham life – that, and the natural passing of the years. The new King had at last found employment and public duties took him away from Norfolk more often and for longer periods that at any time during the previous forty years. Prince George, now Prince of Wales, and his father's successor, took on more engagements. If, at first, he did not relish these incursions into his private life, he committed himself to them conscientiously. Thus the old Queen's death marked a watershed between those carefree days in the '90s and a time of increased responsibilities. Moreover, it was during this later period that Prince Edward and, later, Prince Albert left the secluded schoolroom at York Cottage for the wider, harsher world of Naval Cadets at Osborne. King Edward, failing to persuade any of his relations to accept the great house on the Isle of Wight, left it to the nation to become a convalescent home for officers from the Boer War. The grounds became the site of the new Royal Naval College at a time of expansion of the service. It was initially a lonelier world for the boys: friendships formed slowly and with caution; there was strict segregation between 'terms' or entry groups, so that Prince Albert could only meet his brother on the far side of the sports field. He accepted with seeming equanimity the drill of leaping from his bed, stripping, and jumping into the plunge pool at the end of the dormitory, all in record time and pursued by the Cadet Captain with powers of punishment. He battled with an unfamiliar, crowded environment which would have passed unremarked by any boy from a preparatory school; his stammer was a handicap and he was ill-equipped for the academic challenges. 'My dear boy,' wrote the King, 'this will not do. If you go on like this you will be at the bottom of the class.'

Sheer courage and determination saw him through to Dartmouth and eventually to sea as a midshipman. It was at Osborne that he made some lifelong friendships, among them Miles Reid and Louis Greig, who became his equerry and remained with him for over thirty years as equerry and later, until his marriage, Comptroller of his Household. He also acknowledged the debt he owed to his strict, but fair and friendly term officer, a Lieutenant Phipps. These and several others stood him in good stead for many years. It was noticed that at this time his stammer all but disappeared. Prince Albert was not a natural sportsman, but was a strong cross-country runner, rode, hunted and enjoyed a strenuous game of tennis. He was good company, cheerful, friendly, mischievous and ready to participate in activities. In short, he was a thoroughly agreeable shipmate.

CHAPTER TEN

KING EDWARD VII

After King Edward ascended to the throne in 1901 it was inevitable that his public duties would sometimes force him to curtail the long-established seasonal visits to Sandringham. He spent Christmas and the New Year in Norfolk, with occasional visits to London, with a week's shooting at Chatsworth or Elveden. By the beginning of February he was back at Buckingham Palace, and at the end of March he went abroad, to Paris and Biarritz, and to spend a month cruising, often in the Mediterranean, on board the *Victoria and Albert*. During the summer the King presided over the London Season, with occasional visits to Sandringham, moving to Windsor for Ascot races, then to Goodwood and Cowes. He then spent a month at Marienbad to take the cure – where, it was said, he would painfully lose half a stone, only to add as much on his return to London. There followed a month at Balmoral in October, returning to London via Newmarket, where he stayed in his own quarters at the Jockey Club. The second week in November was spent at Sandringham and, after a fortnight at Windsor, he was back in Norfolk, having completed an unrelenting round which would have exhausted anyone less robust or without such an insatiable capacity for enjoyment.

By the turn of the century Sandringham had matured. The Big House had been rebuilt and extended; the Ballroom had been added, the Royal Stud established and a range of glasshouses built with the proceeds of the King's racing successes in earlier years and fees from the stud. The game preserves were at their best, plantations thriving and the estate buildings in good order. Indoors an immense quantity of souvenirs and gifts had accumulated: whilst there was evidence of restraint in the King's apartments, the Queen could never bring herself to throw anything away which represented, as she put it, 'the kind thoughts of dear friends'. Prince Christopher, her nephew, noted his aunt's 'positive genius':

> ...for collecting trifles of every description and hoarding them long after their origin had been forgotten: books, photos, china, letters, old

programmes, odds and ends of ribbons and laces were heaped together indiscriminately anywhere and everywhere. Beautiful miniatures and Georgian snuff-boxes occupied a table with Earl's Court china pigs and bog-wood charms from Ireland; she kept the fishing-fly given her by a gillie in Scotland as carefully as she kept a brooch from one of the Indian maharajahs.[179]

A zoo had been established in the grounds with its complement of tigers, elephants, kangaroos and bears – gifts acquired over the years by the Royal owners. The kennels often contained as many as 100 dogs, again gifts and acquisitions and strays rounded up on the estate, as well as the Basset hounds which were among the Queen's favourite pets. The model buildings extended to the outlying villages on the estate, having their own social clubs, and the Royal visits to see how they were being used and to maintain contact with their tenants became a common sight:

On November 7th we took His Majesty on a tour of inspection with Mr Beck, his Agent. First we brought him to Flitcham vicarage, that he might see the alterations and improvements which had by his direction been carried out. Thence he went on to an old house at Anmer, which was his property and which he had lent to Captain Hamilton... Here, too, additions had been made to the building, and when he had satisfied himself that all had been done as he wished, he re-entered the car and drove to Shernborne. The village forms part of the Sandringham estate, and the King always took a keen interest in its welfare. Here was an old inn which His Majesty had had converted for the villagers... This was but one of the many surprise visits he paid to the old house. He walked straight in, without any ceremony, chatted to the steward and his wife, and entered the rooms one after another. The blinds were not drawn, and I was watching some old fellows playing a game of dominoes, when the door opened and the King came in. Taken by surprise as they were, there was no awkwardness about the sudden silence in the room, for they were simply delighted to see him, and were one and all familiar with his presence. For years they had seen him about the village and shooting in the neighbouring fields. He was their squire. They all stood up beaming with pleasure, and the cheerful reverence with which they received his nod and smile was perfectly delightful.[180]

Exactly, the King was their Squire. It was a role which he had valued and nurtured for many years, and now he could see the fruition of his earliest dreams. Sandringham represented, above all, stability and security in a world which was rapidly changing. Beyond the boundaries of the estate loomed the prospect of war and a turbulence unimagined in these quiet confines. Even now Haldane and Fisher were planning their reforms of the armed services; women were pressing for emancipation and the cause of suffrage after the manner of Lady Constance Lytton, Mrs Pankhurst and her daughters. Queen Mary was later to express her disapproval of their militancy. There was increasing industrial unrest, too, with strikes and rioting in the mining and manufacturing areas.

It was the age of the Dreadnought and the submarine, of balloons and powered flight, and of the motor car. Though the King was something of a traditionalist, especially as far as his way of life at Sandringham was concerned, he was yet modern in his outlook. In 1900, while he was still Prince of Wales, his first motor car appeared at Sandringham – a 4 horse-power Renault with a high tonneau and complete with chauffeur. 'The man managed it extraordinarily well,' commented Prince George. Before the end of King Edward's reign the travelling time between Sandringham and Newmarket had been considerably reduced. It was a welcome amenity that Prince Albert could never have foreseen. Later, the great high Daimlers, the coachwork finished in claret, with blue morocco leather upholstery, were a familiar sight in the neighbourhood. The King's car was fitted with a special four-note horn which he had adopted after admiring a similar one on the car of his nephew, the Kaiser. Motorists, on hearing the imperious warning, soon learned to pull in to the side of the road, for the King could not bear to be held up by a car ahead of him.

An interested observer of the King's ways was E. W. Stamper, the motor engineer who invariably accompanied him on his journeys by road. In 1905 he wrote:

Christmas Day... was spent at Sandringham. In the afternoon His Majesty asked me to take him for a run which would last about an hour and a half. I worked out a round by way of Hunstanton, Docking and Anmer – twenty-five miles in all. The snow was on the ground at the time and the country looked very pretty... ever afterwards we always went for this run on Christmas Day.[181]

These 'runs' in the car were often memorable. Once, Stamper travelled for miles spreadeagled on the bonnet of the King's car when the gear lever became detached from its socket and could only be held in place manually. Punctures were common on roads that had not been improved by tarmac, and mechanical breakdowns were frequent. Improvisation was the key word: if vital components broke loose or failed to function, they could often be held in place by the judicious use of a piece of bent wire or a collar stud. If they taxed Stamper's ingenuity, it is a measure of his success that he remained in the King's service until the end of the reign. When problems occurred the King, who was not renowned for his patience in the face of adversity, would settle himself in a corner with a look of comical resignation and read the newspaper. Queen Alexandra enjoyed the sensation of speed and wrote delightedly, 'I did so enjoy being driven about in the cool of the evening at fifty miles an hour! – when nothing in the way of course!' but would poke the chauffeur with her umbrella at bends in the road. Even in his late sixties the King showed an energy and zest for life. Though he has been described as 'slow-moving', this could not be said of him as late as 1907. Stamper wrote:

> The King was sprightly – noticeably so. His walk was never leisurely, unless he was out for a stroll pure and simple. If he had a destination of any kind, his pace was invariably brisk. He entered and left the house swiftly, and he was in and out of a car or a train in a moment... He spoke rapidly, ate very fast, thought apace. He even smoked hard. Speed was of the essence of his nature... Moreover, he expected it of others, and... of tardiness under any circumstances he was impatient.[182]

The King took to motoring with a keen enjoyment which was not necessarily shared by members of his Household. In 1907, the King was to tour the estate with Lord Suffield and Mr Beck, the Agent, accompanying him in the car; but Sir Dighton Probyn had ordered his carriage and pair, intending to follow on behind.

'I would rather go with my horses, Sir,' said Sir Dighton. 'I don't like cars very much.'

But the King would have none of it, and insisted on him entering the car, saying, 'You'll have to get used to the cars, Probyn.'

A year or two later, when he was in Scotland, Sir Dighton took to a car, and never used his horses at all.[183]

During his reign King Edward VII ordered a golf course to be made in the Park:

> The putting greens were good though small and the fairways properly mown, but there were no bunkers. To remedy this, the Agent, Mr Frank Beck, had placed wicker hurdles to indicate where the bunkers would

eventually be dug. He argued that they could easily be moved to any position that the King decided upon... Having blinked at the bunkers on the right and left of the fairway, the King proceeded to drive off and of course hit those on the right. The Agent... looked horrified but the King merely said, 'What a silly place to put a bunker! See that it is altered tomorrow; have them put much more to the right, and further off the tee.'

At every other hole the same thing happened, and the King got louder and louder in his denunciation of the person who had placed the hurdles. The second day we played he took the even holes and of course drove into the hurdles again, when precisely the same thing happened and he ordered the hurdles to be moved. The third day was the most unnerving for the Agent, because all the hurdles had been moved to different spots indicated by the King... Again, after viewing them distastefully the King never failed to drive into them and, in a voice of thunder, asked who had been stupid enough to place them there. When the Agent replied by reading his notes which proved that it was the King himself who had selected the spot, the King exploded with rage and ordered all the hurdles to be taken away.[184]

On another occasion:

In the afternoon Queen Alexandra and I played against Princess Victoria and Francis Knollys. The Queen seemed to confuse it with hockey and was under the impression that one had to prevent the opponent putting the ball in the hole. This usually ended by a scrimmage on the green. She also thought that the person who got into the hole first won it, and asked me to hurry up and run between strokes. It was very good fun.[185]

The traditional elements favoured by the King could be seen in the revival of the ceremonial of Court functions, whose brilliance had been dimmed since Queen Victoria's widowhood. He demanded a rigid adherence to the niceties of dress, uniform and the wearing of orders and decorations, and he enjoyed life in the Grand Style no less than his role of country squire. So, in the end, there was no paradox in the arrival of the motor car and electric lighting at Sandringham, and the formality of evening dress, gowns and tiaras worn as a matter of course at the dinner table of the Big House. Visitors to Sandringham often commented on the mixture of formality and ease which they encountered. Admiral of the Fleet Lord Fisher wrote:

I went down to Sandringham with a great party... As I was zero in this grand party, I slunk off to my room to write an important letter; then I took my coat off, got out my keys, unlocked my portmanteau and began unpacking. I had a boot in each hand. I heard somebody fumbling with the door and thinking it was the footman whom Hawkins had allocated to me, I said, 'Come in, don't go humbugging with that door-handle!' and in walked King Edward with a cigar about a yard long in his mouth. He said, (I with a boot in each hand), 'What on earth are you doing?' 'Unpacking, Sir.' 'Where's your servant?' 'Haven't got one, Sir... couldn't afford it.' 'Put those boots down: sit in that armchair.' And he went and sat in the other one, the other side of the fire. I thought to myself, 'This is a rum state of affairs! Here's the King of England sitting in my bedroom on one side of the fire and I'm in my shirtsleeves sitting in an armchair on the other side.'[186]

They talked for some time, until the Admiral was forced to remind the King that they would soon have to change for dinner. In this informal way the King could entertain his guests and keep himself informed about important matters. At this time Lord Fisher was deeply engaged in plans for the development of the Navy, building battleships apace to maintain parity with the German fleet, since the Kaiser's envy of Britain's naval power extended to the Empire as a whole, and was not to be trusted.

The Christmas season was invariably spent at Sandringham. Fritz Ponsonby found that the festivities began on Christmas Eve:

The King and Queen did the presents themselves and spent hours in the Ballroom arranging everything. In the centre of the Ballroom was a large Christmas tree and round this were ranged trestle tables the whole length of the room, covered with a white tablecloth. It was all beautifully done, and the pleasure of giving never seemed to leave Their Majesties. Before dinner on Christmas Eve we all assembled in the corridor outside the Ballroom and one by one we were called in. It was impossible to make a set speech, and most people, including myself, continued gasping 'Thank you so much'.

I was quite overcome at first by the number of presents I received. There were prints, watercolours, silver cigarette-cases, a silver inkstand, pins, studs, and several books. Gottlieb's band played in the gallery, and every evening we went to the Ballroom and looked at everyone else's presents. The King and Queen, of course, received wonderful things from their relations in Europe, the Emperor of Russia sending particularly lovely things by special messenger.

On New Year's Eve all the presents were taken away and the tables were arranged differently and closer to the Christmas tree. All the servants and workers on the estate came in and remained outside the row of tables while the presents were massed round the Christmas tree. Each servant and employee drew two numbers on entering the room, and the Princess and members of the Household took the numbers and found the present. Of course often a present didn't fit the recipient and a housemaid might get a razor and a footman a powder-puff, but these could be exchanged later. Some 800 presents were given in this way and it seemed to give much pleasure. At the conclusion the Christmas tree was stripped and all the toys and sweets were given to the children.[187]

The celebrations marked one of the highlights of the Sandringham year. In principle, the routine varied little, but the King's activities might be modified by the weather, or his inclinations. Hockey was sometimes played on the lawn opposite the front door, and for years there had been skating and ice-hockey on the lake, which was lit in the early days by flaming torches and, later, by floodlights. A tent was erected by the lakeside and hot negus was served to the skaters. The King sometimes played in goal and would stand there, bowler-hatted with the customary large cigar held in a gloved hand which also grasped the hockey stick. His zest for amusement and activity, his capacity for enjoyment, never flagged; his concern for his guests' happiness never diminished.

The shoots on the estate took place both before and after Christmas, and were the central feature of the winter house-parties. They were arranged with the utmost care and attention to detail. 'Luncheon', wrote Fritz Ponsonby, 'was in a large tent and everybody staying in the house had to come no matter what they might have been doing during the morning. Carriages were ordered and we all had to have luncheon in a damp tent. Tea was a full-dress meal with all the women in tea-gowns and the men in short black jackets and black ties.'[188]

The King's birthday shoot in 1909 was marred by tragedy. It was celebrated in the usual festive style in the company of members of the family and some of his oldest friends. The King had decided upon the Ling-House Shoot for the day, rather than the traditional Horse-Shoe and, according to custom, the gentlemen went off to shoot during the morning expecting the ladies to join them for lunch at about 2 p.m. in a big marquee pitched in one of the fields, where carriages and cars waited to take them back to the house afterwards.

'Soon after the guns had taken up their positions for the afternoon's drive,' wrote Stamper:

> The King's pony-boy galloped up with the news that Mr Montague Guest had dropped dead on the shooting field. The King asked for the shooting-brake to be brought to where the body lay. It was a heavy vehicle and the ground was soft after the rain, but Stamper manoeuvred the car across the field. Mr Guest had been a large man and it was found that the shooting-brake was unsuitable, and the horse-drawn ambulance was sent for. Afterwards the King turned to the others and said, 'We'd better all go home.' Mr Guest was taken to the Royal waiting-room at Wolferton station; he had long suffered from a weak heart and no inquest was called for. But the King was very much upset by the loss of his friend, and the fact that it had occurred during one of the highlights of the year intensified the shock.[189]

Discipline was tight during a shoot: on one occasion the King spotted a rare white pheasant flying towards the guns and called out, 'Let it go!' But Prince Edward, then about thirteen, brought it down with a clean shot. The King was very angry and sent him home in disgrace. He missed several shoots before he was allowed out again.

Other events, too, marred the tranquillity of Sandringham: in December 1903 fire broke out under the hearth in Charlotte Knollys' bedroom. It seems that the joists were insufficiently insulated from the newly-installed fireplace; smouldering, they crashed through the ceiling in the Queen's room below. 'Terrible smoke,' wrote Queen Alexandra:

> ...with a terrible crash down came half my ceiling... God saved us. Shock has done no harm to Charlotte... Luckily neither her sitting-room nor my dressing-room were touched... a good many of my precious souvenirs and things, books and photographs, etc. were both burnt or spoilt by fire or water.[190]

In 1908, a storm destroyed a number of trees on the estate. Some of these had stood between the Norwich Gates and the House, which now lay open to the public gaze. The King decided that the wall and gates should be moved 300 yards further from the House, which also meant altering the course of the road outside. Before the days of planning permissions, this was easily achieved.

One of the King's greatest pleasures was to take his guests to visit the stud, where Persimmon, the horse that had won the Derby in 1896 had a special box of his own, and a groom all to himself. 'Many a time,' wrote Stamper, 'as we have been driving past the paddock, there has been Persimmon out at exercise... the King would watch him with great pleasure and "Isn't he beautiful?" he would say. "Isn't he beautiful?" '[191] The Sunday tours continued with visits to the greenhouses or to look at the flock of Southdown sheep which were brought to a high state of perfection in special pens near Commodore Wood by the shepherd, Mr Moulding, and his son, John, who sometimes attended the shoots carrying the King's cartridge bag.

In the early months of 1910, King Edward suffered violent fits of coughing and periodic bouts of bronchitis. Despite these, he continued to smoke his favourite cigars, but his health was being steadily undermined – to a point when his doctors strongly recommended that he should spend the winter abroad in a more congenial climate. But the King was worried by domestic crises and the growing threat of war, and was reluctant to leave. In the event, he was in France early in the new year, and spent much of March and April at Biarritz, where he remained in his rooms for days together. His retiring in a place where he had been known for his conviviality and affability necessitated an announcement that the King was indisposed. At the end of April he returned to London and two days later went to Sandringham. He walked slowly round the gardens before lunch, accompanied by the head gardener and his agent, inspecting work that had been done in his absence. The next day, a Sunday, he went to church, though he did not follow his customary routine of walking across the park, but went round by car. After lunch he walked round the gardens again, despite the cold driving rain. In the evening he worked at his papers with Sir Frederick Ponsonby. The following afternoon he returned to Buckingham Palace. For the next three days he continued to see visitors and sign papers in spite of sleeplessness, shortness of breath and feeling 'wretchedly ill'. 'I shall work to the end,' he declared. 'Of what use is it to be alive if one cannot work?' By this time the King was suffering from terrible fits of coughing, when he would turn black in the face.

In the meantime, Queen Alexandra had heard, whilst on holiday in Corfu, that the King was unwell and decided to return, though she had no premonition that he was, in fact, close to death. He was not well enough to greet her at the station and she was shocked to see him on her arrival at Buckingham Palace, grey in the face and struggling for breath. She noticed an oxygen cylinder standing in the corner of his room. On the next day he dressed in order to receive Sir Ernest Cassel and lit a cigar, which he was, however, unable to finish. He spoke indistinctly, saying: 'I am very seedy, but I wanted to see you.'[192] He could eat little lunch and later he walked to the window of his room to look at his canaries. It was then that he collapsed and fell. Still he refused to go to bed. On being given the news that his horse Witch of the Air had won the 4.15 p.m. at Kempton Park the King replied, 'Yes, I have heard of it. I am very glad.' Soon afterwards he fainted and was assisted to bed. Before he lapsed into a coma, he realised that he was dying. He was heard to murmur, 'I shall not give in. I shall work to the end.'[193] It was then that the Queen showed in its fullest extent her generosity of heart, sending for Mrs Keppel that he might bid her farewell. In the evening, surrounded by his family, he lost consciousness and died peacefully a quarter of an hour before midnight.

Queen Alexandra wrote to Mary Drew, whose husband had died some three months before the King:

I have been wishing to write to you long ago to thank you for your dear letter of true sympathy in my overwhelming sorrow and misery, but somehow I could not summon up courage to do so sooner, which I know you will understand and forgive., Indeed all you say in your despair I feel in mine, and the world can never be the same again in our loneliness. It all seems still like a terrible dream, and I cannot realise that I shall never in this world see his blessed face again or hear his dear voice.[194]

He was sadly missed. Those who knew him recalled with affection his affability and charm, his extraordinary zest for life and untiring energy, his enjoyment of companionship and entertainment. They remembered his contented gurgle of laughter when amused and his kindness. Summing up his life, his biographer wrote:

King Edward was a thoroughly conscientious sovereign who made pleasure his servant and not his master after his accession to the throne. His private life, which was not free from what moralists could term blemishes, included an ideal relationship with his heir; and the dignity of his public life, his immense popularity and charm, and the zest, punctuality and panache with which he performed his duty forcefully and faithfully until the day on which he died, enhanced the prestige of the monarchy. The journey upon which he embarked in boyhood... may be compared with a voyage to the Antipodes. Safe havens were attainable from opposite directions; parents and tutors pointed one way but he found another; and he arrived.[195]

CHAPTER ELEVEN

KING IN A COTTAGE

King George and Queen Mary were confronted by many urgent and important issues in those first exhausting weeks of the new reign. The period between the death and funeral of King Edward VII had been unduly protracted, and now there were questions concerning the Royal residences which had to be addressed. Queen Alexandra, who ten years previously had never wanted to go to Buckingham Palace at all, now did not wish to be dislodged, and her often illogical mind needed some persuading that this was necessary. Somewhat reluctantly then, she moved the few yards down the Mall to Marlborough House and so returned to the scene of those heady days of the 1860s. At Sandringham, King Edward had left her the Big House for her lifetime and King George refused to listen to any suggestions that his mother's intention of remaining there was unreasonable. Meanwhile, the King Emperor remained, while he was in Norfolk, in the cramped conditions at York Cottage. His children were growing up and the family and Household were as uncomfortable as possible, yet a few hundred yards away stood this enormous mansion almost entirely unoccupied. In this Queen Alexandra showed a quite extraordinary lack of consideration for the all-too-obvious needs of her son, the King. Her obstinacy and selfishness, contrasted with her impulsive but quite random kindnesses to anyone who crossed her path, made her seem not quite grown up. There is the well-recorded incident when one Christmas she chanced to meet a young Scottish footman standing pensively by a window. She brought him a pair of gold cuff-links saying; 'Nobody must be lonely in my house. You will get your proper Christmas present later, but these are something personal to you from me.'[196] Her lack of consideration to Princess Victoria was proverbial: she had effectively prevented the Princess's marriage to the Earl of Rosebery. He was, said the

Princess, the only man she had ever really loved; but her mother made it clear that she was needed at home. Queen Alexandra's possessiveness was all too evident; as Princess of Wales she used to keep a bell by her side to summon her daughter. A cousin wrote:

> Poor Toria was just a glorified maid to her mother. Many a time a talk or a game would be broken off by a message from my Aunt Alix, and Toria would run like lightning, often to discover that her mother could not remember why she had sent for her, and it puzzled me because Aunt Alix was so good.[197]

King George himself was not blind to her failings: 'Mama, as I have always said, is one of the most selfish people I know.'[198]

So it was to York Cottage that the King and Queen returned during their visits to Sandringham, which were, alas, somewhat rarer than they had hitherto been. They were much occupied during the first year of the King's reign, not least by preparations for his Coronation, while Queen Mary found relaxation from the many official functions in arranging the King's family possessions at Buckingham Palace. After the ceremony, the King and Queen sailed to India to attend the Durbar – the meeting of the Indian Princes to pay homage to their Emperor. This accomplished, there were state visits to be paid in Germany and France. But already industrial unrest was threatening the country's economic stability. The King and Queen visited the Welsh mining valleys, where they were received enthusiastically. This was followed by a tour of the Yorkshire Coalfield: while they were there an accident occurred underground, in which several miners lost their lives. They at once drove over to condole with the bereaved families and Queen Mary, usually so firmly controlled, could not restrain her tears. Their sympathy and readiness to share in this tragedy meant more to the community than any formal carriage drive and these tours were widely appreciated and set the pattern for the future, ultimately leading to the 'walkabout' later in the century. The contrast between the extraordinary splendour of the Durbar and a King who could talk to his subjects as man-to-man could not have been greater.

Further problems arose at this time over the Suffragette Movement whose activities, fast gathering pace, were to be interrupted only by the outbreak of war in 1914. The old way of life, the certainty of an established order of things, was imperceptibly changing. The King's cousin, Kaiser Wilhelm II, was being dragged towards war by the German military hierarchy. His attitude towards England was ambivalent: he once expressed the wish 'that every drop of his English blood might be drawn from his veins'; he felt that his uncle, King Edward VII, had taken a condescending view of him: when he left Sandringham after attending the Edward VII's birthday celebrations in 1902, the King commented, 'Thank God he has gone.'[199] Yet there had come an easier relationship with his cousin, King George, from which he hoped that the increasing rivalry between the two nations might yet be peacefully resolved. This hope was destroyed by the assassination of Archduke Franz Ferdinand at Sarajevo and the punitive ultimatum delivered by Austria to Serbia. As the countries of Europe arranged themselves into two conflicting camps, there could be no alternative to Britain's declaration of war against Germany on 4 August. It was the end of an era.

At Sandringham York Cottage, standing beside the lake in all its peacefulness, seemed far from the tumultuous events in which the King and Queen were deeply involved. On the night of 4 August, they were repeatedly summoned to the balcony of Buckingham Palace by huge and patriotic crowds. Standing there, on the newly finished balcony, they symbolised the stability and security of England herself, which no enemy forces could dislodge. Deeply saddened as they were by the turn of events, the King and Queen entered a period of intense activity, and there were times when York Cottage must have seemed very far away. Yet somehow they managed to pay fleeting visits when they could briefly recuperate from the constant strain of their public duties and where some semblance of permanence could be found.

Queen Alexandra – who, as we have seen, maintained a long-standing hatred of Prussia – retired to Sandringham on the edge of a nervous breakdown, after a hectic year in which she had thrown herself into the war effort with abandon, visiting hospitals and organisations connected with war work. On these occasions her deafness was no handicap, and her unpunctuality was forgiven, yet it cannot have been an easy task with her disability, and public appearances were becoming an increasing strain on her constitution. She grieved over the huge casualty lists, and only too often went to console tenants on the Sandringham estate who had lost a husband or a son. She left London accompanied only by Charlotte Knollys, declaring 'I shall go mad if not left alone by myself.'[200] Her hatred of the Germans was not untypical: belief in atrocities was widespread and, although her situation enabled her to be better informed than most, her deafness and simple nature scarcely allowed an intellectual approach to the conduct of the war. In any case, her dislike of Germany went back some fifty years to the Schleswig-Holstein affair, which in 1864 had ended disastrously for Denmark. When Zeppelins dropped bombs in the neighbourhood in January 1915, she wrote to 'Jackie' Fisher, the First Sea Lord, asking for 'lots of rockets with spikes or hooks on to defend our Norfolk coast'. There was, at about the same time, an invasion scare on the coast, and a guard of Grenadiers was attached to the King and Queen after Christmas. One bomb dropped on the estate, on the Wolferton flats near The Wash; the crater was afterwards enlarged to form a haunt for wildfowl. The only casualties were at King's Lynn, where four people were killed. Queen Alexandra, in this trying time, felt cut off, as indeed she was, from her family and home in Denmark. The strain of maintaining some contact with her relatives spread widely across Europe was considerable, but she found ways and means of keeping in touch with her nephew, King Christian X of Denmark, and she was able to warn her sister, the Empress Marie Feodorovna, mother of Czar Nicholas II of Russia, that the Germans intended to attack Warsaw, and hoped that she was aware of it.

Towards the end of 1915 the King came to Sandringham as an invalid. Whilst he was inspecting the Royal Flying Corps at Hesdigneul in October, three cheers were called while he was still only a few yards distant. The sound frightened his horse, which reared up: slipping, he fell back on top of the King. For a short time it seemed that he had suffered only minor injuries, and he was supported to his car, but further examination showed that he had broken his pelvis in two places, and he returned to England on a stretcher. For some months he was in considerable pain, and it seems that from this time, his health was never again quite the same. Despite the King's injury, the family Christmas at Sandringham was a comparatively festive affair, with sing-songs at the piano, and all the fun of the gramophone, which was still something of a novelty. 'In the evening after dinner I had to play accompaniment for comic songs,' wrote Lady Bertha Dawkins, 'sung by the Queen, Princess Mary & 3 Princes till we went to bed....The King is ever so much better & looks very well indeed, but his leg still bothers him, as he gets neuralgia in it, & that makes him walk lame at times.'[201]

But there was a darker side, for in 1915 tragedy came to Sandringham. During the year the Allied forces had invaded Turkey in the Gallipoli peninsula, in a campaign that was doomed to failure from the outset and ended in a humiliating withdrawal after suffering heavy casualties. Among the units participating was the King's Own Sandringham Company in the 5th Battalion of the Royal Norfolk Regiment. It was a Territorial unit created in 1909 at the suggestion of King Edward VII, formed and commanded by Captain Frank Beck, the King's agent and son of the

Edmund Beck, who had been such a thorn in the side of Louise Cresswell. One afternoon in August, shortly after disembarking at Suvla Bay, the Company was ordered to advance: it was never seen again. Some, including Beck, were killed by shell-fire or machine-guns during the initial stages of the attack; it was assumed that, of the remainder, some at least had been taken prisoner. The effect on a small community of scores of telegrams arriving simultaneously and containing the ominous word 'missing' was profound. The King personally requested news of the Company but, as it gradually became clear that the Turkish prisoner-of-war camps did not contain any of its members, it was assumed that it had been annihilated. After the war it was revealed that those who had survived the initial advance had found themselves isolated from the rest of the battalion and surrounded, that they had almost certainly surrendered and had all been massacred at a farmstead where their bodies were found in a shallow ravine. How much of the disaster was reported to the Royal family is impossible to say; undoubtedly the sudden and unexplained loss of more than 150 men from local families must have darkened the lives of those living on the estate. In the context of the First World War it was unfortunately a situation which was tragically common to many communities, throughout the country, in the wake of the battles of Ypres and of the Somme. Characteristically, Queen Alexandra unhesitatingly visited all the bereaved families whose sons she had known and watched grow up on the estate.

Zeppelin raids continued intermittently along the Norfolk coast. Early in 1916, Lady Bertha wrote to her daughter:

> We were all, maids included, after tea sitting listening to the gramophone, when Sir Charles Cust put his head in & said: 'Come, a Zepp can be heard', so out of the front door we went into the dark, wrapped up in rugs & coats, the Queen in the King's fur coat, & we did hear a distant dull thudding, but it must have been a long way off, so we came back into the house. Sir Charles had heard 3 bombs fall before he called us, & the detective, Spenser, heard 6. When we got in all the lights went out, & the King was frantic & somebody caught it! [202]

In September of the same year Queen Alexandra wrote to the King:

> We have been living through some gruesome moments here – just a fortnight ago we had those beastly Zepps over us. At 10 o'clock that Saturday evening they began. We were all sitting upstairs in Victoria's room when we were suddenly startled by the awful noise! and lo and

behold, there was the awful monster over our heads. Everybody rushed up and wanted to go downstairs. I must confess I was not a bit afraid – but it was a most uncanny feeling – poor Victoria was quite white in the face and horror-struck – but we all wanted to see it – the house was pitch dark and at last Charlotte and I stumbled down in the darkness and found Colonel Davidson and Hawkins (the butler) scrambling about outside so I also went out, but saw nothing and for the time the Zepps had flown off somewhere but came back about four o'clock in the night and dropped bombs all over the place! [203]

After this raid, Queen Alexandra immediately went to Dodshill where the bombs had fallen, to commiserate with those whose homes had been damaged.

King George and Queen Mary took the wartime food shortages very seriously and rationed themselves and their Household like everyone else. Vegetables were planted and grown at Sandringham where once there had been flower-beds, and much of the produce was diverted to where it was most needed. Meals were always on the dot, and those who were late got nothing:

> One was late if the clock sounded when one was on the stairs, even in a small house like York Cottage...The point was that there was just enough and no more for everyone; but as most people helped themselves too generously, there was nothing left for the person who came last. (Captain) Godfrey-Faussett was kept on the telephone one day and came into the dining-room after everyone else had sat down. He found nothing to eat and immediately rang the bell and asked for a boiled egg. The King accused him of being a slave to his inside, of unpatriotic behaviour, and even went so far as to hint that we should lose the war on account of his gluttony.[204]

At the instigation of Mr Lloyd George, the King announced that he and his Household would renounce alcohol for the duration of the war. 'I hate doing it,' he wrote in his diary, 'but hope it will do good.' [205] Later, he was to express his disappointment in the lack of public response to the real sacrifice he had made. But perhaps his abstinence was not total: years afterwards, the Duke of Windsor suggested that the 'small matter of business' the King attended to after dinner concerned a glass of port. Cider, however, was deemed non-alcoholic.

Some record of the peaceful occasions during those four years of horror was kept by Mrs Nora Wigram, wife of the King's Assistant Private Secretary.

Captain Clive Wigram of the Indian Army had been appointed an Extra Equerry to Prince George when, as Prince of Wales, he visited India in 1905. Four years later, Major Wigram became a member of the Household as an Equerry and Assistant Secretary, deputising for the Private Secretary, Lord Stamfordham, during the latter's illness. The King reported to Lord Stamfordham, 'Wigram has done quite splendidly: never made a mistake: is simply a glutton for work, besides being a charming fellow. I am indeed lucky in having found a man like him.'[206] Mrs Wigram was a frequent visitor to Sandringham, staying at Park House. She herself possessed sterling qualities: such a position required a certain resilience of temperament, and her letters to her mother, Lady Chamberlain, reflect a pleased surprise as she learned that the King and Queen appreciated her on her own merits. 'This is such a charming little house; it gets every ray of sun, and is so beautifully fresh and bright. You would love it,' Mrs Wigram wrote to her mother.

> It is just the sort of house I should love to have for my own. We continue to lead our homely existence. On Wednesday they asked me down to lunch at York Cottage. I rang the front door bell and who should come and open the door to me but the King! I little thought I should live to have the door opened to me by the King of England.
>
> Clive wasn't lunching. The usual homely meal followed. I sat by the King and the conversation was vy general – all the company had table napkin rings – the King said, 'I quite refuse to use one, and I like a clean napkin every day.' Whereupon the Queen remarked rather tartly from her end of the table, 'You don't encourage me at all in my war economies' – Such a simple lunch only pheasant and chocolate soufflé. I shall never have any qualms at inviting T.M.s to any meal.
>
> The Queen carried me off to a village concert with the children and herself, alone. Such a concert, I really think the Castle Knock ones used to be better. However, she was most happy and cheerful over it and was convulsed with joy over the efforts of the funny man – a fat sergt in the Black Watch.
>
> We see the King and Queen every day, one way and another. On Thursday she came over to this house to inspect it all – I was out of doors and returned to find her here and she greeted me with – 'My dear, we have been inspecting your rooms and I do apologise that you have no cushions on your sofa.' Meanwhile, she had bounced into Carrie's room and had a chat to her, sat in her chair and asked her if it was comfortable. Carrie's face was pink with excitement which deepened later in the day when she received a box of chocolates with a

little card attached on which was written by the Queen herself: 'To Mrs Wigram's maid from the Queen, wishing her a happy new year.'

The King and Princess Victoria joined us while C. and I were playing golf yesterday morning, and the King was most helpful in his efforts to find our lost golf balls. Clive thinks they are going to stay here until the end of the month...The Prince of Wales and Prince Albert arrived here last night...I have not seen them yet.[207]

Meanwhile, Queen Alexandra lived on in the Big House nearby in much the same style as before. Generous as ever, despite heavy taxation, she could see no necessity for economies in her establishment. As always, her rooms were filled with flowers but in the grounds, owing to the shortage of staff, some of the old horses, which it had given her great happiness to see retired in the park, had to be put down.

'It breaks my heart that this cruel, wicked, beastly war should be the cause of so many of my precious old friends my horses being slaughtered after all these years,' she declared. But the kennels were left unscathed. 'My kennels and my dogs,' she said firmly, 'I will not have touched: I will rather keep them out of my own pocket.'[208] It did not occur to her that she had always paid for their upkeep. Her generosity was proverbial, and often exploited. Her Controller, Sir Dighton Probyn once expressed a wish to retire but, on being pressed to remain, he agreed, hoping that once 'the Blessed Lady's' affairs were in order the work would become lighter. Alas, he hoped for the impossible: like the Duchess of Teck, Queen Alexandra had no idea of the meaning of money: every applicant for alms was given £10 as a matter of course. Once, when it pointed out that the applicant was serving a prison sentence, her reply was, 'Send the man £10; he will want it when he comes out.'[209] During the war, she gave thousands of pounds to charities. Whenever an attempt was made to explain her financial situation, she feigned deafness. In her youth she had been accustomed to – comparative – poverty; as Princess of Wales she had been accustomed to every luxury, even extravagance, and her artless character rejoiced at what seemed to her a bottomless well of gold. She was uninterested in the acquisition of wealth; for her the sentimental value of an article was everything. It was far too late to try to change her ways.

Down at York Cottage members of the Royal family arrived whenever they could be spared from their war duties. At this new year of 1917 there were times when they were all together.

After lunch Clive and I walked down to York Cottage, and then the walking cavalcade set out – such a party. The King and Queen, Prince of Wales, Princess Mary and Princes Henry, Albert and George. The little P. of W. has filled out a good deal, I think. Nice looking boy and much more talkative, but such a Baby still – he and Prince Albert walking about arm in arm – singing comic songs, and most typically English. Clive says the little Prince thinks fit to use the most appalling language – the correct thing in the Guards, I suppose! Tomorrow we are to have a cinematograph show of the Battle of the Ancre, which ought to be interesting. It seems curious to know the Royal family on such intimate terms – they are always so pleasant and friendly. [210]

Such a horrid day here – series of snow showers – I don't mean it in a blasé way, but really I got rather bored this afternoon! The King asked me to come for a walk with them.... and we all trooped forth – the whole party – and dawdled through the gardens and then on to the stables, and it was bitterly cold. Then the children got lost purposely: the King said they were always trying to evade him (quite true!) and then the dog got lost – then Godfrey-Faussett got lost looking for the dog!! By that time the King was awfully cross – and we were all shuffling around to keep warm – finally the King and Queen said goodbye – and Princess Mary and the Prince of Wales and Prince Albert all walked home with me. They were quite cheerful and entirely flippant! – writing their names in the snow. Poor boys – a very boring afternoon for them. We had rather an interesting man here last night; he is the confidential adviser to the King of Denmark; Mr Anderson. He comes and has long talks with the King about affairs in Germany and elsewhere, for he often goes to Berlin. One is inclined to wonder if he is quite 'all right'. However, I fancy they are careful about what they let him see and hear... He was quite interesting about Russia... says the new Prime Minister is the worst possible selection – he belongs to the Reactionary class, who are all pro-German. He says anything may happen in Russia – a great deal depends on the Czar but he is undependable in that he is so superstitious. If the Empress comes to him and says, 'I dreamt such and such a thing and it succeeded,' the Czar is quite likely to go off and do it. He also said, 'The Empress is mad.' [211]

In fact, Mr Anderson was a reliable source of information. He had built up large business interests in Denmark and had become acquainted with the Danish Royal Family. Through them he was introduced to King George, the German Emperor and the Czar and his business enabled him to travel widely through Europe in the midst of the war; he was thus well placed to assess the situation within Germany and Russia.

Other events during the four years of war disturbed the tranquillity of life at York Cottage. As it was, the King spent little enough time there, but after Christmas in 1915 he broke his holiday to return to London to preside over a crisis within the Government; the issue was concerned with the Military Service Bill under which single men aged between eighteen and forty-one would be compelled to attest their willingness to serve with the colours. The King strongly supported the Prime Minister, Mr Asquith, and the threat of massive resignations of Ministers receded. The following year David Lloyd-George, the War Minister, convinced that the war was not being conducted with sufficient determination – a feeling shared by the general public, who were confused by the terrible losses on the Somme – proposed to establish a War Council over which he would preside. This was unacceptable to the Prime Minister, Mr Asquith who, with several of his Liberal colleagues, tendered their resignation. The King was anxious to avoid a general election in wartime and asked Lloyd-George to form a Government to ensure the survival of the coalition. Shortly after he had come into office, Germany sent a Peace Note to the American Embassy in London, which was a gesture designed to cloak plans for unrestricted submarine warfare to defeat the Allied blockade on Germany. The King, briefed by Mr Anderson and with first-hand knowledge of the effects of this blockade, urged caution in the wording of the reply. In the result, though, the Allies made such demands as to preclude any possibility of a meaningful interchange of views.

Thus the King found himself constantly at the centre of problems of critical national importance, exercising his right, defined by Walter Bagehot, 'to be consulted, to encourage and to warn'. Whether his judgment was always right is arguable. Certainly he supported Sir Douglas Haig, the British Commander-in-Chief replacing Sir John French, when questions of policy or command arose. Haig enjoyed the King's confidence: his wife, Dorothy, had been a Maid of Honour to Queen Alexandra and he had been a visitor to Sandringham for nearly twenty years. When public confidence in his policy of a 'war of attrition' wavered after the Somme and the Third Battle of Ypres (Passchendaele), where a third of a million casualties were suffered for a gain of 4 miles of shell-crater and mud, his conviction that he received 'divine inspiration' was strengthened by the King's support. Detached from political argument and free to travel to mine and munitions factories and service units at home and abroad, together with briefings from war committees, the King was in a unique position to make a personal assessment of public sentiment, rather than military strategy.

Meanwhile, visits, and visiting, continued at Sandringham:

York Cottage, Jan 21, 1917. We have a clergyman staying here today, Mr Temple – of St. James', Piccadilly. He had travelled in Germany a lot previous to the war... on one occasion he was talking to some eminent German scholar, and was saying to him how much better he thought it would be if more powers were delegated to the Reichstag and taken out of the hands of the Emperor. The German said, 'Good gracious! You do not know what you are talking about. Why! more than 2/3 of the members of the Reichstag are Roman Catholics, and we would far rather have an autocratic sovereign than give the government of the country over to the Church of Rome.' It is curious how the Religious question always crops up in every country.

We had quite an interesting experience on Friday. Princess Victoria invited us to come over to Sandringham (the Big House) to see her rooms. All the rooms with the exception of the big Hall and her suite of rooms are shut up. A fine Hall but very early Victorian in the mixture of things; a chandelier which would give one the 'vertigo' – blatant brass, with about 30 electric globes, all covered with bright yellow silk, and on the walls some fine Landseer prints... We went upstairs to her rooms – oh! such a collection of things – a real maiden lady's room. The tables covered with things: little boxes, china rabbits, pigs, penguins, cats – anything you please – photographs galore – all the Royal family and her friends. In her bedroom there is a screen about 5ft high and 4 panels, consisting of nothing but framed photographs let into a white wooden frame. I am sure I have never seen such crowded rooms but she is so proud of them all, showing us everything. She was most affectionate, calling me 'dear' all the time.[212]

'Here I am in regal surroundings once more,' wrote Mrs Wigram blithely in September, 1917:

The King and Queen welcomed me so very kindly at the station, and then Clive and I walked up, had a cup of tea, and then played six holes of golf. I was rather disturbed when going to bed to hear that there was a heavy air 'raid' in progress over London... I am afraid they will come again, this lovely clear evening, the dirty brutes.

We went off to church this morning... and a nice simple service. A quiet lunch which was followed by a strenuously Royal afternoon. Finally we all sat down to a merry tea party in the garden, where light badinage was exchanged all round, both Queens smoking hard. At last we broke up and shortly we are to go and dine at York Cottage. They are very nice and kind to me. Queen Alexandra is just like a child, isn't she – there was one terrible moment when she presented a carrot to the groom who was holding one of the race horses, for him to bite! – she warmly invited me to come to see all over Sandringham House.[213]

At the end of the year Mrs Wigram was again at Sandringham, having recently recovered from chicken-pox. On 26 December she wrote:

I am so glad I managed to struggle down to tea on Christmas Eve to York Cottage for it was quite an experience. We had a select little tea in the drawing room – Their Majesties, Lady Katy, Reggie Seymour and ourselves; the Queen in a very diaphanous green dress with a pretty necklace. I wore my black and blue dress. Toast, biscuits, potato scones, jam and sponge cakes was the fare provided. After tea the Queen rang the bell and when the Page came in she said, 'Tell the children we are ready, please,' whereupon there was an avalanche from all directions. The whole party was marshalled, consisting of P. Mary, Princes Albert, Henry and George – Dr Grey, Mlle Dussau and Mr Watts (the boys' tutor), and we all proceeded into the Billiard Room, where everybody's presents were collected in little heaps. Lady Katy was the first to be given hers: a very nice pair of sauceboats and a quaint jade paper-cutter. Then to my amazement the Queen called me and they gave me a most charming brooch – too kind of them – it is about 1" square. The groundwork blue-grey enamel surrounded with white enamel and little pearls and then in the middle a diamond 'GM' surmounted by a diamond crown; a delightful thing to have and besides that they gave Clive yet another present; a charming coloured reproduction of their picture and that of the Prince of Wales – by Cuye – very nice. Dr Grey and Reggie both received cigarette cases – Mr Watts framed photo of themselves. Mlle. Dussan a gold brooch with enamel decoration and seal coney muff –

Then having bestowed all their generous gifts they opened their own which they were so excited over. The Queen gave him a fine set of sporting books illustrated and a set of black pearl studs, and he got – from Princess Victoria, I think, a sort of china goblet and from Queen

Alexandra 2 horrid little boxes with her and King Edward's picture on the lids. The Queen had some delightful things. I was so amused with her. Like every good wife she said, 'I saw this little box which pleased me and I asked the King to give it to me as his Christmas present.' All her things were objets d'art; little lacquer boxes, jade ornaments and an old Stuart snuff-box. She had carefully chosen her mother-in-law's present to herself – a nice little Chinese ornament. Princess Mary had some nice things – a pair of blonde tortoiseshell and diamond hairpins, an ermine muff and stole, and a pretty little hair wreath – a dreadful brilliant blue inkstand from Queen Alexandra – one or two nice little ornaments including a fascinating little George III work box with the most dainty fittings. The boys all got little articles of jewellery – a little pearl and diamond pin for Prince Henry – besides which they always give them silver so that when they marry they may be suitably equipped. It seemed so funny to see Princes Henry and George staggering off with silver toast-racks, salvers, tea-strainers, etc! – They were a very happy little party and I am so glad I did not miss it all. [214]

For the King and Queen these visits to York Cottage were only brief respites from the growing pressures of the war. Unrest among munitions workers called for tours of industrial areas by members of the Royal family to improve morale; the King visited the Fleet at Scapa Flow; the Queen interested herself especially in the development of artificial limbs at Roehampton for war casualties. The Prince of Wales was begging to be allowed to be of more use on the Western Front, and his disregard for personal safety caused his parents some anxiety. Prince Albert had qualified as a pilot – the first member of the Royal family to do so – and had served in a gun turret in HMS *Collingwood* during the Battle of Jutland in 1916 despite recurring health problems which ultimately necessitated an operation.

October 14, 1917. I had such an interesting afternoon on Saturday. Queen Alexandra asked me to come over to Sandringham and said she would show me over the House. She is very fascinating, I think – and I really enjoyed seeing all the things – some of which were quite beautiful – She kept saying, 'The King used to sit there' or 'The King used to do this' and one pictured all the revels that used to take place. Finally she took me into her own private sitting-room – a truly marvellous room so crowded that one cannot turn round – a bewildering mass of photographs – and every sort of treasure. I don't think I am exaggerating when I tell you that there were over 200 things on her writing table; the only space left being taken up by her blotter... She loves all her little possessions, and kept showing them off. Finally I took my leave, and she embraced me so warmly, murmuring 'My dearrr, do drrrop into teee any afternoon I shall be so pleeesed!' Dear kind little Queen. Princess Victoria then led me into Sir Dighton and Miss Knollys' room – dear old things – they loved showing me their treasures. Sir D. led me by the hand round his room and Charlotte was glorious. 'I must show you my bathroom, Sir Dighton gave it to me and it cost him £100 – and there are seven glasses in it so I am never lonely in my bath as there are 7 other Charlotte Knollys looking on'!! (Charlotte Knollys was remarkably ugly.) It was too nice of Princess Victoria; she sent me 6 vy nice bits of Danish china – as a souvenir of my afternoon.

The King has been in great form lately, and so easy to sit next to at dinner – full of interesting stories about matters grave and gay. (He) is so nice to me and said that Princess Victoria had so enjoyed having me down here, and it had made all the difference to her... They are so dear and kind to me. My riding has been such a source of delight... went for a long ride with Princess Mary and Clive on Saturday. [215]

Even as the struggle for the ridge at Passchendaele in 1917 was creating appalling casualties in the sea of mud, a certain tranquillity was maintained at York Cottage – which was illusory, for the King and Queen suffered the personal worries about their sons which they shared with every family in the country. The Prince of Wales badgered the authorities to be allowed nearer to the front line, though he confessed to a friend that he felt terrified each time he moved forward. He was told that, if it were certain that he would be killed, the risk might be acceptable, but in no circumstances could the possibility that he might be taken prisoner be entertained. For the King and Queen, work never ceased. Quite apart from the constant tours, there were also the red despatch boxes which arrived incessantly on the King's desk, wherever he might be. The abdication of the Czar, the King's cousin, in 1917 came as a shock to them, which turned to horror in the following year as the news of the assassination of the Czar and Czarina and all their children filtered through. On 25 July 1918, the King wrote in his diary: 'May and I attended a service at the Russian Church... in memory of dear Nicky who I fear was shot last month by the Bolsheviks, we can get no details, it was a foul murder, I was devoted to Nicky who was the kindest of men, a thorough gentleman, loved his country and his people.' [216] On the anniversary of his accession he wrote: 'I don't think any Sovereign of these realms has had a more difficult or more troublous 8 years than I have had.' [217]

Early in January 1919, Mrs Wigram wrote to her mother from York Cottage:

> Princess Victoria telephoned asking me to go for a walk with her, and we walked up to 'Appleton' which is Queen Maud's little house. There we found Queen Mary and Queen Maud, the latter most cordial and nice to me – but such a funny, exotic, merry little thing – very minute – rather 'chic' in her way – with very pretty feet, well shod – a neat tweed skirt and rather a rakish black velvet 'Tam'. She looked so tiny beside our Queen. A furious family wrangle then ensued as to how they should all sit in church tomorrow at Prince George's confirmation; Queen Maud's voice rising more and more shrilly: 'Dear Papa used to like it done like this or that' – Queen Mary made some eminently pacific and practical suggestions and the tumult subsided. I was then requested to take a photograph of the two Queens with Princess Victoria in the middle. Then I was conducted over the house – architecturally very nice but some of the things in it too deplorable – the dining room pictures consisting of a series of sort of Christmas number pictures, framed – you know the sort of thing – 'The Gamekeeper's Wife', 'Grandmamma and Baby'... dreadful. Princess Victoria so friendly and nice as usual – she asked after you both – and said she always remembers your seat on a horse. She then said, 'George often tells me how much he likes Nora Wigram'... We met Princess Mary on our way back, she was on her way out to a shooting lunch...[218]

Though the war had drawn to its agonised conclusion on 11 November 1918, the following year was to bring much unrest and a spreading sense of disillusion – and a personal sorrow for King George and Queen Mary. Only a few days after Mrs Wigram's letter, the Queen was informed, by telephone, that her sixth and youngest child, Prince John, had died. Born in 1904 a fine, strong boy, he had from early childhood suffered from epilepsy and other complications, and in 1917 it was judged that he should be brought up separately from the other children. He had his own establishment on the Royal estate, and was seen from time to time in the woods with Mrs Bill, who superintended his household. Though his brothers were deeply attached to him, they were of course separated by age and occupation. 'At 5.30,' wrote Queen Mary in her diary for 18 January:

> Lalla Bill telephoned me from Wood Farm, Wolferton, that our poor darling little Johnnie had passed away suddenly after one of his attacks. The news gave me a great shock, tho' for the poor little boy's restless soul, death came as a great release. I broke the news to George & we motored down to Sandringham. Found poor Lalla very resigned but heartbroken. Little Johnnie looked very peaceful lying there.[219]

'For him it is a great release,' the Queen continued, a few days later:

> as his malady was becoming worse as he grew older, & he has thus been spared much suffering... he just slept quietly into his heavenly home, no pain, no struggle, just peace for the poor little troubled spirit which had been a great anxiety to us... ever since he was four years old – The first break in the family circle is hard to bear but people have been so kind and sympathetic... [220]

There was, too, a sad irony in the event. Like so many mothers all over the Empire the Queen had endured four years of anxiety for her two eldest sons at the front; and now, just as she was beginning to relax, she was shaken by this personal sorrow. It was not her first, nor was it to be her last; and while she would not have wished it otherwise, the death of her youngest son was to cast its shadow. The King, too, was no less saddened: '...dear little Johnnie was laid in the churchyard next to (my) brother (Alexander) John,'[221] he wrote in his diary on 21 January. So the youngest children of King Edward VII and King George V lie side by side at the east end of Sandringham churchyard.

Mrs Wigram had been invited by the King to attend a shoot and described the occasion in a letter to her parents:

> The car comes to fetch me at 1 o'clock and I go down to York Cottage to pick up the Queen, Princess Mary and Lady Mary Trefusis. The dear Queen in a vy long dress with a very unsuitable crimson feather toque! – and wearing an absurd little tiered cloak wrap. Pcess M. and Lady M. quite suitably dressed. We arrive at a field where a tent is pitched and the Royal Standard flying proudly above it – several Royal footmen 6ft high help us to remove our wraps. In due time the King arrives – and greets me warmly, says he is so glad I came, and I find myself sitting

between him and the Duke of York, the rest of the party being Lord
Farquhar, Major Dick Molyneux, Charles Cust and Sir Fritz Ponsonby.
We sit at a narrow trestle table and the menu consists of mulligatawny
soup – a savoury stew of some sort – cold meats and salad – and a rice
pudding, followed... by cheese and a delicious selection of fruit. The
King tells various shooting stories and old 'Battues' of the Edwardian
reign are discussed. The King attacks me at one period and tells me Clive
is tiresomely pessimistic about the general situation, and don't I think
so – a voice at my elbow from the Duke of York consoles me by saying,
'Wiggy knows what he's talking about, that's why.' Lunch at last comes
to an end and the company rises, and we watch the beaters going off, vy
picturesque figures in blue smocks with black soft felt hats with a red
and blue band. Bland, the Head Keeper, mounted on a vy fine animal
tells the guns their numbers. We move on, followed by a sort of escort of
cavalry being 3 of the shaggiest old ponies, that anyone who wants may
climb on to. The King invites me to stand beside him, and the Queen
and I sit on our shooting sticks. Howlett, the King's valet loads for H.M.
A little boy slips in the cartridges. A man with two beautiful Labradors
and Spencer, the detective, completes the party – Bland's horn blows in
the distance and the drive begins. Driven partridges flying like bullets.
The King gets a brilliant right and left; 'Well done, George,' from the
Queen. At the end of the drive everyone looks for the birds, including
the Queen. I sit next to H.M. for the next two drives when the same
process repeats itself, and then have a turn with the Duke of York and
Prince Henry – the latter a fine shot already.... We have a great deal
of walking through turnips – ploughed fields – the Queen stumping
along with the best of them, being pushed through a hedge by 2 of the
keepers, while Charles Cust rolls about on one of the fat ponies and the
King rides too. The afternoon wears on, the light begins to go. We see
the motors waiting for us in the hollow of the road while the last beat
goes on – and the King brings down 6 birds with 6 cartridges at the last
moment. I travel back in the Royal car with the King and Queen and
Princess Mary and so ends a vy pleasant and interesting day. [222]

As time passed, Mrs Wigram found herself increasingly involved in
Royal affairs at York Cottage. As the king's confidence in Major Wigram
increased, so the Queen called on his wife as her lady-in-waiting.

They are being so awfully nice to me...You will be amused to hear that
today I am Lady-in-Waiting to the Queen officially. (She) said to me

yesterday, 'Will you come and be my Lady tomorrow, please, for I have to go to a lecture in the Women's Institute in the afternoon and would like to be accompanied by you.' [223]

In her next letter Mrs Wigram continued:

My waiting on the Queen went off very well. We went out and had a charming lunch with the shooters... Then after lunch we motored to the Women's Institute where all the good dames of the parish were collected, listened to a particularly naive lecture. This was followed by tea, the Queen sitting at a little table, pouring out tea. The Queen sitting down to a game of 'Happy Family' with 3 old ladies: 'Please, Your Majesty, is Mr Bun the Baker at home?' This was varied by a prolonged game of musical chairs... The lecturer narrowly escaped sitting on H.M.'s lap, but delicately extricated himself. Then Sir Roger de Coverly was danced. Meanwhile Queen Alexandra, Queen Maud and Princess Victoria had joined the party. We got home at 6 o'clock.

The Queen telephoned to ask me to go shopping with her in Dersingham. She chose £10 worth of goods for her guilds... After that we went for a long walk together for almost an hour and a half, and she was vy delightful.' [224]

October 17, 1920. I had a nice quiet day yesterday and in the evening we went down to dine at York Cottage with the Bishop of Norwich. I sat next to the King and Fritz Ponsonby. The King was very easy and chatty... he evidently was depressed about this coming coal strike – poor little man, he has had so many strifes during his short reign...

We have just come from church where the Bishop had to dedicate a memorial to King Edward... It was pathetic to see poor old Sir Dighton come into church. He looked so bent, his poor old head more down than ever. [225]

October 19, 1921.– So lovely down here and I am feeling so well, and playing lots of golf which is still improving... Old Miss Charlotte (Knollys) came to call on me yesterday and gratified me by saying that Queen Alexandra thinks I am very nice!... Princess Victoria is in very good form; she has just been away to Harrogate and paying visits for the last two months. [226]

Mrs Wigram, in the course of this letter, mentioned that she was writing a full description of a dinner party she had recently attended:

My selection of dress for the occasion was a pale yellow satin with which I wore a wreath of green leaves in my hair with my pearls and green earrings. We arrived rather early as the motor had to go on to fetch the Queen of Norway (formerly Princess Maud of Wales), so we waited in the drawing room chatting to Lady Bertha Dawkins and Sir Charles Cust; the latter full of speculation as to how a success could be made of the coming evening. The Royal party came into the room simultaneously... Queen Mary was in white satin with her wonderful emeralds... Queen Alexandra, wonderfully striking still was in a black velvet tea-gown, of rather an old-fashioned cut, which showed off her slight figure to perfection. Dinner was announced – no sign of the Prince of Wales, and the King began to get very restive when in rushed H.R.H like a whirlwind, clinging to his left ear, which was bleeding profusely from a fore-dinner shave. This proved a useful diversion and we all went harmoniously in to dinner. I found myself sitting between the Prince of Wales and Sir Charles Cust, which was really not as agreeable as it sounds, for the Prince had Queen Alexandra on his right and our conversation was continually being broken into, for the poor Queen, being very deaf, was always trying to understand what was being said on either side of her, and I saw the Heir Apparent with a fork belonging to the entree course vigorously hitting the salt-cellar, thereby illustrating to his grandmother that he had been playing golf – 'So glad, my dear'. The King would occasionally address remarks to me down the table and the whole of the Royal family sitting between us – would listen to the airy badinage – so embarrassing! The little Prince seemed very low at the idea of going off for such a long time and said he hated leaving his own country, that the endless ceremonials did weary him so, and that the only thing he really liked were children's functions. He loves children but had to draw the line at kissing them – otherwise his embraces would have run to thousands.

Dinner finished with my curtsey to the King... Coffee, cigarettes and chat and much standing in the drawing-room until the King returned... We at last wandered back to the billiard room where the King and Prince of Wales were having a match. They both look delightful types of English gentlemen, each wearing white carnation buttonholes and were on such good terms with one another. Queen Alexandra did not leave until 11.15. The first time she has dined out for a year; she wanted to make the most of the Prince of Wales, to whom she is quite devoted. [227]

Mrs Wigram was by this time well aware of the King's strict adherence to routine and his extreme punctuality. At Sandringham he rose early to get through some business and saw his keepers before breakfasting at 9 a.m. with the Queen and other Royal guests:

> Immediately after breakfast he would walk out of the front door, with a cigarette (in holder) in his mouth and Charlotte, his grey-pink parrot, on his left wrist, his dog following him, to examine the sky and judge of the weather. Wet or fine, winter or summer, he never varied this procedure at Balmoral, Sandringham or Windsor, and indeed, he usually followed it at Buckingham Palace. At Balmoral and Sandringham the guests and Households, as well as the Royal visitors, had luncheon, tea and dinner with the King and Queen. A guest, strange to the ways of the house and to Court life, was very soon put at his ease when he found that essential formalities were few and easy, and that life at Sandringham was but country-house life all over England. Teatime was a friendly, informal meal even for an arriving guest introduced straight from the car into the Royal circle, and when the Royal family greeted the guests, assembled in the drawing-room before dinner, it was a prelude to another, quite informal occasion. The fare was never elaborate, and swift service shortened the meal still more. When the Queen rose and the ladies followed her out, each curtseying to the King as she retired and receiving a bow in return, he would beckon the latest guest and, summing up his potentialities, put him instantly at his ease with a suitable gambit in his kindly way. And after dinner he would turn on his gramophone, in his last years perhaps his favourite relaxation after conversation and philately. [228]

The seemingly tranquil life at York Cottage, where the King was certainly happiest, was seriously marred at this time by the social and industrial unrest during the demobilisation of the armed forces, which had not been organised on a fair basis. Though the Victory Parade of 1919 and the news of the signing of the Treaty of Versailles, which effectively ended the First World War, had drawn cheering crowds to Buckingham Palace, the post-war boom was all too short-lived: unemployment increased rapidly and a sense of disillusion spread among the men who had been living dangerously for the past four years. The King's prerogative 'to advise and to warn' was often exercised during these difficult times; David Lloyd George, the Prime Minister, was asked to exercise restraint after he had promised to prosecute the Kaiser, the king's cousin. In the end, Wilhelm was permitted to remain in Holland, which had offered him asylum after Germany's defeat. The King was greatly concerned by the effects of unemployment and recession and was worried by the emergence in Ireland of the Irish Republican Party, writing to Lord Stamfordham, his Private Secretary, that 'each year my responsibilities increase'.

Family problems, too, disturbed the illusion of tranquillity at York Cottage. Happy though he was in those familiar surroundings, his children were beginning to cause him anxiety – in fact, they were growing up and developing minds of their own. The King wrote confidently in 1911, 'my sons have begun well, especially the eldest...' But he spoke too soon. The Prince of Wales, released from the Army, was now a well-to-do young man about town, with modern ideas and interests and with no intention of allowing old-fashioned protocol to interfere with his enjoyment. The Prince, in common with many of his contemporaries, was making the most of the freedom which he had gained during the war, dancing the night away in nightclubs and enjoying the latest jazz and ragtime. The King observed this with increasing irritation and bewilderment, feeling that his own standards of duty were threatened and did not hesitate to criticise him loudly and in front of others. He was loud in his denunciation of the Prince's dress: for wearing turned-down collars (New Zealand); for wearing blue overalls with white tunics – 'a most extraordinary ugly uniform' – (India), combined with relentless exhortation to improve his riding. The Prince must have felt confused and defeated by the barrage of criticism which lacked any tempering of warmth or approval, and which could only widen the gap between father and son. He was naturally shy and under-confident, and disliked the tours of the empire which had been arranged with the King's approval to express the gratitude of the nation for their support and sacrifice. His visit to India was controversial: the British were not generally popular; there was strong indignation at the massacre at AmriCzar, and Mahatma Gandhi was leading the movement for independence. He scored some personal successes: his enjoyment of riding made him popular and his win at a difficult and dangerous race at the Meerut Tent Club brought him recognition. He was a reckless rider, though, and known for the ease with which he and his horse parted company. Later, he resented official duties and engagements which intruded on his freedom. There were other signs. But at York Cottage, surrounded by all that had been familiar and cherished for twenty-five year, the King found a measure of peace and relaxation.

The young Prince of Wales was susceptible and attractive to women and often chose as his companions older, married women. The relationship with Lady Furness did not last but he was certainly deeply in love with

Mrs Dudley Ward, the wife of a Member of Parliament who was much involved with Parliamentary affairs. Lord Esher, a relative of hers, had warned the Prince to be discreet, but within society it was widely spoken of. After fifteen years Wallis Simpson, an American and already divorced, replaced Mrs Ward and dominated him by the ease with which she was able to satisfy him – by the use, it was said, of skills acquired in the Far East. It was a relationship that endured for the remainder of his life.

Prince Henry, after preparatory school and Eton, attended Cambridge briefly with his brother before embarking on an army career at Sandhurst. Created Duke of Gloucester by his father, he spent the war visiting army units at home and overseas, afterwards serving a term as Governor General of Australia. As a younger man he had caused gossip by his weakness for drink, but it had not affected the decision to offer him the post. He was supported in his role by his Duchess, a daughter of the Duke of Buccleuch, and they continued to carry out public engagements.

The behaviour of Prince George, too young to have taken part in the war, was worrying; at this time there seemed little direction in his life other than a penchant for the unconventional. He left the Navy in 1929 and briefly became a civil servant. His association with louche young men – and his penchant for living on the fringes of the drugs scene – made it was advisable to remove him from the capital. Accordingly, the Prince of Wales brought him to Sandringham for a respite. In 1934, he married Princess Marina, daughter of Prince Paul of Greece. They, and later their children, played an active part in public life. Tragically he was killed when his aircraft crashed in 1942.

Princess Mary, who had so easily disturbed the composure of Mr Hansell's classes, somehow acquired fluency in French and German – and a love of horses and horse-racing. Clearly a strong character, she was actively occupied during both world wars, supporting the women's services, and training as a nurse. In 1922, she married Viscount Lascelles, heir to a titled family in Yorkshire, and bore him two sons. After his death the Princess Royal, as she was known, continued her activities, sometimes representing the Queen and participating in Yorkshire affairs until her death in 1965.

Prince Albert remained compliant and dutiful. His health had improved since the problems encountered during his war service and he enjoyed his golf and tennis and setting up the boys' camps named after him. He was deeply interested, in a practical and intelligent way, in the welfare of young people, especially those in industry. He had fallen in love with Lady Elizabeth Bowes- Lyon. The King dreaded the idea of their marrying but accepted their choice and was an affectionate father-in-law. It was noticed that he was often at his best, cheerful and good-natured, when the Yorks visited. From King George V's diary of 15 January 1923: 'At Sandringham. Bertie with Grieg arrived after tea and informed us that he was engaged to Elizabeth Bowes-Lyon, to which we gladly gave our consent. I trust they will be very happy.' Queen Mary noted: 'We are delighted and he looks beaming.'[229]

After his visit the Duke wrote to Queen Mary:

> You & Papa were both so charming to me yesterday about my engagement, & I can never thank you properly for giving your consent to it. I am very happy & I can only hope Elizabeth feels the same as I do. I know I am very lucky to have won her over at last. [230]

Lady Elizabeth, later to become Queen Elizabeth, the Queen Mother, wrote 'I was never afraid of him (King George) as his children were.'

The penultimate sentence needs a little explanation. The Duke had known Lady Elizabeth Bowes-Lyon since childhood, but fell in love with her in 1920. The children of Lord and Lady Strathmore were a close-knit and loving family. Lady Elizabeth, the ninth of ten children, became a close friend of Princess Mary, the Princess Royal, and was one of her bridesmaids. The Duke of York was not only greatly attracted to his prospective bride, but also to the open and happy family life he experienced at their homes at Glamis Castle in Scotland, and St Paul's, Walden Bury. It represented a cheerful and unfettered style which he had never encountered at York Cottage – but there were difficulties. Lady Elizabeth understood exactly what would be required of her were she to join the innermost circles of the Royal family, the surrender of that very freedom which she had hitherto enjoyed. In 1921, she had refused the Duke's proposals, but for two years he persisted and eventually won her hand. For nearly thirty years, and throughout a world war, their marriage represented to the nation an example of comfortable and devoted domesticity.

On 20 January, Lady Elizabeth and her parents arrived at York Cottage to meet the King and Queen and – a much greater ordeal – Queen Alexandra. The Royal parents were enthusiastic as they wrote up their journals that night. 'Elizabeth is charming, so pretty and engaging and natural. Bertie is supremely happy,' Queen Mary wrote. The King was quite captivated by her: '...a pretty and charming girl & Bertie is a very lucky fellow.'[231]

The record of the meeting between the aged Queen Alexandra and the future Duchess at the Big House has not been published, but it cannot have been altogether easy. By now Queen Alexandra was extremely deaf: by 1922 she was complaining of 'everlasting pain and noises in my wretched old head'; her eyesight was seriously impaired. Even the King, who was one of her most frequent visitors, was unable to make 'Motherdear' hear the news he would bring her – for she liked to be kept abreast of current affairs. It is certain, though, that she approved of the match, and wished that the Prince of Wales, too, would find himself a wife. Like all elderly people her mind tended to dwell on the past. When the Duke of York's engagement was announced she clearly recalled the circumstances of her own, though her memory was by now unreliable. More than sixty years ago another Bertie had proposed to her: 'We were walking together in the pretty garden (at Laeken) following my mother and the late Queen of the Belgians when he suddenly proposed to me! My surprise was great and I accepted him with greatest delight!' [232]

There remained the matter of a home for the Duke and Duchess after their wedding on 26 April 1923. It was Queen Mary who suggested that they should move into White Lodge, in Richmond Park. It had been her parents' home for many years and Prince Edward, now Prince of Wales, had been born there. It seemed eminently suitable, and the King, whose gift it was, approved the plan. There was much refurbishing and decorating to be done but Queen Mary, no doubt recalling her dismay on finding York Cottage completely 'done up' by her husband and sister-in-law, left the arrangements to the young couple. Later, King George and Queen Mary were invited to see what they had made of it. 'May & I paid a visit to Bertie & Elizabeth at White Lodge and had luncheon with them,' the King recorded. 'They have made the house so nice with all their presents.'

Unfortunately, unforeseen problems arose: with the advent of the motor car Richmond Park had become easily accessible to the public, and the privacy of the Duke and Duchess was threatened. Conversely, it was inconveniently far from London for their numerous public engagements; it was too large and too expensive to maintain. Eventually, another home was found for them in London, at No. 145 Piccadilly. By the time they were settled, Queen Alexandra had died, and the King and Queen moved into the Big House at Sandringham, where there was plenty of room for visiting in-laws, and York Cottage was converted into estate offices and staff flats.

CHAPTER TWELVE

MOVING HOUSE

When, in 1915, Queen Alexandra retired to Sandringham, exclaiming that she would go mad if she could not be alone, she largely turned her back on public life. Her deafness was now more marked than ever, seriously impairing her ability to absorb and assimilate facts: her views on international affairs were less than rational, caused in part by her 'everlasting pain' in her ears[233] and also to the fixation of ideas in her mind, unalterable by any persuasion. King George used to return to York Cottage from the Big House in despair: 'I simply cannot make Motherdear hear, much less understand, anything at all about Greece,'[234] for she was trying to make the King interfere on behalf of her nephew, the ex-King. A broken blood vessel in her eye also left her, for a time, half-blinded. She was deeply depressed by her situation, but could be helped by visits from her family and, though many of her old friends had died, including de Soveral, that tireless member of the Sandringham house parties, there were still others who were made most welcome. Her two faithful companions, Charlotte Knollys and Sir Dighton Probyn, remained with her. Probyn's death in June 1924 came as a severe blow to her; for more than fifty years he had given all in his power in the service of his 'Blessed Lady.'

On her eightieth birthday, 20 December 1924, Queen Alexandra wrote, 'I feel completely collapsed; I shall soon go.' She was to linger on for another year: she knew she was 'breaking up'[235] – her memory had gone. Very late one night, Princess Victoria became alarmed by the silence in the house. She went downstairs and found the two old ladies sitting on either side of the fire, sound asleep. In March 1925, Queen Alexandra wrote her last letter to King George: 'You and my darling May are in my thoughts all day long, and all your children.'[236] In November she had a heart attack sitting on a settee in her room. She died the next day, the 20 November, with the King and Queen beside her. Two days later her body was taken to the church in the park before being taken to London and Windsor for her funeral. 'Although the afternoon was cold and cheerless

Charlotte Knollys had flung a window wide open, the better to watch the little procession. As the bearers crossed the wintry lawns they heard her crying aloud, like a little child.' [237]

So at last Queen Alexandra, the life-tenant of the Big House, had left it vacant for its occupation by King George V and Queen Mary. If George V's move there seems overdue, it must be recalled that he himself had never questioned his mother's continuing tenancy by the terms of Edward VII's will, and that he himself preferred the cramped quarters of York Cottage. If his loyalty was sometimes sorely tried, he gave no sign of it to 'Motherdear', who had been at once the most generous and most selfish of mortals.

Queen Alexandra had inhabited Sandringham since its earliest days as a Royal residence, regarding it as more completely 'home' than Marlborough House or Buckingham Palace, and for more than sixty years had assembled her possessions here. The task of dismantling the contents of the house and the possessions of an acquisitive old lady who 'loved to have her things round her' was immense. Even Queen Mary, who had a natural talent for the work, and who had spent half a lifetime gathering together the Royal collections of works of art of every kind, was somewhat daunted – and there was really no one who could be of much help.

'We have just been lunching with Princess Victoria at the Big House,' Mrs Wigram wrote to her mother on 10 December 1925.

> Really I think she is looking better than she did in October – but what a business to tackle the contents of that House. She took us into the Queen's sitting-room – I had been in there before, but I had forgotten how impossibly crowded it was – not a single inch of space. Rather pathetic Princess Victoria pointed to such an uncomfortable-looking little settee saying, 'This is where she was sitting when she had her first heart attack.' Streaty says that poor Princess V. is perfectly hopeless – doesn't know how or where to begin to tackle things, just moves them from one table to another and then says, 'Oh, the Queen would not like that to have been touched.' [238]

It was clearly a task that would have to be tackled with thought and care, and by degrees. In January 1926, the King and Queen visited Sandringham to see what could be done. 'Such a bewildering lot of things and pictures,' Queen Mary noted. [239] Having collected up and put aside the Crown Jewels, which the Queen Dowager had kept for her own use during her lifetime, they then divided up her personal jewellery. 'At 11 to S. where Toria and Maud with George & me divided dear Mama's jewels – it was interesting but sad.' [240]

But there was a more urgent concern than mere possessions. Charlotte Knollys lived on in the house, almost alone and bereft of her companion and mistress of more than half a lifetime. In the same letter to her mother Mrs Wigram wrote:

> After lunch poor old Charlotte said she would like to see us – and we went up to her overheated, overcrowded room. I don't think I have ever seen anything so pathetic. She said, 'Oh dear, isn't it terrible, for 63 years I have been with the Queen, and now I have nowhere to lay my head. What are they going to do with me – And then my letters' (and she showed me heaps of them). 'I can't answer them; I feel so bewildered – and yet I must answer them.' The one thing that cheers her is a long string of pearls which she clutches continually. In the Queen's dressing-table drawer was found a memorandum saying that she wished these pearls to be at once given to Charlotte. They were the pearls she wore every single day of her life – She looks about 1,000 years old – and yet is all there, but she cannot be long for this world.★ She kept talking of Sir Dighton and then turning to me and saying, 'He was always so fond of you.' Poor old lady. Princess Victoria is going to live in a house near the Teddy Seymours at Iver, near Windsor. [241]

August 1926 found Queen Mary again at Sandringham, prepared to be busy during the London Season after clearing up Queen Alexandra's things at Marlborough House. 'You never saw such a mass of things,' she wrote. 'A warning to one not to keep too much as nothing was ever thrown away in those 60 years!' [242] Apart from its sheer magnitude, it was a task after her own heart. For the most part she worked alone. There was some irony, and the Queen herself must have been aware of it, in her new responsibility for the Big House when, thirty-three years previously, she had arrived as a bride at York Cottage, which now she was about to leave, to find all the furnishings chosen for her and installed:

★ After leaving Sandringham, Charlotte lived at South Audley Street, London, until her death in 1930, aged 95. She never married.

You cannot think how terribly I miss you here, yr rooms seem so empty
& desolate & make me feel quite sad & lonely. It was a good thing for
me that David came down for 2 nights & he was simply enchanted with
Sandringham in the summer, and with the lovely flower beds in front
of the house and with the garden. I don't think he had ever been here
in the summer since he was a child... Really this place is too lovely just
now & I am so glad to see it once in all its beauty.[243]

The King replied from London: 'I am delighted you and David were both
pleased with the dear place, in summer it is lovely, we must really try & see
if we could not go there for a few days in the summer.' [244] He agreed that
the pictures would require sorting and arranging and, in a sudden access of
domesticity, feared that the unfaded areas behind the pictures would show.

Queen Mary worked rapidly, and at the end of the fortnight's visit she
was able to report to the King: '...Everything is as nice as I can make it at
S. and I hope that all will meet with yr approval... Of course some of the
curtains and carpets are faded as well as wall papers but all this can be put
right some day and at our leisure...' [245]

With the Big House now ready for occupation by the King and Queen,
they were ready to leave York Cottage. Inconvenient and highly unsuitable as
their country residence as it had been, there were real pangs at the moment
of parting. 'I fear this will be my last letter to you from our dear little old
home where we have been for thirty-three years,' the Queen wrote; 'I am sad
at leaving it with all its many memories & old associations.' [246]

Thus, in August 1926, the King and Queen moved into the refurbished
Big House, full of memories as it was of his childhood with Prince Eddy and
'Motherdear', and the genial, bluff old King. From here he had set out on
the road to Wolferton Station and his journey to HMS *Britannia*; here he had
watched, appalled, the death throes of his elder brother, with the realisation
that all the responsibilities of the Monarchy would one day, in all likelihood,
be his; and from its doors he had set out to follow his mother's coffin only
the previous autumn on its journey across the park to the church.

After this, York Cottage remained empty until the Second World War.
It might have passed to the Prince of Wales but, though he recorded many
happy memories of his childhood there, divergences of outlook with his
father, and his own inclination to be nearer good hunting country and the
diverse attractions of the capital left his childhood home untenanted. But
this is not quite the end of the story: during the war a detachment of the
Guards occupied the Cottage under a Major Coates. 'Coates' Mission', as
it was called, was given an important directive: if the safety of the Royal

Family were threatened as a result of invasion by Germany, they were to be taken to Scotland, and thence to Canada. A fleet of armoured trucks stood ready in the yard but, as the threat of invasion receded, 'Coates' Mission was disbanded and the Cottage was again deserted until, after the war, it became the Estate Office. Reminders of its historic past are still very much in evidence: the red cloth which adorned the walls of King George V's study is still in place, as is the mirror from which the King, reading in his armchair, could observe callers as they arrived at the door – 'Forewarned is forearmed'. Queen Mary's safe, which contained in its time some fabulous jewellery, remains in her dressing-room, discreetly concealed by a very ordinary door, doubtless the work of 'the man from Maples'. The wing which was added for the then Duke and Duchess of York has been converted into staff flats, but the plaque on the wall remains, dated 1893, the year of their marriage. The timber boathouse on the edge of the lake has now gone, but the forlorn pelican fountain which, when the water was turned on, caused the Duchess so much amusement is still there. York Cottage, with all its architectural surprises, its narrow winding passages, small rooms and a staircase that would not have excited remark in any Victorian villa, remains a memorial to the simplicity of the King who was also Emperor of India and, dynastically, the most powerful Monarch in the world in the years after the First World War.

This was the first year that King George and Queen Mary were able to celebrate Christmas in the Big House in their own way. The year before, Queen Alexandra had been dead little more than a month and major alterations were in progress. In the event, this Christmas at Sandringham differed little from those enjoyed by King Edward VII. 'Life still pursued its cosy informal pattern...' wrote Lady Airlie; '...country walks, going out with the guns, enormous teas by the fire; very much the routine of any country house, except for the orders and decorations which were worn at dinner. The guests were usually personal friends of the King and Queen who contributed to the homely intimacy of the atmosphere.' [248]

For this, his first Christmas in the refurbished House, the King invited Mrs Wigram and her children to stay. As Assistant Private Secretary, Major Wigram took turn and turn about with Private Secretary Lord Stamfordham, and had always been on duty in December. Perhaps someone had reminded the King that Major Wigram was a family man, and must have missed his own Christmas at home.

Mrs Wigram wrote to her father on 26 December 1926:

I wrote on Christmas Eve. Well, we had tea, and then the children were summoned, the King and Queen saying, 'The children must come first' and they went off into the Ballroom with the King and Queen and we followed. They were led up to their respective tables which were simply smothered in gifts! Francis' eyes jumping out of his head when he saw the most marvellous fort, from all the Princes. A huge thing, and a marvellous battleship, and endless small things. Neville with a gold watch from the King and a hunting crop from the Princes and again many other things. Anne with every sort of thing – books – ornaments. Each child was given an ashtray!! (Most pernicious.) Their three dear faces were one huge glow of joy, but they were very sedate. Then Clive and I were smothered in gifts. Clive got a set of silver cruets and various books while I was given an Indian 'shawl' (like a Persian rug)... a lovely old tortoise-shell tea caddy box, a mirror, a flower bowl, an evening bag etc. Just too generous and kind. We all went about examining each other's presents, and then all the Princes showed us their presents and finally the Queen. The King gave her a diamond brooch about the size of a cake of soap, combining all the badges of the Guards Brigade... We finally dispersed but our gifts are all left there for days! The children hurry off and gaze at their treasures occasionally... Christmas Day dawned early for me, and the creatures all trooped into my room where I had their presents; they were very happy... Good little souls, they galloped off to start writing their letters and had already accomplished 2 before church. The children and I all sat in one pew. Clive took them out playing golf after lunch and then they spent the rest of the day playing with their things till the great moment came for dinner... Neville of course came out with the ladies. Had to walk all by himself and bow to the King. He did it perfectly naturally. After dinner the Queen said to the children, 'Come and talk to me.' She was so nice to them. The evenings here are killing. The last two nights I've never sat down between 9.30 and 11 o'clock...[249]

December 30, 1926.– Well, we are alive and still very happy. The King has asked us to stay on till Monday... The children are enchanted. We had such a jolly day on Monday. Squeaks and Anne acted as Beaters. You can imagine how they loved it. Tumbling through the bracken – and then the Shooting lunch. They astound me with their 'savoir faire', no gaucheries of any description. They always talk when talked to and dissolve away when not wanted... Anne had to come in to tea one day to make up 13.

She was rather alarmed at the prospect and confided this to Tids who replied, 'Pouf! You oughtn't to be frightened by the King of your country'...There was the big Christmas tree last night for all the people on the estate and Tids was splendid, tearing round distributing things and throwing crackers at them, and not dreaming of wanting anything for himself.Anne and I went out to the shooting lunch yesterday, but left directly afterwards as the Queen wanted to go to King's Lynn, so Anne and I drove behind her in the 2nd car, with everybody taking their hats off, to my young friend's great joy. Lady Airlie and the Prince departed this morning. I have found him easier than I thought. He certainly is attractive...The Queen showed us all round her Sitting-Room, Bedroom etc. She has some lovely things, but I much prefer my own rooms![249]

It was sad that the King was not destined to enjoy the property without the increasing effects of ill-health and age. In November 1928 he returned to London from Sandringham, and two days later became seriously unwell. His condition deteriorated and on 12 December, his doctors operated in order to drain an abscess on his lung. In those days before antibiotics, the King had few resources to fight a widespread septicaemia and after his operation his reserves of strength were very seriously depleted. From February to May 1929, the King and Queen stayed at Bognor. In July he attended a Thanksgiving Service in Westminster Abbey for his recovery, although there were still complications from the abscess. It was not until 24 August that he returned to Sandringham after an absence of some ten months. He did not go out shooting for a further two months, and even then it was with a twenty-bore gun made specially by Purdey in place of his usual, heavier twelve-bore.

In fact, the King spent less than ten years of his reign in the Big House and they were tinged with anxiety for the future: in the early thirties there was massive unemployment at home; abroad, the threat implicit in the rise of the dictators Adolf Hitler and Benito Mussolini and Germany's rearmament became ever more evident. The King was a pacifist at heart but he was also a realist and urged that the country should not be taken unawares. His views on modern weapons were based more perhaps upon his conservatism than reason; he especially doubted the potential of the Air Force and disliked the concept of flight. Throughout all this he continued to drive himself hard, devoting himself conscientiously to the contents of the despatch boxes which arrived daily on his desk.

On Christmas Day 1932 at Sandringham, the King made his first broadcast to the Empire. He had first spoken on the radio in 1924 when he opened the Empire Exhibition at Wembley; since then, the size of the potential audience and the range of the transmission had increased greatly. The King initially expressed reluctance to participate in this venture but, after he had been given a radio and understood its value as a means of communication with his people, he prepared for the broadcast with the greatest care and considerable nervousness, which subsequent broadcasts did nothing to diminish. In his diary he wrote: 'At 3.35 I broadcasted a short message of 251 words to the whole Empire from Francis' room.' This was a small room on the ground floor, overlooking the drive, and had once been used by Lord Knollys. His message was simple: he was the father to a family but, in a wider context, also to a family of nations – and it held an enormous appeal for those who heard him. Speaking of past difficulties and future trials and the efforts made towards a lasting peace, he concluded:

> My life's aim has been to serve as I might towards those ends. Your loyalty, your confidence in me, has been my abundant reward. I speak now from my home and my heart to you all; to men and women so cut off by the snows, the desert or the sea that only voices out of the air can reach them; to those cut off from fuller life by blindness, sickness or infirmity, and to those who are celebrating this day with their children and their grandchildren – to all, to each, I wish a happy Christmas. God bless you.

It was a message which could not fail to move and he was immensely gratified by the knowledge that it had been so favourably received. Nevertheless, he dreaded these Christmas broadcasts and said that they spoiled his day. It is a measure of his sense of duty that he nevertheless continued with them to the end of his reign.

The King enjoyed these family gatherings at Sandringham with his children and the young grandchildren who delighted him. The eldest was Princess Elizabeth who, aged twenty-one months, 'perched on a little chair between the King and me, and the King gave her biscuits to eat and to feed his little dog with, the King chortling with little jokes with her...'[250] The last years of his reign these reunions brought the wives of Prince George and Prince Henry; Princess Mary had married Viscount Lascelles in 1922; only the Prince of Wales remained single.

CHAPTER THIRTEEN

THREE KINGS IN ONE YEAR

In December 1934, the King caught a bad cough and cold whilst at Sandringham and, rather than face the February fogs in London, he went with the Queen to Eastbourne to stay at Compton Place, a property belonging to the Duke of Devonshire. He took some time to recover and was easily tired. In terms of his health the turning point in the King's life was the fall from his horse at Hesdigneul in 1915: certainly after his illness in 1928, when an abscess formed at the base of his lung, he was never again the same and had the air of a man much older. Now, at the age of seventy and far from robust, there loomed ahead all the strain and fatigue of his Silver Jubilee celebrations.

On 6 May, the King and Queen drove to St Paul's Cathedral for a service of thanksgiving, and they were evidently moved by the enormous crowds that turned out to greet them. For over a month the celebrations continued, and on the 3 June they went to Sandringham to rest for a week, but a few days later the weary King caught a cold and was advised to remain in Norfolk for the time being. In August he was able to enjoy Cowes week and, although his yacht *Britannia* won no races, the King regained some of his former vitality. Perhaps he realised that the end was not very far off, for he decided to lay the yacht up permanently at the end of the season.

In the autumn the King was not well enough to attend the annual Armistice service at the Cenotaph in Whitehall, and immediately afterwards left for Sandringham. His last pheasant shoot was held on 14 November. It was at about this time, too, that he went out shooting for the last time with his old friend George Brereton. They had been shooting in Parson's Clump when the King turned to him and said: 'Well, Mr Brereton, I think I must go home.' 'Yes, go, Sir, we've had a nice morning's sport.'[251]

After their return they visited Princess Victoria, who had been unwell for some time. Her condition continued to deteriorate and she died at her Buckinghamshire home on 3 December. The King himself was far from well and the death of his favourite sister came as a terrible blow to him: 'How I shall miss her and our daily talks on the telephone,' he wrote in his diary, 'No one ever had a sister like her.' [252] A story which the King much enjoyed telling reveals something of their relationship: 'Every morning I ring up my sister at half past nine, just to have a chat. Of course, we're not always too polite. One morning her telephone rang at the usual time and she took up the receiver and said, "Hullo, you old fool." And the voice of the operator broke in and said, "Beg pardon, Your Royal Highness, His Majesty is not yet on the line"'

Never before had he felt unable to undertake a public duty, but he cancelled the State Opening of Parliament due on the day of his sister's death: it would have been his last. On 21 December the King and Queen returned to Sandringham for Christmas, when all the usual traditions were observed, with the giving of presents to family and Household, and to all the staff. The weather was bitterly cold and there was no shooting. For the last time he made his usual Christmas broadcast to his people, an occasion which always worried him, and he continued to deal with State affairs.

In the New Year, the King still went out in favourable weather to drive with the Queen, or on his favourite white pony, Jock, and he planted a cedar tree in the garden at Sandringham. He tended to fall asleep during the day, and even at meals, which distressed him. He enjoyed watching films but they began to seem unnecessarily long. Walking tired him quickly; he had to stop for breath frequently. On 15 January he remained in his room and retired early to bed. 'Poor George,' Queen Mary wrote, 'who had not been feeling well for some days, felt worse, & had to go to bed before dinner.' [253] Only the day before he had been busy with the Queen arranging the Fabergé collection which had passed from Queen Alexandra to Princess Victoria, and now, to him: they had come back, in the end, to Sandringham. He had not been out recently; the weather was bleak, and snow lay thinly on the ground. On the 17th, Queen Mary realised that the King was seriously ill and sent for the Prince of Wales: 'I think you ought to know,' she wrote, 'that Papa is not very well.' [254] Lord Dawson of Penn, his personal physician, whom she had summoned, was 'not too pleased with Papa's state at the present moment.'

The Prince of Wales arrived by aeroplane and from then on, the family began to gather at the Big House. Sadly, the King was unable to continue with his diary: the last entry, on 17 January, reads: 'A little snow and wind. Dawson arrived this evening, I saw him & feel rotten.' [255] The next word is but half-formed; he could write no more. On the 19th, the Archbishop of Canterbury and the Duke of Kent arrived. By now the public had been informed of the King's condition and reporters began to congregate around the estate. The Prince travelled to London to inform the Prime Minister of the

King's condition and then returned to Sandringham. 'G. about the same,' Queen Mary wrote, 'sat with him from time to time – Did not go to church as the place was surrounded by reporters and photographers, too heartless – Walked with Mary morning & afternoon…' [256]

On the next day, 20 January, at about eleven 11 a.m. on an intensely cold morning, Lord Wigram was summoned to the King and found him with a copy of *The Times*. 'He whispered something about the Empire, and I replied that "all is well, Sir, with the Empire."…The King said, "I feel very tired. Go and carry on with your work. I will see you later."' [257]

Ramsay MacDonald, Lord Hailsham and Sir John Simon, members of the Privy Council, with Sir Maurice Hankey as Clerk, arrived half an hour later, and went upstairs to join three other members, the Archbishop, Lord Dawson and Lord Wigram, in a sitting-room adjacent to the King's bedroom. They found the King in a dressing-gown, sitting in a chair. He was suffering from increasing breathlessness and had lost the use of his right arm. He greeted them with his friendly smile and in a firm voice approved the setting up of the Council of State, but was unable to make more than two shaky marks on the paper saying, 'I am sorry to keep you waiting, gentlemen, but I find it difficult to concentrate.' The Archbishop had seen him before the Council and had recalled the long years of their friendship: 'More than forty years, Sir,' he said, and the King replied, 'Yes, yes, a long time; more than forty years.' The Archbishop asked if he might give the King his blessing, and he had answered, 'Yes, do give me your blessing,' and thereafter had tried to repeat the Lord's Prayer, but sleep closed down on his mind again.

By evening the Prince of Wales had returned to the Big House with the Duke of York, and the Duchess of Kent had also arrived. That night Queen Mary was looking drawn and tired and the Royal Family dined alone. While the Household were at dinner Lord Dawson was asked for the wording of the 9 p.m. bulletin. Lord Dawson consulted Lord Wigram, who sat next to him, and said to the company: 'I think the time is past for details.' Then he wrote on the back of a menu card, which Lord Wigram handed him, the doctors' last and beautifully worded message: 'The King's life is drawing peacefully towards its close.' [258]

Outside, the weather had broken and given way to rain which fell softly on the crowd of reporters at the gates. Indoors, in the King's room, the Queen and the family were gathered round the bed while the Archbishop said the commendatory prayers. Afterwards, because there was 'a little evidence of struggle', an injection of morphine was administered at which the King roused, said, 'God damn you', and settled down to sleep.

Earlier, the Queen and the Prince of Wales had told Dawson that 'they had no wish for the King's life to be prolonged if the illness were judged to be mortal but that, having made their view known, they left the decision in the doctors' hands.' Dawson agreed to direct the treatment accordingly. The physician's own view on euthanasia was clear. Later in the year, he was to vote against a Bill to introduce voluntary euthanasia on the grounds that it was something 'which belongs to the wisdom and conscience of the medical profession and not to the realm of law.'[259] He recorded his own decision in his private Sandringham notebook:

At about 11 o'clock it was evident that the last stage might endure for many hours, unknown to the Patient but little comporting with that dignity and serenity which he so richly merited and which demanded a brief final scene. Hours of waiting just for the mechanical end when all that is really life has departed only exhausts the onlookers & keeps them so strained that they cannot avail themselves of the solace of thought, communion or prayer. I therefore decided to determine the end and injected (myself) morphia gr.3/4 and shortly afterwards cocaine gr.1 into the distended jugular vein:'myself' because it was obvious that Sister B. was disturbed by this procedure. In about 1/4 an hour – breathing quieter – appearance more placid – physical struggle gone.[260]

The Queen and family returned and stood round the bedside – the Queen dignified and controlled – others with tears, gentle but not noisy... Intervals between respirations lengthened, and life passed so quietly and gently that it was difficult to determine the actual moment.

But there had been another consideration, perhaps a shade less worthy than the alleviation of suffering. Lord Dawson admitted that he had also weighed up 'the importance of the death receiving its first announcement in the morning papers rather than the less appropriate evening journals', and had telephoned his wife in London to advise *The Times* to hold back publication as the announcement could be expected.[261]

Queen Mary herself wrote: 'At 5 to 12 my darling husband passed peacefully away – my children were angelic.'[262] It was then that she, sensing the importance of the succession, stooped and kissed the hand of her eldest son – a gesture of affection and of homage to the new King.[262]

Lord Wigram, who was present when the King died, recorded that the Prince of Wales 'became hysterical, cried loudly, and kept on embracing the Queen'.[263] Dawson commented more moderately, putting the Prince's state down to 'an emotional outburst at the realisation & following strain of studies and preparation for what must follow the King's death. A little later on he returned – stood quietly by his dead father's bedside & went out to the anteroom & sd. "I hope I will make good as he has made good."'[264] But there was little respite for grief: the continuation of the Monarchy was essential and the new King must be proclaimed. 'David and Bertie,' Queen Mary wrote, 'went to London for the Proclamation,' which, with Mrs Simpson, he watched from a window at St James' Palace. 'David very brave & helpful – for he has a difficult task before him – Answered endless telegrams – the doctors and the Archbishop left.'[265]

For some years a post office had been established at Sandringham, separated from the Chinese Room only by a thin partition, so that the clerks were sometimes admonished to make less noise. At the time of King George V's death four additional teleprinters were installed to cope with the flow of cables from all over the world, and the clerks were kept busy taking them to the footmen, who would deliver them.

For a little while the King's coffin, made of oak from the Sandringham estate, lay upstairs and members of the Household were able to pay their last respects. Late in the afternoon the King's coffin was carried out of the main door and brought on a bier, preceded by the King's Piper and escorted by Grenadier Guards and Queen Mary, together with the family and some of the Household, to the church in the park. It was cold and dark, and someone with a torch guided the little procession along the paths until they could see the lych-gate brilliantly lit, where the rector in his robes awaited them. 'The Guardsmen, with scarcely a sound, slung the coffin on their shoulders and laid it before the altar, and there, after a very brief service, we left it to be watched for thirty-six hours by the men of the Sandringham estate.'[261] 'We had a very comforting short service,' Queen Mary recorded, '– the church full of our own kind people – Such a sad sad day – It is curious my having been present in this house at the deathbeds of 2 brothers Eddy & George.'[267] The following day Queen Mary returned: 'Went to the Church after luncheon,' she wrote. 'It all looked very peaceful – but so sad.'[268]

Two days later the body of King George left Sandringham. The weather was fine and clear as the new King and his brothers, accompanied by members of the Household followed the coffin to Wolferton station and thence to the Royal vault at Windsor. As the cortège wound through the woods where the young Prince George and his brothers had played as boys, Tommy Lascelles saw a cock pheasant fly directly over the gun-carriage. It was the end of a long chapter in the history of Sandringham.

Queen Mary's eldest son, whose hand she had kissed at his father's deathbed, was proclaimed King Edward VIII. As Prince of Wales he had been enormously popular; energetic, charming and with a large capacity for enjoyment, he symbolised the modern age. His arrival by air at Sandringham was in itself symbolic; his father had never been in an aeroplane. His brief reign was marked by the idea of change – indeed, it was the keynote. One of his first orders was to have Greenwich time restored, an act that caused some dismay among the Household, for 'the order for it was given while his father lay dying, and carried out while his body was still warm.' [269]

Other, larger changes were in the air. Since 1930, the Prince of Wales had regarded Fort Belvedere at Sunningdale, on the edge of Windsor Great Park, as his real home. Sandringham had been the home of his father, of whom he had been so much in awe, and who had openly disapproved of his 'modern ways'. Now, King Edward looked at the accounts of the Sandringham estate with dissatisfaction and sought more economical methods of running it. Accordingly, he asked the Duke of York to visit Sandringham and advise him on how the expense of running it might reasonably be reduced. In his mind the estate had become a 'voracious white elephant', and substantial reforms must be made. The Duke spent a fortnight in Norfolk touring the estate with a close friend, the Earl of Radnor, who was the owner of a very large and successful estate. The completed report was a masterpiece of good sense, written largely by the Duke himself, and some of his suggestions must have caused him distress. His feeling for Sandringham was greater than his brother's, and with his own conservative outlook, he had been the closer to his father. The report consisted of an analysis of the cost of running the estate in 1935, with suggestions for possible reductions in 1936 and 1937. These included giving up some shootings and other economies in the game department; for instance, that no pheasants should be reared in 1936, that deer should be sold. There were also suggested reductions of staff in the house and gardens and various economies in the running of both and of the estate's farms. Emphasis was laid on the need to avoid creating hardship among staff likely to be dismissed: they should be found other jobs first. The report ended by emphasising that the expenses of the estate, reputed to be £50,000 in 1935, were much increased by the services carried out for the house, and commented that although other expenses were also high, this reflected the late King's insistence on Sandringham being a model estate, which could not be achieved without expense. [270]

The Duke's suggestions were made in good faith, and, although King Edward's reign was too short to see them carried out, the majority were implemented during his own reign. The new King, however, revealed an extraordinary concern for his financial security: at the time of his abdication the sale of two large areas of the estate at Flitcham and Anmer was in hand, but cancelled by King George VI. In the event, only 25 per cent of the staff were laid off, rather than nearly half which had been rumoured. He had caused consternation by enquiring whether the late King's will could be altered – he had asked in an aggrieved tone 'Where do I come in?' [271] He himself had been left nothing, as his father had provided for him amply in his lifetime and expected that he would have been able to save a considerable sum from his revenue from the Duchy of Cornwall. (In fact, he had privately amassed approximately 1 million pounds.)

King George V's staunch conservatism reached its zenith at Sandringham, and 'his love for it had defied the encroachments of time. There... his private war with the twentieth century had ended with the almost complete repulse of the latter.' [272] This outlook found its sympathetic echo, fainter perhaps but still recognisable, in the Duke of York. The Duke of Windsor was to write that his brother 'was in outlook and temperament very much like my father. The patterns of their lives were much the same, with the steady swing of habit taking them both year after year to the same places at the same time and with the same associates.' [273] Both the new King and the Duke of York had stood in considerable awe of their father, who was a somewhat exacting arbiter of their destinies and often successfully concealed his real affection for his children. Towards the end of his reign King George V sensed the significance of the appearance of Wallis Simpson upon the scene, though it was a subject which neither he nor the Prince of Wales could bring themselves to discuss such was the gulf between them. Not only was the King aware of this dangerous relationship but it caused him great anxiety. He met Wallis only once, in 1934, at Buckingham Palace. The King was furious: 'That woman in my own house!' [274] he exclaimed. He challenged the Prince directly about his relations with Mrs Simpson and was unlikely to have been mollified by his son's assurance that he had never had any immoral relations with her. The King accepted this at its face value and Wallis was invited to a Jubilee Ball at the Palace. The Prince cannot have made the last years of his father's reign easy or peaceful: their lifestyles were diametrically opposed and there was no indication that he had detached himself from Wallis. He told the Prime Minister, Stanley Baldwin: 'After I am dead the boy will ruin himself in twelve months' [275] and a few weeks before his death he said, 'I pray to God that my eldest son will never marry and have children, and that nothing will come between Bertie and Lilibet and the throne.' [276]

Thus it was not to Norfolk, but to Sunningdale that the King brought Mrs Simpson. During his brief reign he visited the estate only to bring a party of friends for the shooting from time to time. In mid-October 1936, the King was at Sandringham with friends, shooting partridge and noting the changes which were in progress following his brother's report. But the visit was cut short; on his arrival he found a message from his Private Secretary asking the King to telephone him. The Prime Minister was seeking an audience to discuss the King's growing friendship with Mrs Simpson and to apprise him of the rumours in the foreign press which might, if continued, endanger the Monarchy. Mr Baldwin might have come to Sandringham, but fears of further rumours brought the King to London for the interview. He left the Big House after only one night – his only period of residence there as King.

Although the first hints of a crisis in the monarchy had been published in the provincial press on 2 December, the full impact did not reach the country as a whole until the following day. In fact, the Press had been effectively muzzled: as early as October the King's friendship with Mrs Simpson had been the subject of comment in the American press; on 13 November Tom Jones, Deputy Secretary to the Cabinet, wrote: 'There is only one topic of conversation in London – Mrs Simpson.' [277] A cynical note was sounded, predictably perhaps, by Evelyn Waugh on 8 December:

> The Simpson crisis has been a great delight to everyone. At Maidie's nursing home they report a pronounced turn for the better in all adult patients. There can seldom have been an event which caused so much general delight and so little pain. Reading the papers and even listening to announcements that there is no news took up most of the week. [278]

Events moved swiftly. The King, advised that a twice-divorced woman would be unacceptable to the country and unwilling to relinquish her – it was impossible, he said, 'to discharge his duties as King without the help and support of the woman he loved' – made the decision to abdicate in favour of the Duke of York.

The abdication created a number of problems for which there was no precedent: an appropriate title for the ex-King had to be devised – and rapidly, too, for he was to broadcast a message to the nation that evening, and would be introduced by Sir John Reith, Director-General of the BBC. (For this occasion he was announced as His Royal Highness Prince Edward.) One of King George VI's first acts was to proclaim the ex-King the Duke of Windsor, though his title was not legalised until the following May. Then there was the matter of Balmoral and Sandringham, of which Edward VIII was the life tenant. It was impossible that he could retain any interest in these Royal properties, and therefore necessary that they should be transferred to his successor. Informed guesses put the figure for Sandringham and Balmoral at one million pounds and the yearly income paid by King George to his brother at £60,000. Such was the speed of events surrounding the abdication that it seems these transactions were only agreed on 10 December, the day on which the King signed the Instrument of his Abdication in favour of his brother, the Duke of York, and not completed until after the Duke of Windsor, as he was created, had sailed for France on board the destroyer *Fury*.

Thus, by Christmas, another King was on the throne and the Duke of Windsor was in Austria preparing for his marriage with Mrs Simpson.

CHAPTER FOURTEEN

KING GEORGE VI

The new King was physically and emotionally exhausted by the abdication crisis. He had been dismayed by the prospect of his succession, fearful of the inherent danger to the Constitution of an abdication and unprepared for his responsibilities as sovereign. On the afternoon before King Edward signed the Instrument of Abdication, the Duke visited Queen Mary at Marlborough House. 'He was devoted to his brother,' Queen Mary told Sir Harold Nicholson, 'and the whole abdication crisis made him miserable. He sobbed on my shoulder –'[279]

In addition he had to survive his ordeal alone, because the Duchess was ill with influenza at their home at No. 145 Piccadilly. But there was some consolation. History has a way of repeating itself: when the new King protested, 'David has been trained for this all his life. I've never even seen a State paper. I'm only a Naval officer, it's the only thing I know about,'[280] Lord Louis Mountbatten replied:

> This is a very curious coincidence. My father once told me that, when the Duke of Clarence died, your father came to him and said almost the same things that you have said to me now, and my father answered: 'George, you're wrong. There is no more fitting preparation for a King than to have been trained in the Navy.'

After the initial shock of his succession, the new King accepted his role with courage and dignity. While reconstructing the temporarily tarnished image of the monarchy, he was busy mastering the intricacies of his role, achieved through his qualities of endurance, industry and integrity, which stood him in good stead throughout his short reign. The new King, lacking in experience and confidence, and strongly supported by the Duchess, now Queen Elizabeth, showed his true mettle as he picked up the threads of kingship. The young boy who had pulled M. Hua's beard in the schoolroom in York Cottage had turned into a young man with a sense of humour and a capacity for enjoyment. What he may have seemed to lack of his elder brother's undoubted charm and superficial brilliance, he made up for with moral integrity, determination and with a quality that was almost wholly wanting in his predecessor – a strong committment to duty. Subsequent memories of him tended perhaps to be overshadowed by the vitality of the Queen Mother, whose activities never ceased to fascinate people, and who remained very much in the public eye during the nearly fifty years of her widowhood. Only since her death in 2001 has his sterling contribution to the monarchy become more fully appreciated. Despite a serious stomach complaint he had served courageously as a midshipman at the Battle of Jutland in 1916. He played a hard game of tennis, enjoyed golf, hunted and shot with the rest of the family and spoke his mind with firmness and authority. At the time of his accession, Sir Claude Schuster asked the new King what his brother would be known as after his abdication. It had been suggested that prior to his abdication broadcast he would be introduced as Mr Edward Windsor.

> I replied:– That is quite wrong. Before going any further I would ask what has he given up on his abdication? S. said I am not sure. I said, it would be a good thing to find out before coming to me. Now as to his name. I suggest HRH D of W[indsor]...' and in a few decisive sentences he showed Schuster that for a variety of reasons any other title would be inappropriate.[281]

King George VI and Queen Elizabeth and the two Princesses journeyed to Sandringham for Christmas with a sense of heartfelt relief from the enormous publicity that had recently surrounded them all. There was in 1936 to be no Christmas broadcast: too much had happened too recently, though shortly afterwards the King broadcast a New Year Message to the people of the Empire and Commonwealth. The nation had reacted to the abdication with a kind of shocked disillusionment which was followed by a wave of sympathy for King Edward's successor. On Christmas Day, more than 6,000 well-wishers turned out to greet the King and his family as they left the little church in the park. This year Queen Mary joined the family party for Christmas and her presence there symbolised a kind of permanence which the nation, having undergone so much turmoil, greeted with great satisfaction. She had left Buckingham Palace in July to spend a month at Sandringham in preparation for her move to Marlborough House, which was to be her home until her death. On her arrival she wrote to King Edward:

It is very nice here and peaceful & I am sure I shall like it, but I miss dear Papa quite dreadfully, even more than in London & his rooms look so empty and deserted without him; I forced myself to go in & look round but felt very sad. Papa adored this place & I love it, it is full of so many happy memories of my whole married life, though of course Papa & I went through sad times too – especially when Grannie became so frail those last two years. [282]

Since that visit in the summer Queen Mary, too, had endured the strain of the abdication. For one whose whole life had been ordered and governed by a sense of duty and service to the monarchy, her eldest son's decision to give up the throne in order to devote his life to Mrs Simpson was shattering. She wrote bitterly to her eldest son that she did not think it possible that he would be able to return to England 'for a very long time.' But there was something reassuring in the traditional return of the Royal family to Sandringham. On 22 December, Queen Mary wrote: 'Left London with Bertie, E. & their children for dear Sandringham to spend Christmas there, my staff running it this year... Happy to be back in the old home.' [283] But for the elderly Queen the strain had been too much. She became unwell and spent Christmas Day and much of the following week in her room. She came downstairs on New Year's Eve to watch an amusing film. 'Thank God,' she wrote that day, 'this sad year is over.'

Queen Mary was still at Sandringham on the occasion of the first anniversary of King George's death. 'Many letters and flowers & was glad to be surrounded by the family – Went into his room.' [284] The familiar rooms and the gardens were a reassurance after a year of violent change. Though she no longer wore mourning, she felt his loss as keenly as ever and she was perhaps uncertain of the role that would be left for her to play with the accession of the new King. Her instinct, however, was unerring: having consulted with her son she decided to attend the coronation service in Westminster Abbey, which broke with tradition. Her reception by the enormous crowds along the coronation route assured her that not only had she done the right thing, but that her presence symbolised the enduring quality of the British monarchy – an institution which had been battered by the abdication crisis.

The following year the Royal Family were once again at Sandringham, grateful for a respite from the arduous coronation celebrations, and on Christmas Day the King broadcast to his people. It seemed that the earlier traditions established by King George V were being maintained; to a large extent this was true, but the King was his own man and the changes to the estate which he had recommended to his brother were being planned with a view to the property becoming economically self-sufficient. Like his brother, now Duke of Windsor, his boyhood had been spent in the shadow of his father, of whom he was considerably in awe; but he, too, was very much part of the twentieth century, moving with the times – he was the first member of the Royal Family to learn (with some reluctance) to fly – respecting the traditions of the past, though ready to adapt them to the present. His independence of spirit won him the admiration of his father, who recognised in him the virtues he himself admired and cherished, in contrast to his eldest son whose interests and views seemed so exactly contrary to his own. 'You have always been so sensible and easy to work with and you have always been ready to listen to any advice and to agree with my opinion about people and things, that I feel we have always got on very well together (very different to dear David),' [285] he wrote.

But change was in the air: though King George VI respected tradition, the yachting his father loved did not appeal to him and the attention he paid to the Royal stamp collection was more dutiful than enthusiastic. He shared, however, with the Queen a sense of companionship and affection within the family circle which he cherished above all else. It differed from 'the Waleses', which had been inward-looking and uncritical, and from that of his own childhood with parents of whom he was much in awe. Though a close affection and mutual respect developed as Prince Albert grew into manhood, biographers of King George V and Queen Mary consider that they failed as parents of young children. King George VI, though, enjoyed the company of his daughters and admired their attributes; there was a confidence and trust within the family which brought great happiness to them all.

The new King turned his attention to the Sandringham estate with a zeal that would certainly have won his father's approval, though he would have hesitated over the changes which were about to take place. But the threat of war, and war itself, intervened. Queen Mary was at Sandringham on the day war was declared. At morning service in the little church in the park she listened on the wireless which the rector had set up in the nave to the momentous words of the Prime Minister, Neville Chamberlain, telling the nation that Germany had not replied to the British ultimatum and that 'consequently, this country is at war with Germany.'

On the following morning the air-raid siren sounded and she and the children of the Duke of Kent, who were also staying at Sandringham, took refuge in the basement. Later she regretfully left the house for Badminton, in Gloucestershire, where she was to spend the war, and did not return for five years. Although she felt that her place should be in London, she understood that her presence there would an avoidable anxiety for the King. The Big House was shut up, and on their rare visits to Sandringham, the Royal Family stayed at Appleton where Princess Maud and, before her, Louise Cresswell had lived. York Cottage, which had remained empty since King George V and Queen Mary moved into the Big House, became the base for Coates' Mission, the small Army team prepared to move the Royal Family from Norfolk in a crisis. In the meantime, whilst enjoying those cherished visits to Norfolk, the Princesses sometimes worked on the estate, helping with the harvest; it was a pleasant interlude from Windsor, where they spent much of the war. The King continued to keep in close touch with affairs on the estate, and in September 1941, during a brief rest, he was able to arrange some highly successful partridge shooting but, with the Queen, he was almost constantly engaged in visiting units of all the armed forces and civilian services. Their interest and support were widely appreciated, especially during the 'Blitz', when major cities had been bombed and Buckingham Palace was also damaged. The King's relationship with the Prime Minister, Winston Churchill, which had not initially been easy, developed into a warm friendship enhanced by their great responsibilities and strong mutual respect. The King started a tradition of a weekly informal lunch where they could discuss the war situation without risk of interruption. In June 1944 both leaders had desperately wanted to be present at the D-Day landings on the French coast; each had to dissuade the other to their great regret; each in his own way was indispensable to the country.

After the end of the war the family were together again at Sandringham for Christmas – the first time for six years. Lady Airlie went into waiting early in January 1946: 'I travelled up on the King's train,' she wrote:

...in the familiar little compartment always used by the ladies-in-waiting, which brought back many memories. At teatime the King sent his equerry to fetch me for tea with him, Princess Elizabeth, and her cousin Lady Mary Cambridge, who were on the train. We all arrived at Sandringham House together, where we were met at the door by the Queen, Princess Margaret and Queen Mary.

I thought – regretfully at first – how much the atmosphere of Sandringham had changed, but then I realised that this was inevitable, for a new generation had grown up since I had last seen it. In the entrance hall there now stood a baize-covered table on which jig-saw puzzles were set out. The younger members of the party – the Princesses, Lady Mary Cambridge, Mrs Gibbs (Princess Elizabeth's lady-in-waiting) and several young Guardsmen – congregated round them from morning till night. The radio, worked by Princess Elizabeth, blared incessantly.

Only in Queen Mary's room – the one which she had always occupied, with its lovely collection of small treasures – was it possible to recapture the past. I felt as I sat reading to her that King George might come in at any moment with some letter about which he wished to consult her.

Before the end of a week I revised my impressions... There was no denying the fact that the new atmosphere of Sandringham was very much more friendly than in the old days, more like that of any home. We still assembled in the drawing-room in the traditional way, but no orders or medals were worn, not even badges. One sensed far more the ordinary setting of family life in this generation than in the last. It was in the way in which the King said, 'You must ask Mummy,' when his daughters wanted to do something – just as any father would do; in Princess Margaret's pout when the Queen sent her back to the house to put on a thicker coat – like any fifteen-year-old girl's; in the way both sisters teased, and were teased by, the young Guardsmen, to whom Queen Mary referred when we were alone as 'The Body Guard'.

At dinner on the first evening I sat next to the King. His face was tired and strained and he ate practically nothing. I knew that he was forcing himself to talk and entertain me... The King had worked on his Boxes until just before dinner and was going to work again afterwards. Looking at him and realising how hard he was driving himself I felt a cold fear of the probability of another short reign – and a great personal love for him.

At about 11.30 that evening dancing began. We all danced, Queen Mary and myself included... At the end of an hour I stopped... but Queen Mary kept on until we went up to bed at nearly 1 a.m.

...The King was a devoted father to both his daughters. He spoiled Princess Margaret and still continued to treat her as an *enfant terrible*, but Princess Elizabeth was his constant companion in shooting, walking, riding – in fact in everything. His affection for her was touching...[286]

He was aware of her destiny as the future sovereign and felt the poignancy of the passing of her youth. In February 1947, the Royal Family left England in HMS *Vanguard* for a tour of South Africa. It was a tour which recognised the importance of the Union's support during the war, and a respite from the gruelling year, with its shortages of food and commodities, and a feeling of unrest and disillusion. The massive Labour majority in the General Election of the previous year was evidence of a strong desire for change.

A few years later the joy in family relationships extended to his grandchildren and when Princess Elizabeth and the Duke of Edinburgh spent Christmas in Malta, the King wrote to her of her eldest son, Prince Charles: 'He is too sweet stumping around the room & we shall love having him at Sandringham. He is the fifth generation to live there & and I hope he will get to love the place.'[287]

King George and his father were both keen and skilful shots: with a lifetime's knowledge of the Sandringham estate they planned their shoots with great care and in close collaboration with their game-keepers, but in one respect they differed. King George V inherited from his father the love of very large shoots of driven birds reared on estates when the bags could be numbered in thousands; as Louise Cresswell testified, the provision of ideal conditions for the rearing of game birds in the early days at Sandringham was given absolute priority. The size of the bag was the main attraction, irrespective of skill and awareness. For King Edward VII shooting was a means of providing entertainment for his guests: the huge number of birds reared and the size of his game larder simply ensured that in making such provision his hospitality would not be outdone by his neighbours. It was shooting on a scale that derived from the battue prevalent in Europe in the nineteenth century. He opposed any scheme which might have resulted in birds flying high. Dersingham Wood, for example, had 'consisted of a dense semi-circular thicket around which were planted at intervals wide screens of clipped evergreens about seven feet high.[288] After the war conditions had changed: there were fewer keepers, rearing was expensive and the King's tastes veered towards the challenge presented by a wide variety of birds and wildfowl. He was content to be in the right place at the right time – numbers were not important. The King's whole attitude to the sport can be understood from his insistence that a drive was not completed until every bird had been picked up. 'He had not finished his shoot, and was not ready for conversation, until the birds were found. Picking up was an inseparable part of the shoot itself.' It was, after all, as Buxton commented, 'nothing more than common humanity.'[289]

Until his health deteriorated in 1949, the King was almost irresistibly drawn to Sandringham when he heard that there were plenty of duck in. It was for him a new aspect of shooting and, as its possibilities became evident, much care was given to improving wildfowl haunts. Reeds were cleared, islands were created and barrels were sunk. In 1937, he began a 'duck book', separate from his game book, in which he could observe the habits of the birds: Wolferton Splash, Frankfort Pool, Park Ponds – he knew them all. He was often in place by 6 a.m. and his brief comments vividly conjure up the scene: 'Misty and damp. No wind. 6.0 - 8.0 a.m.'; 'Wet and dark. Strong S.W. wind 6.45 – 7.30 a.m. Quite a lot of duck came in large lots. Rather chary.' [290] The bag for that morning flight at half a dozen pools was 113 birds with eight guns, including the King and the Duke of Gloucester. We can picture it all: a dark October dawn, the reeds and rushes rustling in the wind and the marksmen, muffled in coats and jerseys against the cold, and wearing waders, crouched in their barrels waiting silently for the beating of wings in a sky that was beginning to lighten. That morning flight was to be the King's last – and he was accompanied for the first time by Princess Elizabeth.

The King was a knowledgeable and enthusiastic gardener and he designed and supervised the creation of a series of plots, protected by hedges, on a site overlooked by his own rooms so that he could enjoy looking out over them. He took the keenest interest in the work, invariably writing suggestions in his own hand from wherever he happened to be, and was delighted to see it taking shape over the years. He acquired a specialist's knowledge of rhododendrons and was able to discuss with authority the development of the Savile Garden at Windsor Great Park. It was tragic that he was not to see this project reach full maturity. He also reshaped the approach to the house from the Norwich Gates, creating a bank to screen the house from the road to ensure greater privacy.

Since 1948 the King's health had been causing concern: in that year he was diagnosed as suffering from arteriosclerosis which, if not treated promptly, would have led to gangrene developing in his legs and inevitably requiring amputation. The King deeply resented an enforced rest and the cancellation of an overseas tour, but the condition appeared at first to respond. The Royal Family went to Sandringham for the New Year and the King was allowed to go shooting a fortnight later, provided he spent the afternoon in bed. His condition did not improve, though, and he underwent an operation in March 1949. In 1951, he was found to be suffering from cancer of the left lung, which was successfully removed in a further operation in September 1951. There remained, however, a risk of coronary thrombosis, from which he was, in fact, eventually to die. On 21 December he returned to Sandringham for Christmas. It was a happy family holiday and he was well enough to be able to take part in the shooting. On 1 January 1952 at Heath Farm, with six other guns, the bag was 121 head, with 101 pheasant.

At the end of January the King and Queen were back in London to bid farewell to Princess Elizabeth and the Duke of Edinburgh, who were flying to Kenya for the first stage of a tour that was planned to take them to Australia and New Zealand. He had a check-up with his doctors, who were pleased with his progress, and returned with the Queen to Sandringham.

On 5 February he enjoyed a 'Keepers' Day', shooting with some twenty guns. Though it was as carefully planned as ever, it was a day of informal sport after hares – ending, to the King's satisfaction, with three hares with his last three shots. [291] It had been a fine, sunny day, but with a cold wind, and one that he had greatly enjoyed. That evening he sent a message of congratulation to each of the keepers, and after a happy domestic evening, he retired to his room at about 10.30 p.m. At about midnight a night-watchman in the garden saw him 'afixing the latch of his bedroom window, to which a new fastening had lately been attached.' [292] He did not write up his game book that evening.

The next morning, when the King's valet came into his bedroom to awaken him, he found that the King had died in his sleep.

It was said that, as his coffin was borne, like his father and grandmother and two uncles before him, from the Big House to the church beyond the gardens, a cock pheasant crowed in the park.

King George VI came to the throne by default, like his father, and similarly, at a time when the country was preparing for war with Germany. It was also a time of constitutional turmoil following an uneasy and short-lived reign. To him and to his family must be given the credit for the restoration of stability to the country, and the return of a monarchy which was traditional but tempered by having shared with his people the ravages of war. It was enhanced by the emphasis on family values and exemplified by the visible presence of his wife and daughters to a degree that had not been seen before.

AFTERWORD

In the course of more than 150 years and five monarchs, Sandringham has undergone striking changes, from the rebuilding of the old Hall to the modern and highly efficient estate it is today. The trim hedges, the rows of immaculate fruit trees and currant bushes, the air of prosperity that begins to make itself felt even at the approaches to the estate, all are a far cry from the run-down, rabbit-ridden, neglected acres which the young Prince of Wales surveyed with such enthusiasm in 1862. These changes reflect not only the modern agricultural techniques of the last century but also, the individual tastes and interests of successive Royal owners.

For some seventy-five years the programme at Sandringham was one of improvement and expansion. At the end of the nineteenth century, the Prince of Wales delighted in taking the members of his house-parties round the rows of greenhouses: 'All Persimmon!' he would say proudly, for the earnings in stud fees from this horse were enormous. King Edward VIII spoke truly when he said that Sandringham was 'voracious', but only in his mind was it a 'white elephant'. Had he been so minded, he would have spared no expense in its upkeep, but his affections were clouded by memories of the lack of communication and understanding between himself and his father and, besides, he found much greater happiness at Fort Belvedere, the property on the edge of Windsor Great Park given to him by his father and which he had made very much his own. Apart from the shooting, the attractions of a largely agricultural estate in Norfolk, remote from the fast-paced activity of the metropolis, were, he felt, strictly limited. Like his grandfather, King Edward VII before him, Edward VIII was powerfully drawn to the hedonistic life of the capital. The retrenchment which was undoubtedly necessary at Sandringham led to more efficient use of the land and greater productivity. But there was another reason: the new King displayed an obsessive concern about money. It showed, perhaps not for the first time, at the reading of his father's will, as its terms were read out at a family gathering. In response to the King's enquiry, 'Where do I come in?' the solicitor commented drily that King George had considered that his heir was already sufficiently provided for.

King George VI loved Sandringham and the first family Christmas of his reign was spent there, which restored the sense of continuity with the past. It was a feeling shared by the country as a whole, for it marked a return to stability and tradition. There was comfort in the idea that the sovereign was in his own home with his family around him: almost it might seem as though the awful events of the last few weeks had not taken place. Sandringham had been his childhood home, as it had been his father's before him, and he brought to the estate a respect for all the memories it held for him but tempered by its need for a modern system of estate management that would transform it into a highly successful business venture. The second phase, one in which economy and shrewd management were paramount, may be said to have begun with the survey carried out by him, when Duke of York, in 1936.

The Queen's early life, especially during the Second World War, was spent largely at Windsor, but there is no doubt of her affection for Sandringham. She has memories of those Christmases before the war, when her grandfather was King in the Big House and the family arrived by steam train at Wolferton. There were other Christmases, too, if only a few, when her father lived in the Big House and there were house parties with large numbers of young men in attendance, dancing in the corridors and shoots on those winter days in the cold of Norfolk, so deplored many years before by Lady Macclesfield.

The Queen and members of the Royal family traditionally arrive for Christmas for the shooting and remain until the first week of February. Then the house is full, with much of the atmosphere of former house-parties. The hospitality is legendary: the service is unobtrusively perfect, from the 'wellies' of the correct size for the guest to the comprehensive provision of stationery in every room. Entertainments may be less boisterous than they were in Sandringham's early days, but there is riding, shooting and bird-watching or a tour of the stud. In the evening there are entertainments and activities for the young, dancing and discos as well as pictures, the collection of guns, or the Fabergé ornaments which had been given to Queen Alexandra to be inspected.

The Studs at Sandringham are among the Queen's greatest interests, and she makes a number of private visits during the course of the year, staying at a farmhouse on the estate, finding the enjoyment and relaxation which comes from following a personal hobby. If her greatest interest lies in the breeding of bloodstock, there are many other happy memories which reach back to her early childhood; the grounds are beautiful, and at heart she is a countrywoman. She enjoys walking over the countryside with her dogs, and maintains a close interest in all the activities on the estate, where the Duke of Edinburgh has overall responsibility for its management, which is under the general supervision of her agent, to whom each of the Heads of Department report.

The Queen's paramount interest was shared to a great extent by Queen Elizabeth, the Queen Mother. Widowed by the death of King George VI, she took stock of her situation and found a new interest in the purchase and restoration of a remote castle in the extreme north of Scotland. The Castle of Mey was her personal link with the Scotland she loved, and in which she had been brought up. She also became engrossed in the turf; she bred and ran her own horses and seldom failed to attend the major race meetings. She supported the King staunchly during his reign; after his death she emerged as a strong, even dominant, personality, an active participant on Royal occasions, presenting a smiling and benevolent image and dressed so often in pastel shades with off-the-face hats. Now her life was her own, but she was often seen at Royal occasions and her annual appearances with members of her family at the gates of Clarence House in London, where she celebrated her birthday, ensured a crowd of well-wishers and a continuing interest in her life and activities until her death at the age of 101.

The estate today comprises about 20,000 acres, of which more than half are let to tenant farmers: the remainder include forestry land, the land actually farmed at Sandringham, the gardens and park, and saltings. Only the studs are managed separately. The Duke of Edinburgh is very interested in the farm, the improvement of stock and all projected innovations. For many years he has enjoyed watching and painting the prolific birdlife on the salt marshes bordering the Wash and, despite a programme of reclamation of 700 acres of the saltings included in the farm, forty-five acres were retained as a wildfowl reserve. When in residence, the Queen involves herself in local functions, just as Queen Mary before her visited the Women's Institutes and presented the prizes for village schoolchildren. Prince Charles, too, makes two visits during the year and is Patron, with the Queen, of the Sandringham Flower Show in mid-summer.

After the war the gardens of Sandringham were opened to the public for the first time, a Country Park was established in 1968 and the House itself in Jubilee Year, 1977. In a programme of economy and refurbishment, ninety-one rooms in the south-east corner of the house were demolished, the Queen herself symbolically starting the work. Those rooms, built to accommodate the ever-increasing numbers of staff at the turn of the century, will never be missed. Park House, built by Albert Edward for his Comptroller, Sir William Knollys, and the childhood home of Diana, Princess of Wales, was given by the Queen to the Cheshire Foundation as a hotel adapted for use by people with disabilities.

Increasing mechanisation in agriculture brought a reduction in the number of employees and surplus properties have been sold off. Appleton, where Gerald and Louise Cresswell struggled in vain against the depredations of the Royal game-keepers and, later, the English home of Queen Maud of Norway and wartime residence in Norfolk of King George VI and his family, has been demolished.

The long road downhill through the pine-trees and bracken to Wolferton is full of memories: the sons of King George V racing on their bicycles; the carriages bringing the house party guests from the station; the funeral processions setting out from the church in the park, the Royal coffins on gun-carriages on the long journey to Windsor. At the end of the road is Wolferton Station: the 'up', or London-bound side is unremarkable – passengers had only to board the 'special' before it steamed away. We must remember the disconsolate Princess May's parting from her husband and driving back in a closed carriage through the rain to York Cottage to stick photographs in her album with her sisters-in-law; the formal departure of Kaiser Wilhelm II after a difficult visit; Prince Edward and Prince Albert setting out for a new term at the Royal Naval College, Osborne, and the ceremonious leave-taking following Queen Victoria's second visit. The 'down-side' is more elaborate: here Royal guests were met and entertained by the Prince and Princess of Wales while the wagon-loads of trunks and hat-boxes of their visitors were taken up to the house. Here, in her own room, the Princess of Wales presided over the ladies' teacups, while on the other side of the entrance hall the Prince offered whisky and the air was redolent of cigars. 'Down-side' was for some years a museum which, with its costumes and memorabilia, was a poignant reminder of a past age, for the single track of rusty rails ends among the silver birches beyond the platform.

Sandringham is on the road to nowhere, and separated from much of the rest of the country by the vast expanse of flat, almost featureless Fens, yet some 100,000 visitors annually are attracted to this Royal home and many more enjoy the amenities of the Country Park. Once the joy of Albert Edward's heart, and of his son, King George V, and grandson, King George VI, Sandringham remains a Royal home, mature now, carefully-tended and efficiently-managed. Lady Macclesfield – who, we remember, deplored the lack of 'attraction of any sort' – would have approved of the developments over the past century with mixed feelings. While she might have regarded the present accessibility of Sandringham to the public with something like concern, she could no longer have denied the existence of 'attractions' at this Royal estate.

THE FAMILY OF KING EDWARD VII AND QUEEN ALEXANDRA

THE ANCESTRY OF QUEEN MARY (Inset)

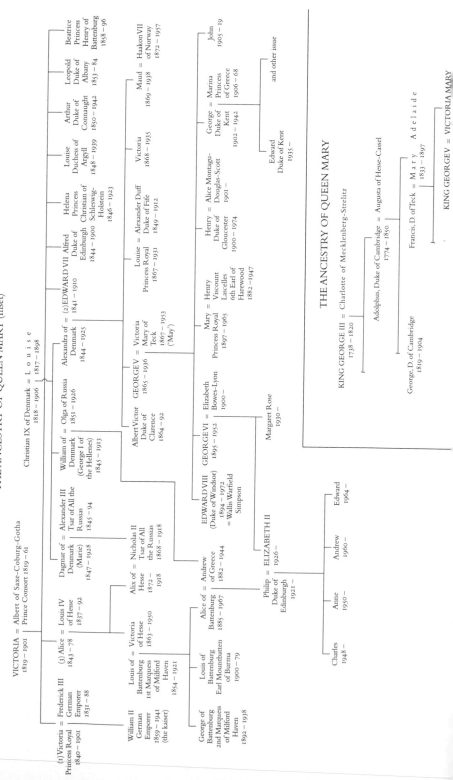

BIBLIOGRAPHY

Books:

Airlie, M., Countess of, *Thatched with Gold: Memoirs* (Hutchinson & Co., 1962)

Allfrey, A., *Edward VII and his Jewish Court* (Weidenfeld & Nicolson, 1991)

Aronson, T., *Princess Alice, Countess of Athlone* (Cassell, 1981)

Barstow, P., *The English Country House Party* (Thorsons, 1989)

Battiscombe, G., *Queen Alexandra* (Constable, 1969)

Benson, E.F., *King Edward VII* (Longmans, Green & Co., 1933)

Blyth, H., *The Pocket Venus: a Victorian Scandal* (Weidenfeld & Nicolson, 1966)

Bradford, S., *George VI* (Weidenfeld & Nicolson, 1989)

Buxton, A., *The King in his Country* (Longmans, 1955)

De Courcey, A., *The Viceroy's Daughters* (Weidenfeld & Nicholson, 2000)

Cowles, V., *Edward VII and His Circle* (Hamilton, 1956)

Cresswell, Mrs G., *Eighteen Years on the Sandringham Estate* (Temple, 1887)

Cathcart, H., *Sandringham* (W.H. Allen, 1964)

Darbyshire, T., *King George VI* (Hutchinson & Co., 1937)

Donaldson, F., *Edward VIII* (Weidenfeld & Nicolson, 1974)

Duff, D., *Whisper Louise* (Muller, 1974)

Esher, 2nd Viscount, *Journals and Letters*, (4 Vols), Nicholson & Watson, 1934-38

Fulford, R. (Ed.), *Dearest Child. Private Correspondence of Queen Victoria and the Crown Princess of Prussia, 1858-61*, Evans, 1964
—— *Dearest Mama, Private Correspondence of Queen Victoria and the Crown Princess of Prussia 1861-64*, Evans, 1968
—— *Your Dear Letter, Private Correspondence of Queen Victoria and the Crown Princess of Prussia 1865-71*, Evans, 1971
—— *Darling Child, Private Correspondence of Queen Victoria and the Crown Princess of Prussia 1871-78*, Evans, 1976
—— *Beloved Mama, Private Correspondence of Queen Victoria and the Crown Princess of Prussia 1878-1885*, Evans, 1981

—— Royal Dukes, Duckworth, 1933

Gladstone, M., *Diaries and Letters* (Methuen, 1930)

Gloucester, H.R.H., *Princess Alice, the Duchess of, Memoirs* (Collins, 1983)

Gore, J., *King George V: A Personal Memoir* (John Murray, 1941)

Grey, Lt. Gen the Hon. C., *The Early Years of the Prince Consort*, (Smith, Elder & Co, 1867)

Hart-Davis, D. (Ed.), *In Royal Service. Letters & Journals of Sir Alan Lascelles, 1920-36* (Hamilton, 1989)

Hedley-Walker R., *Wolferton Station Museum Guide* (Unknown, rev. 1993)

Hepworth, P., *Royal Sandringham* (Wensum, 1978)

Hibbert, C., *Edward VII* (Allen Lane, 1976)

—— *The Court of St. James's* (Weidenfeld & Nicolson, 1979)

Higham, C., *Wallis. Sidgwick & Jackson* (Pan ed., 1988)

Holden, A., *Charles, a Biography* (Bantam Press, 1998)

van der Kiste, J., *Edward VII's Children* (Alan Sutton, 1989)

Lacey, R., *Majesty* (Hutchinson & Co., 1977)

Lee, Sir S., *King Edward VII, A Biography* (Macmillan 1925)

Leslie, A., *Edwardians in Love* (Hutchinson & Co., 1972)

Londonderry, Marchioness of, *Henry Chaplin, A Memoir* (Macmillan, 1926)

Longford, E., *Victoria R.I.* (Weidenfeld & Nicolson, 1964)

—— *Darling Loosy* (Weidenfeld & Nicolson, 1991)

Madol, H., *The Private Life of Queen Alexandra* (Hutchinson & Co., 1940)

Magnus, P., *King Edward the Seventh* (John Murray, 1964)

Marie Louise, H.H., Princess, *My Memories of Six Reigns* (Evans, 1956)

Matson, J., *Dear Osborne,* (Hamilton, 1978)

Nicolson, H., *King George V, His Life and Reign* (Constable, 1952)

Pearson, J., *Edward the Rake* (Weidenfeld & Nicolson, 1975)

Picard, L., *Victorian London* (Weidenfeld & Nicolson, 2005)

Plumptre, G., *The Fast Set; The World of Edwardian Racing* (Andre Deutsch, 1985)

Ponsonby, A., *Henry Ponsonby, His Life from His Letters* (Macmillan, 1943)

Ponsonby, F., *Recollections of Three Reigns* (Eyre, Spottiswoode, 1957)

Pope-Hennessey, J., *Queen Mary* (George Allen & Unwin, 1959)

Reid, M., *Ask Sir James* (Hodder & Stoughton, 1987)

Rhodes James, R., *A Spirit Undaunted, The Political Role of George VI* (Little, Brown & Co, 1998)

Rohl, J.C.G., *The Kaiser and His Court* (Cambridge, 1994)

Rose, K., *King George V* (Weidenfeld & Nicolson, 1983)

St Aubyn, G., *Edward VII, Prince and King* (HarperCollins, 1979)

—— *Queen Victoria, A Portrait* (Atheneum, 1992)

Stamper, C.W., *What I Know* (Mills & Boon, 1913)

Wheeler-Bennett, J.W., *King George VI, His Life and Reign* (Macmillan, 1958)
Williamson, Mrs C.N., *Queen Alexandra* (S.W. Partridge, 1902)
Windsor, H.R.H. the Duke of, *A King's Story* (Cassell, 1951)

Letters:

Wallis and Edward, 1931–37 (Ed. Michael Bloch) (Weidenfeld & Nicolson, 1986)
Wigram Family Papers, Letters from Lady Wigram to her mother, 1917–26
Verner-Jeffreys Family Papers

Newspapers:

Daily Mail
Eastern Daily Press
History Today
Illustrated London News
The Graphic
The Times

REFERENCES

Abbreviations:

Airlie	Mabell, Countess of
Batt.	Georgina Battiscombe
Buxton	Aubrey Buxton
Cambridge	HRH George, Duke of Cambridge
Cathcart	Helen Cathcart
Cresswell	Louise Cresswell
Donaldson	Frances Donaldson
Fulford	Roger Fulford
Gore	John Gore
Hibbert	Christopher Hibbert
Lee	Sir Sidney Lee
Longford	Elizabeth Longford
Magnus	Sir Philip Magnus
Nicholson	Sir Harold Nicholson
P-H	James Pope-Hennessy
Rose	Kenneth Rose
St. A.	Giles St Aubyn
W-B	Sir John Wheeler-Bennett

See 'Works Consulted'

Chapter One: Early Days of a Prince

1. Stockmar, Memorandum, 1842
2. Magnus, p. 5
3. Gibbs, Diary.
4. Ibid.
5. Magnus, p. 14
6. Gibbs, Diary, Magnus, p. 10
7. Gibbs, Papers, Magnus p. 10
7a. Gibbs, Diaries, Magnus, p. 16
8. Magnus, p. 15
9. Gibbs Papers, January 1856, Magnus, p. 14
10. Queen Victoria to Queen Augusta of Prussia, 1856
11. Queen Victoria's Journal, Magnus, p. 23
12. Hon. E. Stanley, Letters, 27/7/48

13. Queen Victoria, Magnus, p. 26
14. Ibid.
15 The English Empress, p. 81
16. Batt., p. 28
17. Fulford, Dearest Child, p. 356
18. Batt. 28, Dearest Mama, p. 213
19. Queen Victoria, Letters, Vol. I, III
20. Magnus, p. 53
21. Queen Victoria, Idem
22. Fulford, Dearest Mama, p. 38
23. Fulford, Batt. p. 58-9
24. Magnus, p. 53
25.
26. T3 88, Batt., p. 36
27. Fulford, Dearest Child, p. 337-8.
28. Ibid.
29. QV Journal, p. 38
30. Fulford, Dearest Mama, p.186
31. Batt. p. 38

Chapter Two: Marriage

32. QV Journal, 5 Nov 1862
33. Magnus, p. 62
34. Batt., p. 41
35. Batt., p. 43
36. Ibid.
37. Ibid.
38. Londonderry, M'ness of, Henry Chaplin, A Memoir, p. 22
39. Fulford, Dearest Mama, p.180
40. Quoted St Aubyn, p. 83
41. Macclesfield Papers., Batt., p. 55/6
42. Longford, p. 391
43. Queen Victoria to Theodore Martin, 1863. Martin V
44. A Victorian Dean, Quoted Batt., p. 56
45. Batt. p. 59,
46. Fulford, *Dearest Mama*, p. 186
47. Dearest Mama, p. 212

Chapter 3: Children

48 The Aristocracy, Lee, p. 170
49. Batt. p.58
50. QV to George, D of Cambridge, 8/7/1864. Private.
51. Ponsonby, p. 101
52. W.E Gladstone, Letters, Quoted Ponsonby, p. 101
53. Fulford, Dearest Mama, p. 278
54. Batt., p. 63

55. Batt., 65
56. Batt., p. 99
57. Batt., p. 79
58. Batt., p. 80.
59 9/11/1866. Batt., p. 81
60. 14/11/1866. Batt., p. 81
61. Macclesfield Papers. Batt., p. 83.
62. Pcess of W. to Gd. Dss of Mecklenburg-Strelitz, 14/3/09. P-H 328.
63. QA to Pcess of W. 21/1/08 P-H 328
64. Esher. I, p. 345
65. Batt., p. 122–3
66.17/4/1871. Batt., p. 123
67. Somerset. 16/4/1871. Ibid.
68. Marie of Roumania, I, 43
69. Batt. p. 122
70. Dalton to QV., Gore, p. 24.
71. Dalton Papers, Batt. p. 140
72. Ibid. Batt., p. 140
73. Magnus, p. 158
74. Batt., p. 141
75. 108
76. Magnus, p. 194
77. Recorded by Sir Owen Morshead, q Gore, pp. 32–33
77. Creig, The Rebel Cadets, 1908
78. Dalton
79. Magnus, p. 178
80. Cambridge, A Memoir II, p. 139
81 Pcess of W. To Mrs Walkley ,as dated. Wolferton Station Museum [letter]

Chapter Four: The House Party
82. Lee, p. 179 & n.
83. Lee
84. Quoted in Barstow, Games of Chance
85 Cathcart, p. 123.
86 Cresswell. Quoted Duff, p. 75.
87. Cambridge II, xiv, p.6
88 A King's Story, p. 89
89. Wolferton Station Museum
90. Cresswell, p.69–70
91. H. Marchant: Daily Express, 21/1138. Quoted Duff, p. 151
92. Lee, I, 181
93. Games of Chance, Ibid.
94. Diana Cooper. Ziegler, p. 26
95 St A. 131

Chapter Five: Queen Victoria' First Visit

96. Macclesfield Papers. Batt., p. 114
97. Ibid. Batt., p. 114
98. Ibid. Batt., p. 115
99. Ibid. Batt., p.116
100 RA., QV Journal. As dated
101. Macclesfield Papers. Batt. p. 116
102. QV Journal, as dated
103. Cambridge, I, p. 302-3
104. Ponsonby, p. 99
105. Fulford. Darling Child, p. 19.
106. Fulford; Ibid., p. 20
107. Ponsonby, p. 98
108. Cambridge, I, p. 303
109. Ibid.
110. Martin V, p. 411
111. QV Journal. As dated
112. Ibid.
113. Alfred Austin
114. QV Journal. As dated
115. Ponsonby, p. 99
116 Fulford. Darling Child, p. 20
117 Ibid., p. 21
118. Dalton Papers, 23 Dec 1871, Batt. p. 119
119. Pcess of W to Pcess Louise
120. Cambridge, I , p. 307
121. Fulford. Darling Child, p. 28
122. QV to D of Cambridge, 26 Feb 1871, Cambridge, p. 3080

Chapter Six: Marriages

123. P.of W. to QV. Quoted Batt, p. 200
124 QV. Letters, Quoted in Cathcart
125. QV; Journal, as dated
126. P -H 181
127. Magnus 221
128. D of Clarence to Lady S. St Clair Erskine, 21 June 1891. P-H 200
129. P-H 193
130. Salisbury Papers. Magnus, p. 238
131. Magnus, p. 238
132. Ibid.
133 Dec.1867, P-H 31.
134. Quoted P-H 222

Chapter Seven: Troubled Years - 1890-92

135. P of W to Lady Brooke, June 1897, Hibbert, p. 164-5
136. QV Quoted in Longford, p. 441

137. K. George V; Diary. Gore, p. 97
138. K.Geo V; Diary,.P-H 222
139. Quoted P-H 222
140 Pcess of Wales to her parents, quoted in Batt., p. 189
141. P-H 226
142. Pons, p. 359
143. Arthur QA 180-1

Chapter Eight: Princess May

144. P-H 226
145. P-H 228
146. D. of Teck, 29/2/92. P-H 231.
147. P-H 248
148. Quoted Nicolson, p. 38
149. Q. Mary, diary, 3/5/93. P-H259
150. Airlie
151. Gore, KGV, p. 128-9
152. Gore, KGV, p 113-4
153. Quoted P-H, p. 279
154. Dss of Meckleberg-Strelitz to D. of Cambridge, P-H 278
154. P-H 280
155. Ibid.
156. P-H 215

Chapter Nine: Fallow Years

157. P-H 302
158. P-H 315
159. W-B 8
160. A King's Story, p. 20
161. P-H 308
162. Airlie p. 148
163. Ibid., p. 150
164. Gore, p. 368
165. P-H 18
166. Bradford, p. 22
167. A King's Story p32
168. Donaldson, p. 19
169. Hansell. Report Book. WB 25
170. A King's Story, p. 39
171. .Hansell Report Book. WB 26n
172. Quoted, Bradford, p. 29
173. H.P. Hansell. Quoted, Bradford, p. 31
174. Ibid.
175. A King's Story, p. 63
176. K. George VI's Game Book, Buxton, p. 3
177. Kings Story

178. A Family Album, p. 61

Chapter Ten: King Edward VII
179. Cathcart, p. 148
180. Stamper, p. 32
181. Stamper, p. 33-4
182. Ibid.
183. Ibid., p. 98-9
184. Ponsonby, Recollections, p. 135-6
185. Ibid., p.136-7
186. Cowles, Edward VII, p. 315-6
187. Ponsonby, Recollections, p. 139
188. Ibid.
189. Stamper, p. 312
190. Batt. p. 253
191. Ibid.
192. Lee. Ed.VII, ii, p. 717
193. Hibbert, Ed.VII, p. 290
194. Gladstone, M., Diaries and Letters, p. 40.
195. Magnus, p. 457

Chapter Eleven: King in a Cottage
196. Batt., p. 202
197. Ibid, p. 201
198. Batt 240
199. Cathcart p. 153
200. Batt. 289
201 P-Hennessey, p. 502
202. F. Ponsonby,.Recollections, p. 329
203. Batt. 291
204. F. Ponsonby,.Recollections, p. 329
205. K Geo V, Diary. Nicholson, p. 347
206. Bigge Papers, Nicholson, p. 264.
207. Mrs Wigram. Letters, 9/1/17
208. Batt. p. 294
209. Cathcart, p. 169
210. Mrs Wigram, Letters
211. Ibid., Letters
212. Ibid., Letters
213. Ibid., Letters
214. Ibid., Letters
215. Ibid.. Letters
216. K.George V's Diary, Gore, p. 307
217. Ibid., Gore, p. 306
218. Ibid., Letters
219. Q. Mary's Diary, P-H 511

220. Ibid., p. 511.
221. K. George V's Diary
222. Mrs Wigram. Letters
223. Ibid., Letters
224. Ibid., Letters
225. Ibid., Letters
226. Ibid., Letters
227. Ibid., Letters
228. Gore, 378
229. George V's Diary, WB 150
230. D. of York's Papers, WB 150
231. Quoted in WB, p. 151
232. Batt. 300

Chapter Twelve: Moving House

233. Quoted in Batt., p. 298
234. Batt., p. 299
235. Knutsford Papers, Ibid., p. 302
236. Ibid.
237. Batt., p. 302
238. Mrs Wigram, Letters.
239. Q. Mary's Diary, 30/1/26. P-H 540
240. Q. Mary's Diary. 9/1/26. Quoted P-H 540
241. Mrs Wigram, Letters
242. Q. Mary to Marquess of Cambridge, 10/2/26. P-H 540
243. P-H 541
244. Ibid.
245. P-H 542
246. Ibid.
247. Lady Wigram, Letters, as dated
248. Airlie, p. 298.
249. Lady Wigram. Letters
250. Woods Papers, Quoted in Rose, p. 389

Chapter Thirteen: Three Kings in One year

251. Gore, p. 438
252. K. George V. Diary, in Nicholson, p. 676.
253. Q. Mary, Diary, P-H 558
254. HRH D of Windsor, p. 261
255. K. George V, Diary, in Nicholson, p. 676
256. Queen Mary's Diary. P-H
257. Gore, 295
258. F. Ponsonby
259. Watson, History Today, p. 29
260. Ibid., No. 28
261. Ibid.

275. Q. Mary's Diary. P-H 559.
276. Watson, History Today, p 28
277. Ibid.
278. Ibid., p. 28-9
279. Q. Mary's Diary. P-H 559
280. Sir A. Lascelles, 21/1/36.P-H 560
281. Q. Mary's Diary, 21/1/36, P-H 560
282. Ibid., p. 22/1/36.

Chapter Fourteen: King George VI

283. Donaldson, p. 187
284. Quoted in Higham, p. 169
285. Summarised by the Registrar, RA
286. A King's Story, p. 270
287. Ibid., p. 258
288. Rose, p. 392.
289. Donaldson, p. 173 and Baldwin, Middelmas and Barnes, p. 976.
290. Ibid., p. 174 and Thatched with Gold, p. 197
291. A Diary with Letters, T. Jones, quoted in Donaldson, p. 243.
292. Diaries, Evelyn Waugh, as dated
293. Sir Harold Nicholson
294. Quoted in WB 293-4
295. Quoted in Wheeler-Bennett, p. 295
296. D. of Windsor, 30/7/36, P-H 567
297. Q. Mary's Diary. P-H 583
298. Q. Mary's Diary. P-H 587
299. Wheeler-Bennett, p. 154
300. Airlie, p. 357ff
301. Quoted in W-B, p. 740
302. Buxton, p. 2
303. Buxton, p. 91
304. Ibid. K. Geo VI. Duck book,
305. Buxton, p. 138
306. W-B, p 803.
307. Buxton, p. 139.

Afterword

308. Lacey, p 410

INDEX